CHRISTIANA SOULOU

ΔΕΣΤΕ

DESTE Foundation for Contemporary Art

CHRISTIANA SOULOU

2000 WORDS

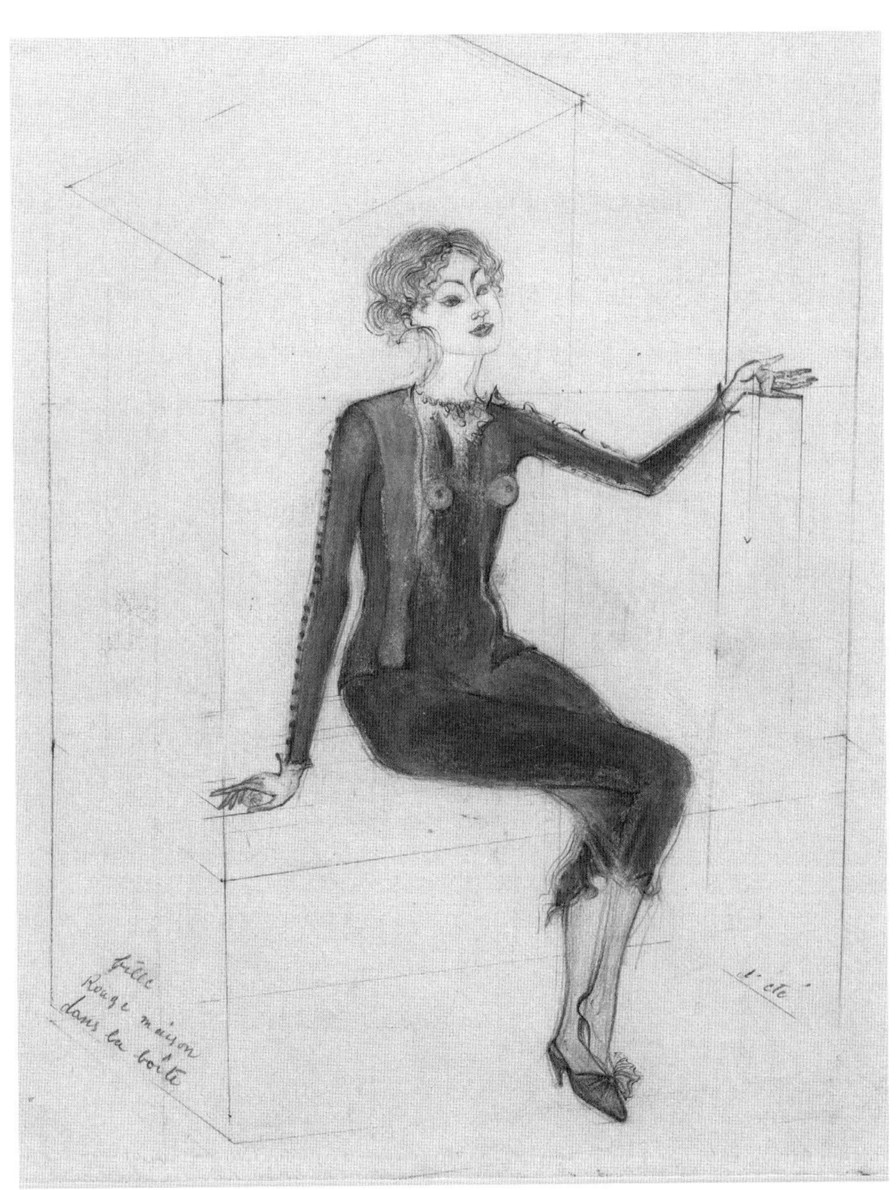
fille
Rouge maison
dans la boîte
1·cte

TOWARDS DRAWING

Claire Gilman

Few artists display a passion for drawing as single-minded in its intensity as that of Christiana Soulou, who has been pursuing the medium from her native Greece since the early eighties. Her resolutely figurative drawings are restrained in their palette and choice of drawing materials (generally pencil or colored pencil on paper), uniformly small in scale, and hesitant in style. Drawing may constitute a restriction for Soulou but it is a fecund one. As the artist says, "drawing is like making plans all your life long."[1] By its nature, drawing permits access to the space of desire and the imagination as no other medium can, its foundational purpose being to envision that which cannot be otherwise realized. Applying pencil to paper is to posit without fixing; it is to reveal the trace or path of motion as it comes into being. In the words of philosopher Jean-Luc Nancy, "'to draw' is at once to give birth to form—to *give* birth in *letting* it be born—and thus to show it, to bring it to light;"[2] just as "to exist is to sketch oneself...to open oneself to a form which shows itself in the movement of its uprising."[3]

Soulou typically works in series, grounding her drawings in specific literary texts and producing scores of images. Emily Dickinson, William Shakespeare, Jean Cocteau, and Heinrich von Kleist are among the heavy hitters whose texts Soulou has engaged with. Indeed, although intimate in approach, the sheer volume of her drawings, and the erudition of their references, signal an equally ambitious undergirding concept. Her figures sometimes evoke specific personages and even precise scenes—as in her careful cataloguing of the characters from *A Midsummer Night's Dream* (2008), complete with accompanying explanatory text—but they are meant to represent universal moral archetypes that echo their source texts while raising larger questions about the nature of what it means to be human.

Most recently, in a seeming departure from the reflective figures that typically populate her work, Soulou contributed twenty-three drawings inspired by Jorge Luis Borges's *Book of Imaginary Beings*—including a growling Chinese dragon (*Chien Dragon*, 2013) and a half-crocodile/half-lion (*Le Dévoreur d'ombres*, 2013)—to the *Encyclopedic Palace* at the 55th Venice Biennale. And yet, what are Borges's creatures if not crystallizations of human dreams and fantasies, a subject that lies at the core of the artist's work? In fact, Soulou has asserted that what is important in her drawings is not so much the story depicted but the fact "that there is someone there telling a story. It is this presence that matters. The... real subject could be more about the correspondence or reflection of what you're seeing,"[4] or, put differently, the projections and desires with which we move through the world.

This motion towards form—or "birth to presence"[5]—is manifest in the ways in which faces, arms, and legs well up from within mottled grounds, or frayed and fragmented contours go in and out of visibility. Consider an early untitled composition from 1982 in which the barely delineated torso of a girl, her eyes wistfully upturned, is borne aloft by an upward sweep of translucent watercolor stains, or the mysteriously titled *Montre ta montre monstre* (Watch your monster shows, 1982) in which a seminude figure embossed with leaves and flowers spins into our field of vision on the spokes of a lightly sketched compass-type wheel. Similarly, in *At the House of the Mournful Man* (2005), a faceless figure, his or her arms and legs outstretched and hands groping for the surface, rises up from beneath some kind of watery depths. Alongside this figure, water bubbles, the head of a sea creature, and faintly delineated flowers and birds replace the abstract blotches and stains that populate Soulou's earlier drawings. Whether figurative or not, these background marks are not incidental gestures. Rather, they read as an extension of the figures themselves, part of a larger field of matter against which the bodies take shape and from which they cannot be completely distinguished.

Identity, in Soulou's drawings, is an open condition, one that necessarily incorporates fragmentation. In the artist's words, "[physical and ethical integrity] is not the result of some addition or other, still less of cooperation or apposition: it is the product of juncture." It "is not a matter of a synthetic act; it is the accomplishment of a rift."[6] Hence the pink frock-coated twins who link arms in *Untitled* (2005) and *La Liaison engagée* (The committed liaison, 2006). Like the body that is carried forth by the rotating wheel, the figures in the latter composition appear to emerge from a network of pencil lines and geometric shapes. So too the naked woman in *Only I Know How Very Much I Loved You* (2005) who is spirited forth by disembodied hands from whose fingertips extend wispy disconnected traces. Here self-identity is identity in union, wherein union implies not fusion but rather "juncture"; that is, the awkward coming-up-against-each-other of form; the urge to fit together even as a "rift" remains. As Soulou observes, "the 'Other' is an inseparable element of the 'same' and even a condition of the identity of the same, that guides from difference to similarity,"[7] and, one might add, back again.

If literature is important for Soulou, so too is

theater and role-playing in its many guises. In addition to her response to *A Midsummer Night's Dream*, acrobats and elaborately costumed players regularly feature, as in the 1983–85 series *Water* in which tightrope-walking and jump rope–wielding ladies join winged fairies, lute players, and grandes dames with Gigot sleeves. Exotics in harem pants step out of seashells in one drawing, while in another a mismatched collection of brightly colored Warholian shoes explodes onto the page. In 2009, Soulou dedicated an entire series to the solitary figures of the tarot ("The Emperor," "The High Priestess," etc.). In stagey poses reminiscent of a circus or magic show, "The Magician" leans forward on his cane, while "Strength" sparkles in a rose-colored jacket and top hat. It is not accidental that Soulou chose to focus on the tarot as a game comprised of allegorical figures rather than as a tool of divination as it is principally known today. Just as Soulou's characters are both distinct and inextricably connected, so too is the tarot comprised of diverse yet interrelated archetypes that are meaningless outside of the system as a whole.

This is not to say that Soulou's drawings invoke an image of humanity as neatly packaged and encapsulated as it is in the tarot. By contrast, her "actors," like her drawings in general, are haunted by what they leave unsaid, by the residue or remainder that resists formation. We see this residue in the blotches and flecks of matter that populate her early images and encroach on the people within. And we see it too in the line's fragility, the way in which the figures, however overwhelmed their bodies are by constraining hoop skirts or lacy doublets, are nonetheless barely there, their limbs and faces fading off into the background, their expressions impenetrable. Indeed, to attempt to plumb the surface is to meet with resistance, as Soulou demonstrates in one of her most powerful drawings, *I Accept, If You Can Tolerate Me Silently* (1982), in which a washy skeleton hovers on top of cream-colored lined paper, its rib bones parallel to the light-blue ruled lines beneath. Here surface adornment is stripped away. What remains, however, is not some kind of essential truth but yet another surface. What emerges when costumes are cast aside is the body without qualities, the silence of death.

Where then does humanity reside in Soulou's work? To return to the beginning of this essay, it resides in the drawn line itself, in the ungraspable motion towards being that this line enacts. It manifests itself in the sweep of a woman's upturned gaze, in the tentative extension of an arm or leg. Her characters are creatures of action, like the masked figure in *The Open Dancer, The Knight* (from the *Water* series) who lunges forward, his skeletal arm outstretched, and like the dancer who occupies the same page, her tilted shoulders little more than a torqued pencil line. These figures are part of a verbal phrase—girl who dances, man who defends himself—that can be read through their actions; actions, however, that are frozen on the page, never complete. Speaking about this phenomenon, Soulou observes, "In my drawings, you see people in constant movement, but you do not know exactly what they are doing.... The result in drawing has the form of an object, it is a visual composition of curves and surfaces, on which any part of the body may shift, move and vibrate,"[8] and which, despite endless mutations, never settles into a fixed or stable whole.

Of all her archetypes, Soulou's favorite is the dancer. *There are Triangle Dancer, Sitting Dancer, Dancer with Ribbon,* and *Red Dancer, Green Dancer* (both slightly bolder in color than their companions), as well as *Dancer with Playing Card*, who, standing jauntily hand on hip and card in hand, is a hybrid of the dancer and the tarot. The dancer appears in various forms: every character in the *Tarot* series, for example, is for all intents and

purposes, a dancer. In 2010, Soulou created a
portfolio titled *Dancers*, fifteen or so drawings
of solitary ballerinas in simple leotards with
nearly identical facial features, their contours
executed in pencil on otherwise blank pages.
Above all, what registers about Soulou's
dancers is the awkwardness with which they
assume their positions. All knobbly knees
and elbows and semi-pointed toes, they are
unstable figures who are emphatically un-self-
contained. In *Triangle Dancer*, the protagonist
balances on one foot, her opposite arm and
leg outstretched. It is evident that the gesture
depicted is fleeting and that at any moment
the leg will drop and the pose will come undone.
This posture is but a temporary consolidation
of form, one pose among the endlessly
substitutable poses that this dancer and her
doppelgangers assume.

Here, as in other of Soulou's drawings, a
wayward pencil line accompanies the composition. Extending from the dancer's fingertips
to the toes of her raised leg, the line could be
explained as the means by which she performs
her arabesque. But it also registers as just what
it is: a diagonal trace that echoes the thrust
of the extended leg, like some surrogate limb.
About her fascination with dance, Soulou has
observed: "the cause of dance itself is to suc-

ceed that state where gravity appears absent, or better to say, where materiality is transformed—with all its weight, into something immaterial."[9] It is this tension between materiality and immateriality that Soulou's work strives to sustain; the ceaseless struggle of an endless becoming that defines both drawing and humanity itself.

1 Christiana Soulou quoted in Maurizio Cattelan, "A World of Silence: A Conversation in Two Parts between Maurizio Cattelan and Christiana Soulou," *Work* (Summer 2008), p. 71.
2 Jean-Luc Nancy, *The Pleasure in Drawing*, trans. Philip Armstrong (New York: Fordham University Press, 2013), p. 22.
3 Ibid., p. xiii.
4 Soulou quoted in Cattelan, p. 71.
5 *The Birth to Presence* is the title of a book by Nancy. *The Birth to Presence*, trans. Brian Holmes, et al (California: Stanford University Press, 1994).
6 Soulou, *Fractures* (Athens: DESTE Foundation for Contemporary Art, 2007), pp. 31–33.
7 Excerpt from Soulou's handwritten notes, "Choreography a4," in *Water* (London: Sadie Coles HQ, 2008).
8 Soulou in Augustine Zenakos, "Christiana Soulou," *To Vima tis Kyriakis* (The Tribute on Sunday), 12 March 2006.
9 Soulou quoted in the press release accompanying *Dancers* at Friedrich Petzel Gallery, New York, 10/29–12/22/2010.

WORK

I Accept, If You Can Tolerate Me Silently, 1982

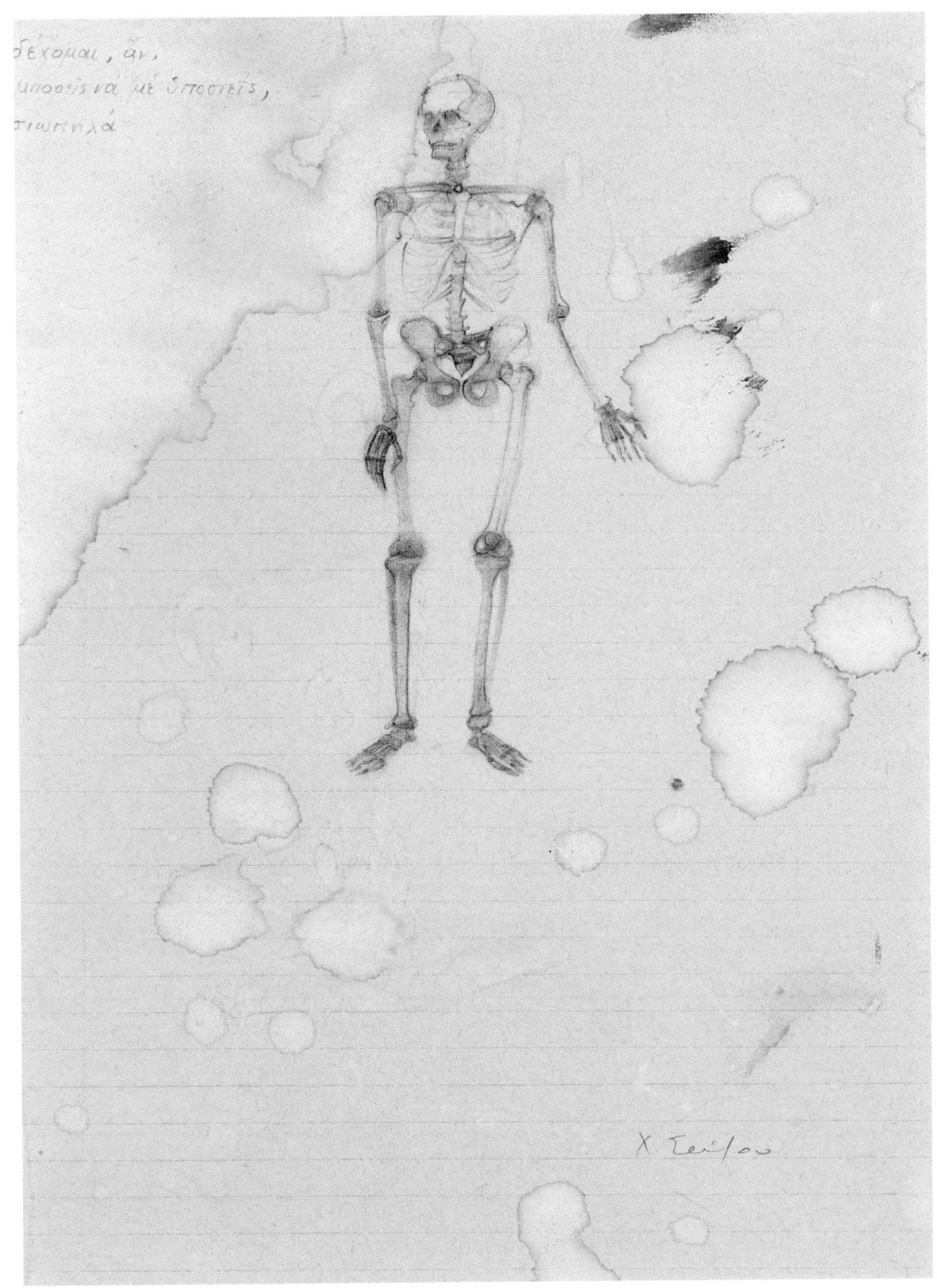
δέχομαι, ἄν,
...μέ ὑποστείς,
σιωπηλά
Χ. Σείβου

Written on the left-hand side of a piece of paper—one of my old drawings from 1982, showing the figure of a human skeleton—are the words, "I accept if you can tolerate me silently."

This phrase, which is also the title of the drawing, may be read in a circular fashion: I accept if—if you can tolerate me—silently I accept—, etc.

We might believe that this phrase written above the drawing refers to an exchange—a dialogue—between two beings who establish an agreement (of love) between themselves, accepting, for example, the proposition of an affair, but only under calculated conditions: (1) if you can, (2) if you can tolerate me, (3) if you can tolerate me silently. We can conclude that there are two people engaged in this dialogue, since, logically, the phrase addresses a question that has been asked. We also assume that two people are involved by the presence of the words "I" and "you" (I accept [me], if you can tolerate me [you]).

And yet, in truth, only one person features in this scene. Still, we immediately accept the amorous character of these words as an invitation extended from me to the other.

And indeed, this drawing is about questioning an amorous proposition, except that the question raised addresses the credibility of one's own love. In truth, the drawing asks, "Am I right to love as I love?"

And yet, it is Love that raises the question: "I, Love, am possible only if you, who is in love, can tolerate me within you."

Thus the skeleton in the drawing is a staged representation of unconditional love, which situates itself as the "I" (me).

To "tolerate silently" in no way means to suffer, but rather becomes "to no longer have to tolerate." It is to gain the strength—the power—of tolerance.

"If you can (tolerate me)" has nothing to do with an ability to stand the test of some kind of torture; it does not mean that one should "endure the blow," but rather asks, "Can you lift away your doubts so that love can become a possibility?"

Ultimately, the "if" (in "if you can") is not a condition here (on the condition that you can...). By "if you can," one must understand, "Are you strong enough, are you able, to lift away your doubts, so that I, Love, can become possible?"

These kinds of demands are what the drawing is all about, and therefore the title of the work can be translated to mean "Am I enough for you?"

The drawing is talking about—or better, *questioning*—self-importance.

All drawing is a kind of questioning of self-importance.

Thus, very strangely, what we find intolerable is also that which is insufficient.

Christiana Soulou
(2012)

Girl, 1982

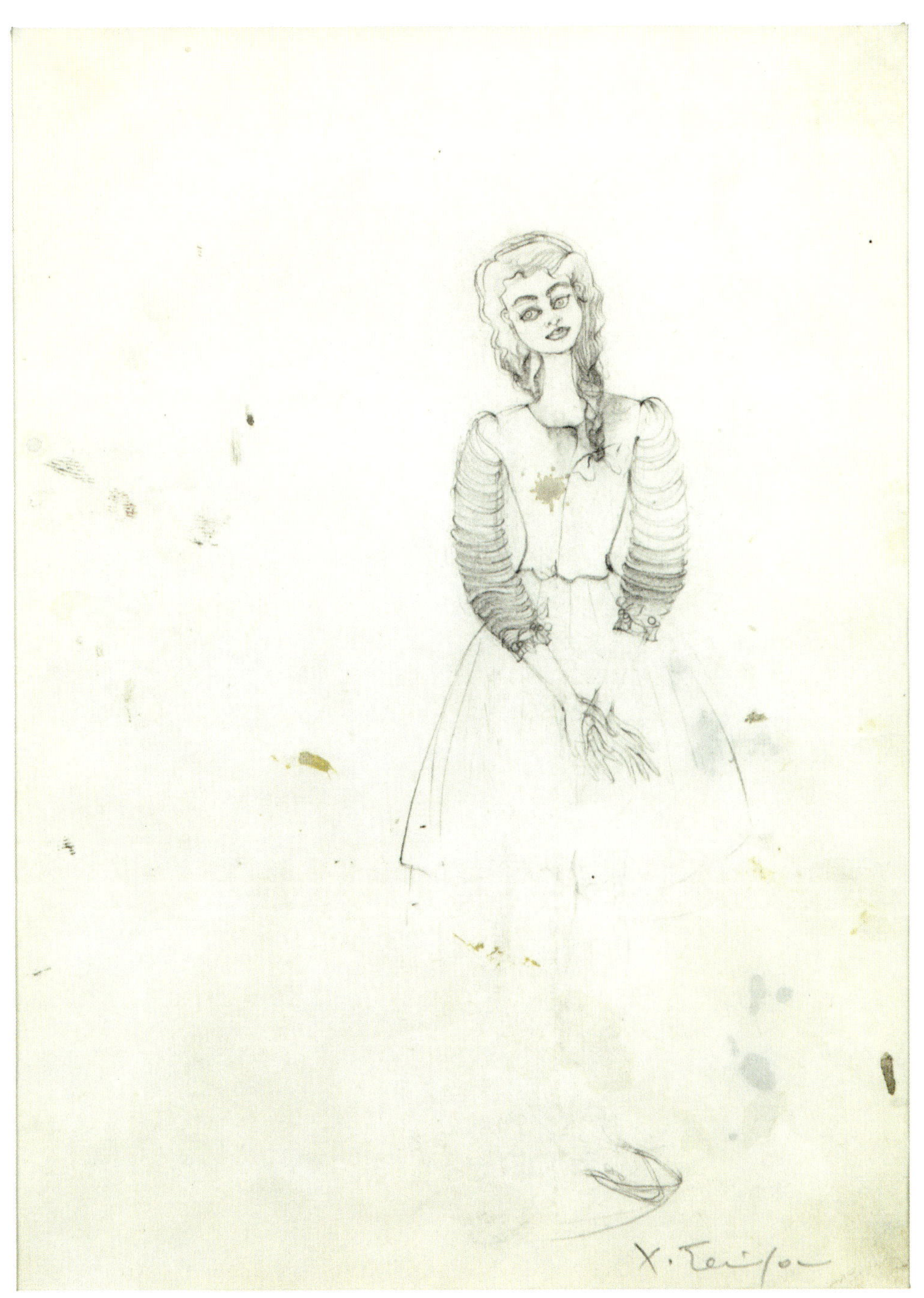

Girl, 1982

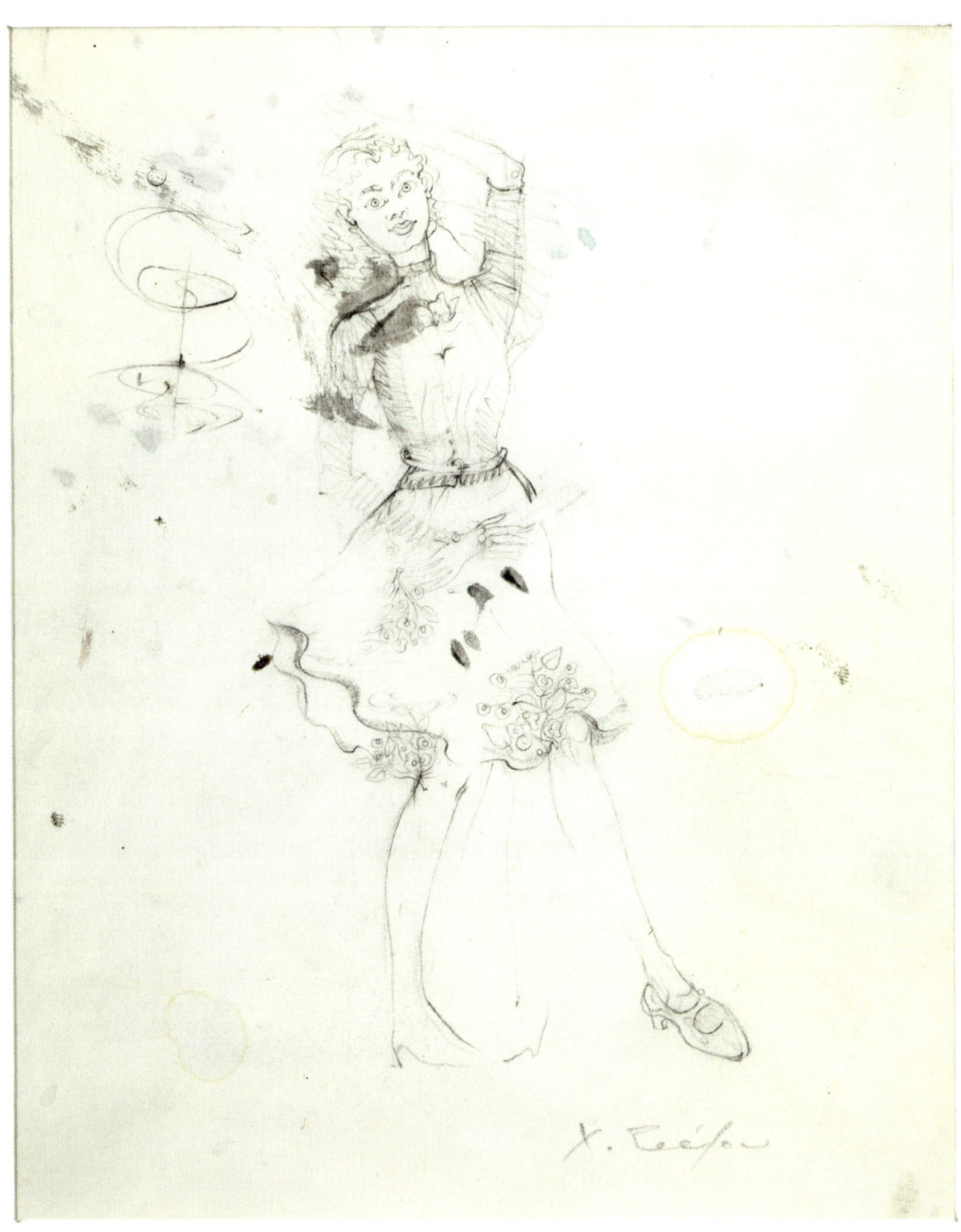

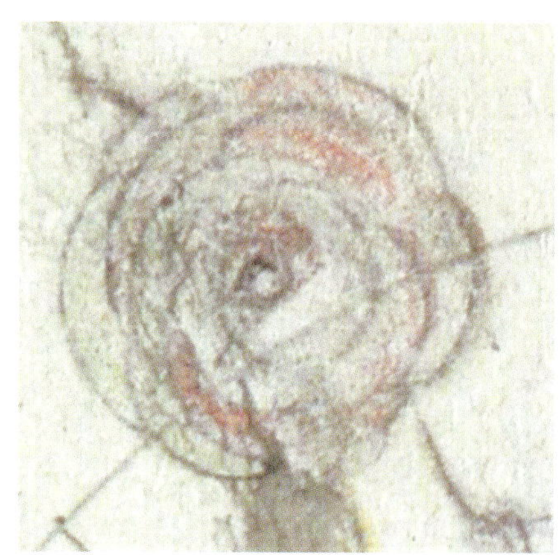

Montre ta montre monstre, 1982

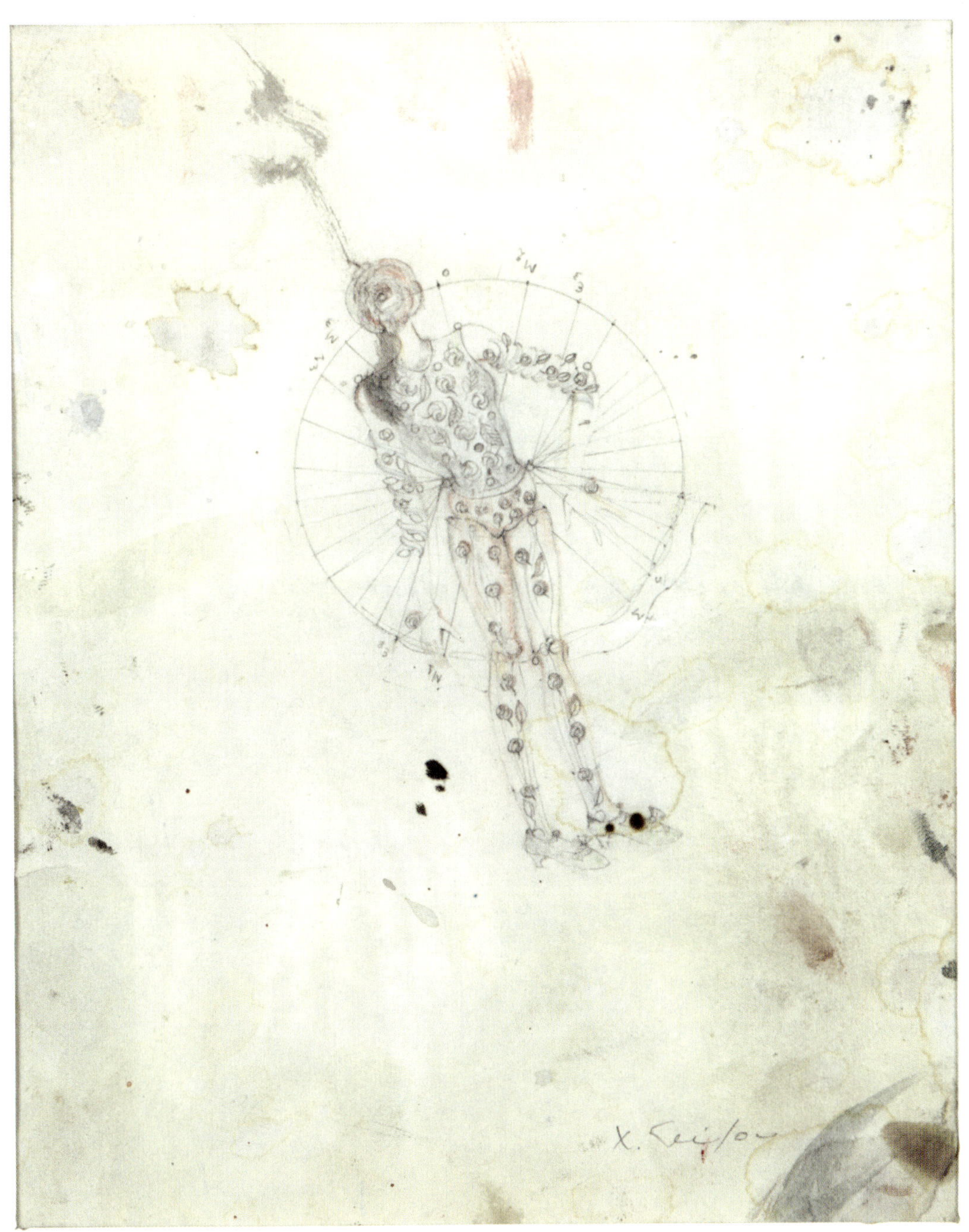

The Letter, 1982

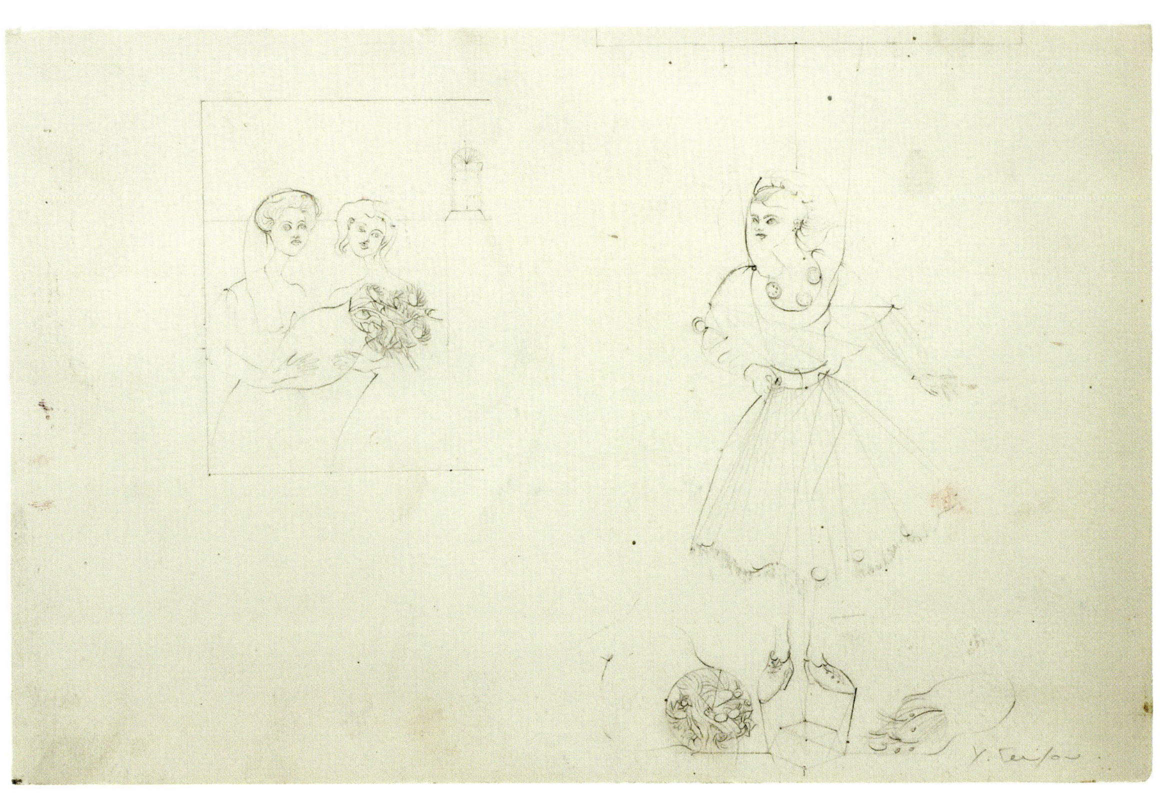

... And You a Coffee House – The Nut in the Cage, 1982

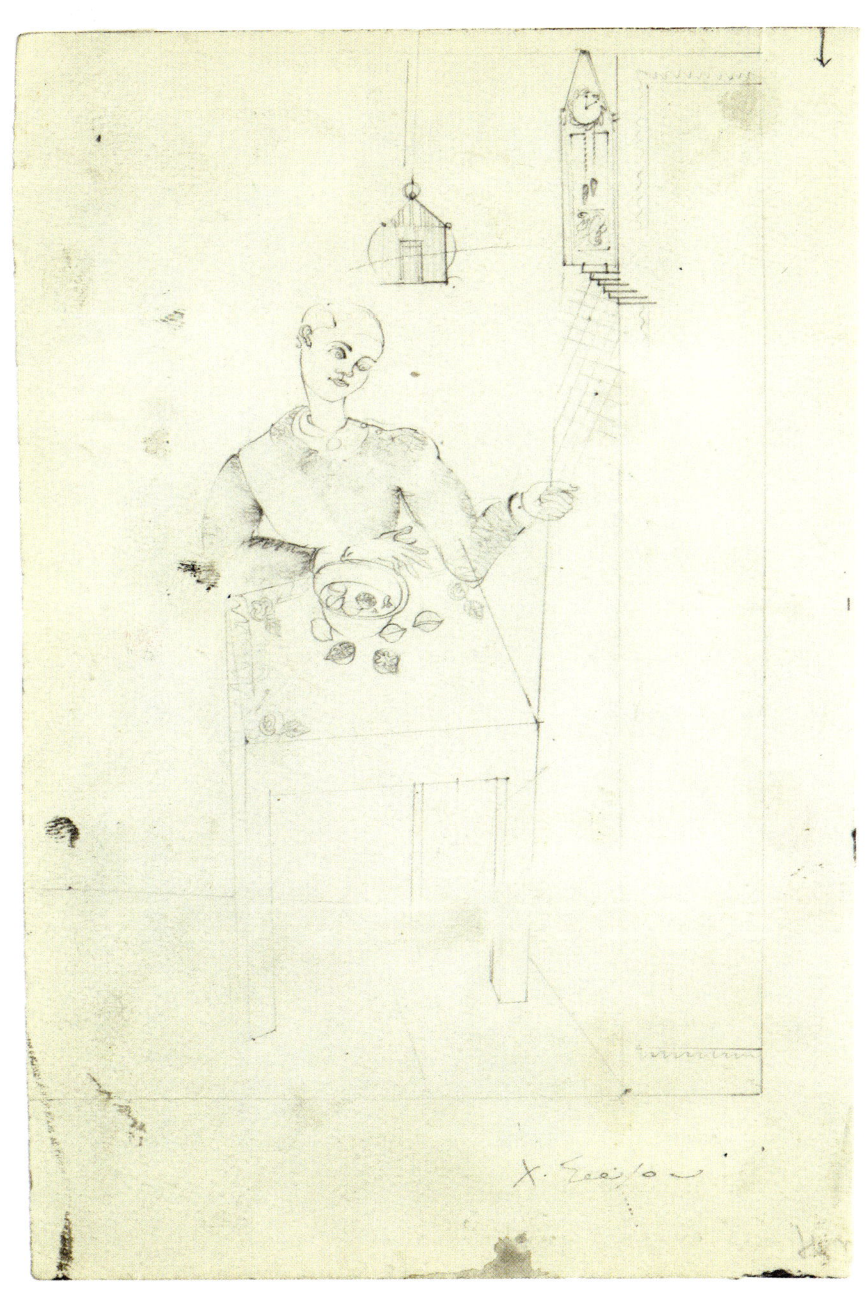

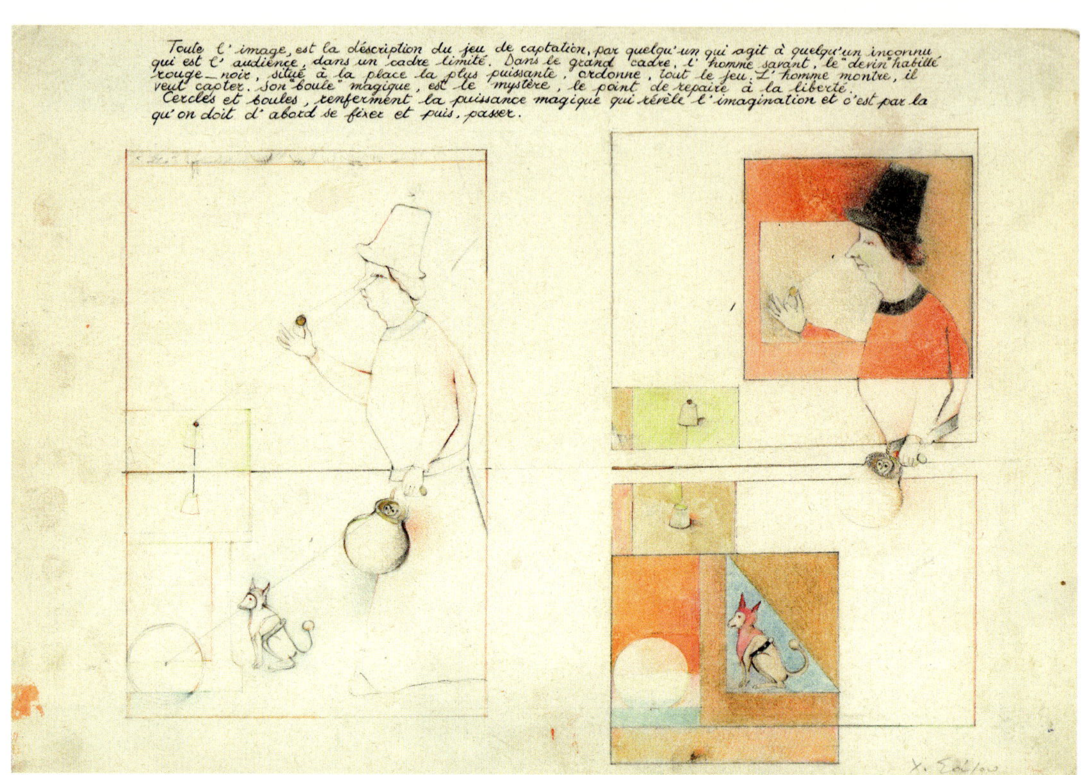

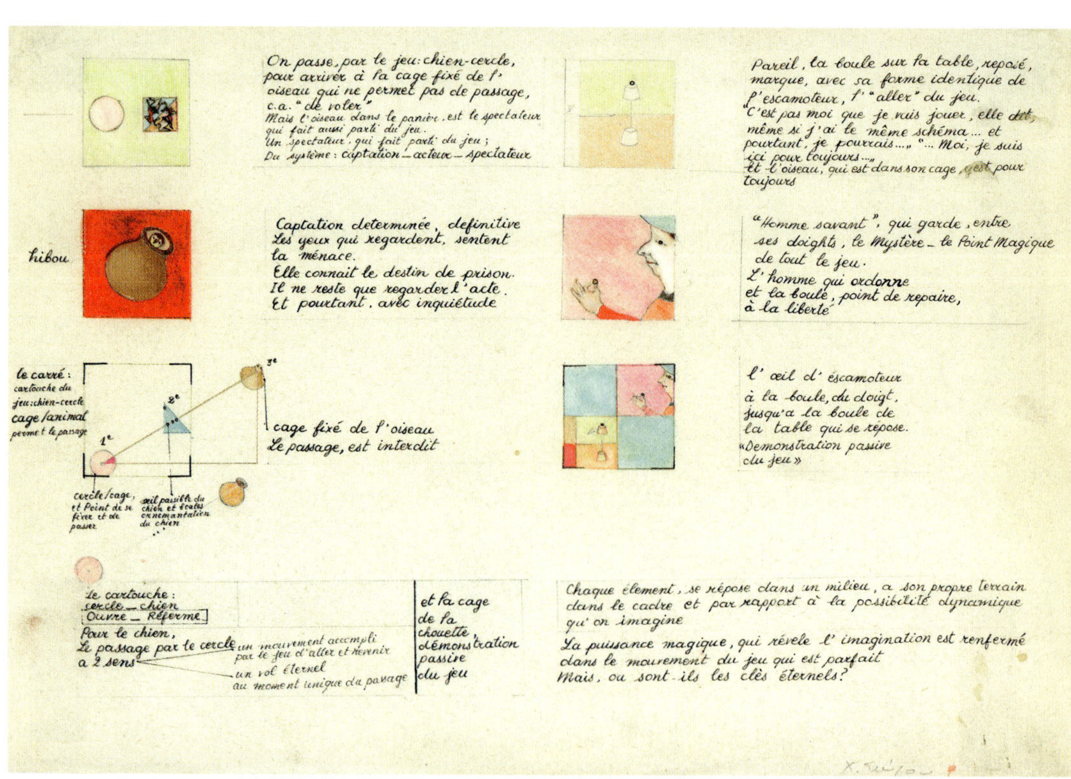

L'escamoteur (after Hieronymus Bosch) 1–4, 1982

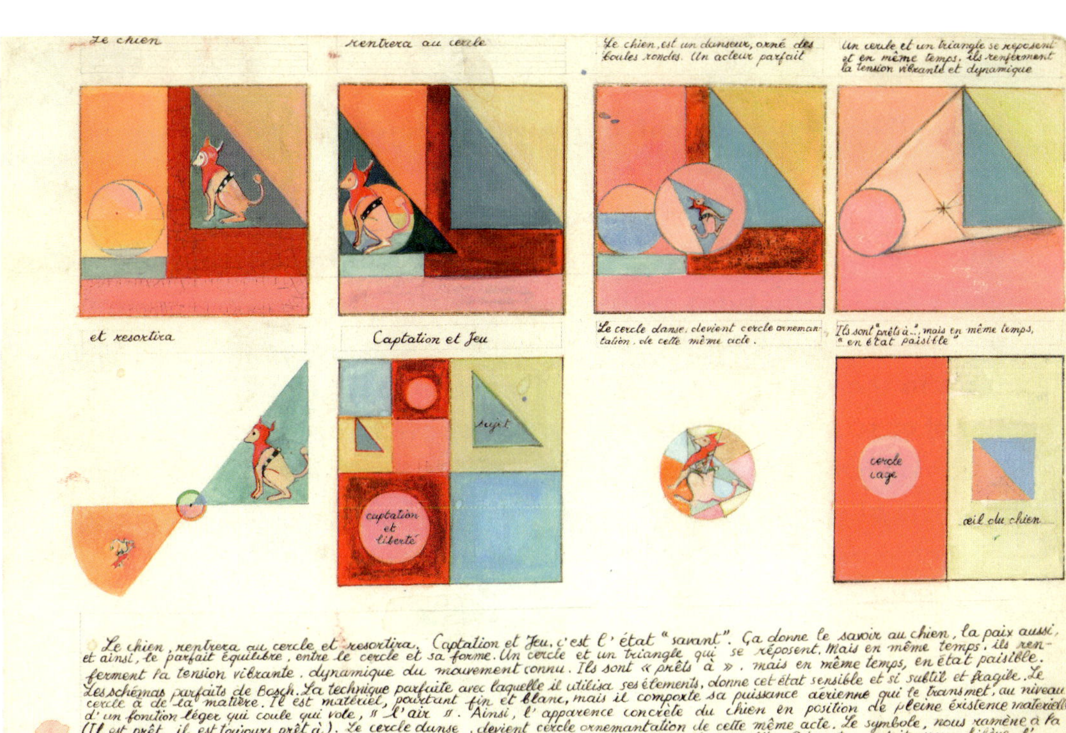

Le chien, rentrera au cercle et ressortira. Captation et Jeu, c'est l'état "savant". Ça donne le savoir au chien, la paix aussi, et ainsi, le parfait équilibre, entre le cercle et sa forme. Un cercle et un triangle qui se reposent. Mais en même temps, ils renferment la tension vibrante, dynamique du mouvement connu. Ils sont « prêts à ». mais en même temps, en état paisible. Les schémas parfaits de Bosch. La technique parfaite avec laquelle il utilisa ses éléments, donne cet état sensible et si subtil et fragile. Le cercle a de la matière. Il est matériel, pourtant fin et blanc, mais il comporte sa puissance aérienne qui le transmet, au niveau d'un fonction léger qui coule qui vole, " l'air ". Ainsi, l'apparence concrète du chien en position de pleine existence matérielle (Il est prêt, il est toujours prêt à). Le cercle danse, devient cercle ornementation de cette même acte. Le symbole, nous ramène à la réalité global de la matière. Ce prêt a... est, qui comporte son complement qui le complit. Cet acte parfait, nous libère l'imagination. C'est l'action. Le chien est orné. Le chien, est un danseur, orné des boules rondes. Un acteur parfait.

X. Tsoclis

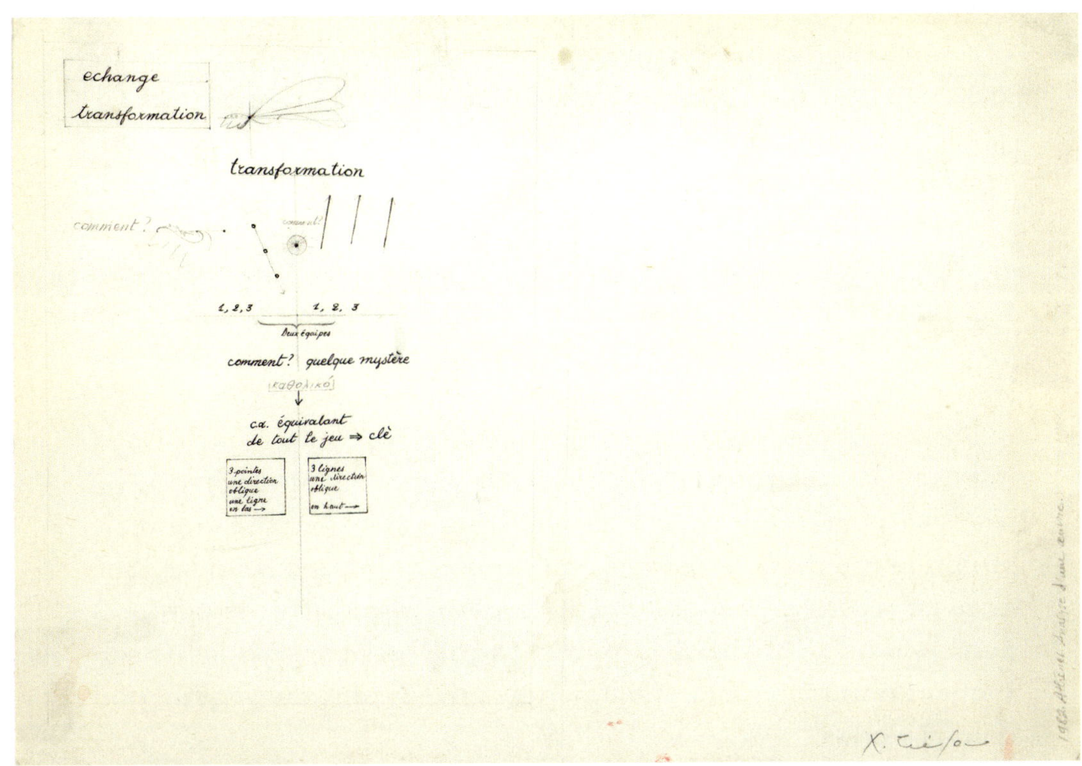

X. Tsoclis

Water (1983–85), together with my drawings from 1982, constitute works devoid of a natural model. In this sense, I consider them more to be works of an ornamental style. They are studies of form, the motif being inorganic structures in the case of the 1982 drawings, and organic structures in the case of *Water*. The drawings from 1982 are works of stylization and an abstract slant. My desire to raise form to the level of ruthless clarity, far removed from its conventional obscurity and temporality, forces me to accommodate organic form into geometrical, crystalline lines. The process that consists of suppressing every element of the organic by approximating pure linear regularity rests on the drawing's two-dimensionality. As it cannot be accomplished by means of the outline alone, construction of the image must be understood as the transformation of depth relations into planar relations, which results in "distorted form." The outline of flowers in the figure's dress in *Montre ta montre monstre*, for example, is made up of regular curves. The lines of the figure's limbs are drawn absolutely straight in response to the requirements of a maximum crystalline regularity. In all the drawings from that period it is the inorganic structure of the organic form that prevails. The colors of the skeleton in *I Accept, If You Can Tolerate Me Silently* are not those of the bones, but those of their structure.

The end of that tendency marks the beginning of *Water*. *Water* responds with a reverse process focusing on the organic structure of form, which is most purely and perceptibly observed in the structures of plants, shells, and animals. Throughout this series of drawings, the motif is organic regularity. A figure is perceived not as a living natural model but as an ensemble of organic laws, with everything that laws imply. All the elements of the organic structure are there: regularity, arrangement around a center, balance between centrifugal and centripetal forces. This structure is perceived as an abstract form and the process consists, in its subsequent naturalization, of elements derived from the vegetal and animal worlds.

In *Water* it is not the natural model that is reproduced; it is the projection of organic structure that is animated. Some of the drawings, though, especially toward the end of the series as it is presented in this book, still employ the "distorted form" process. ... *And You a Coffee House – The Nut in the Cage* (1982) is identical to these works.

Christiana Soulou
(2014)

Water, 1983–1985

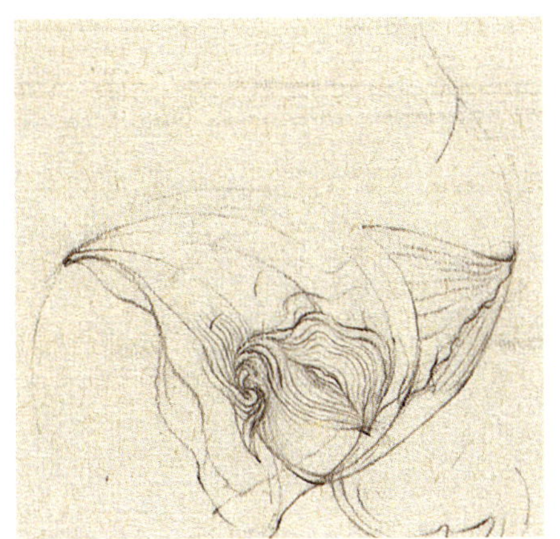

Untitled (detail)

Artemis Polumastos

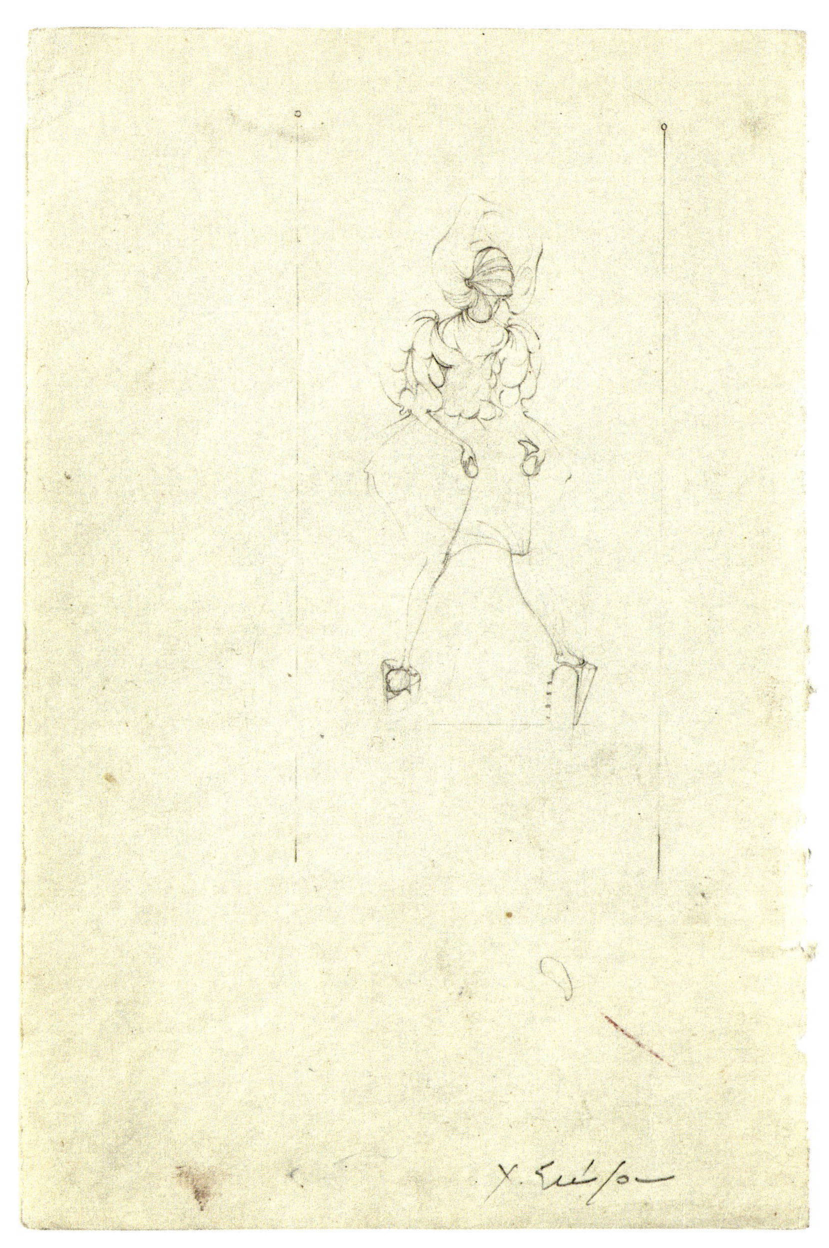

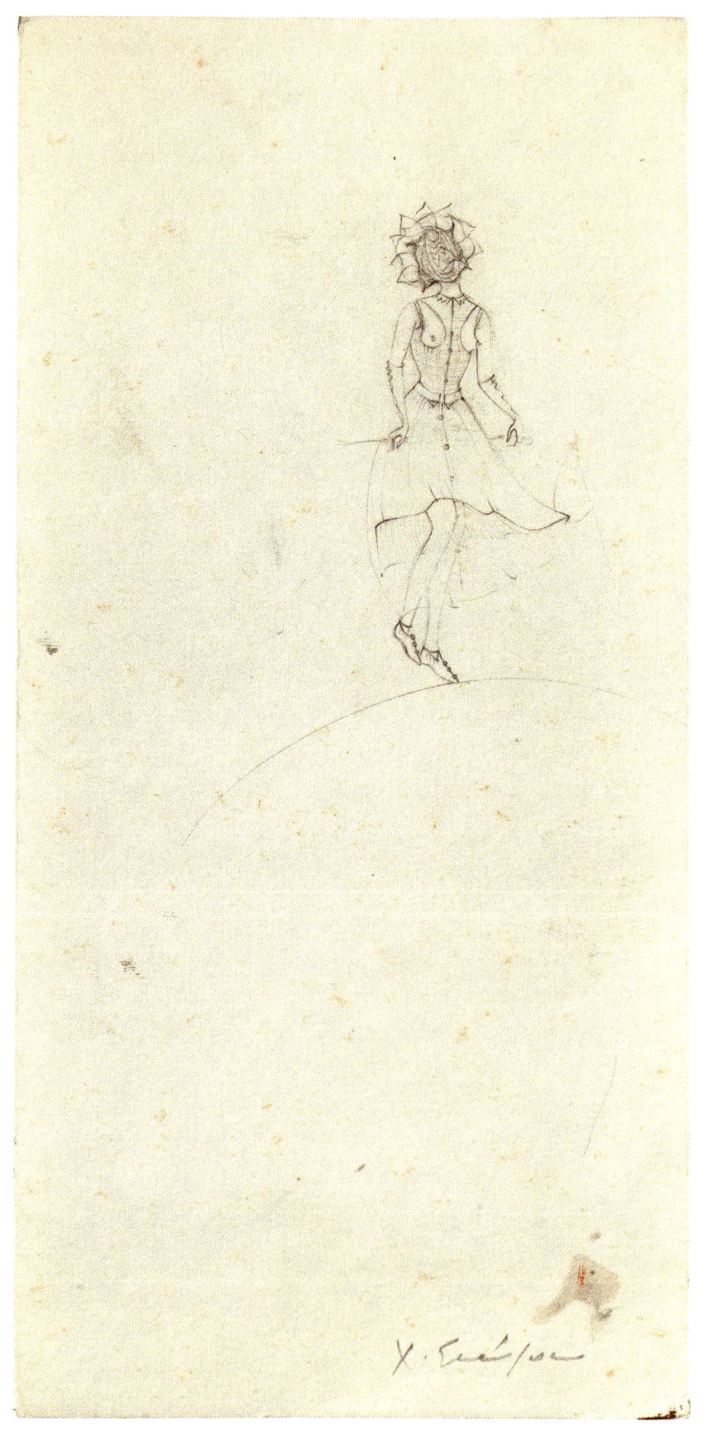

Untitled

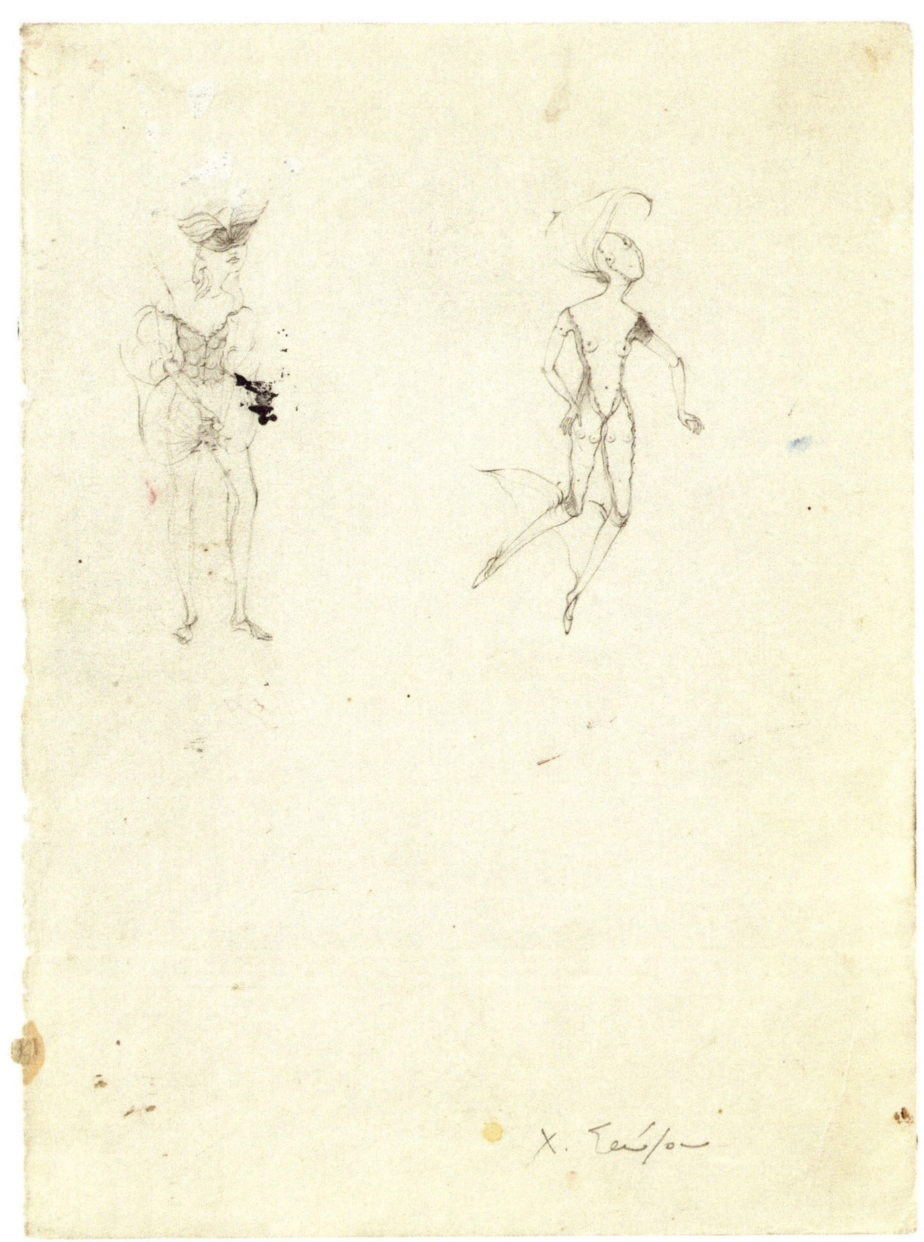

Untitled

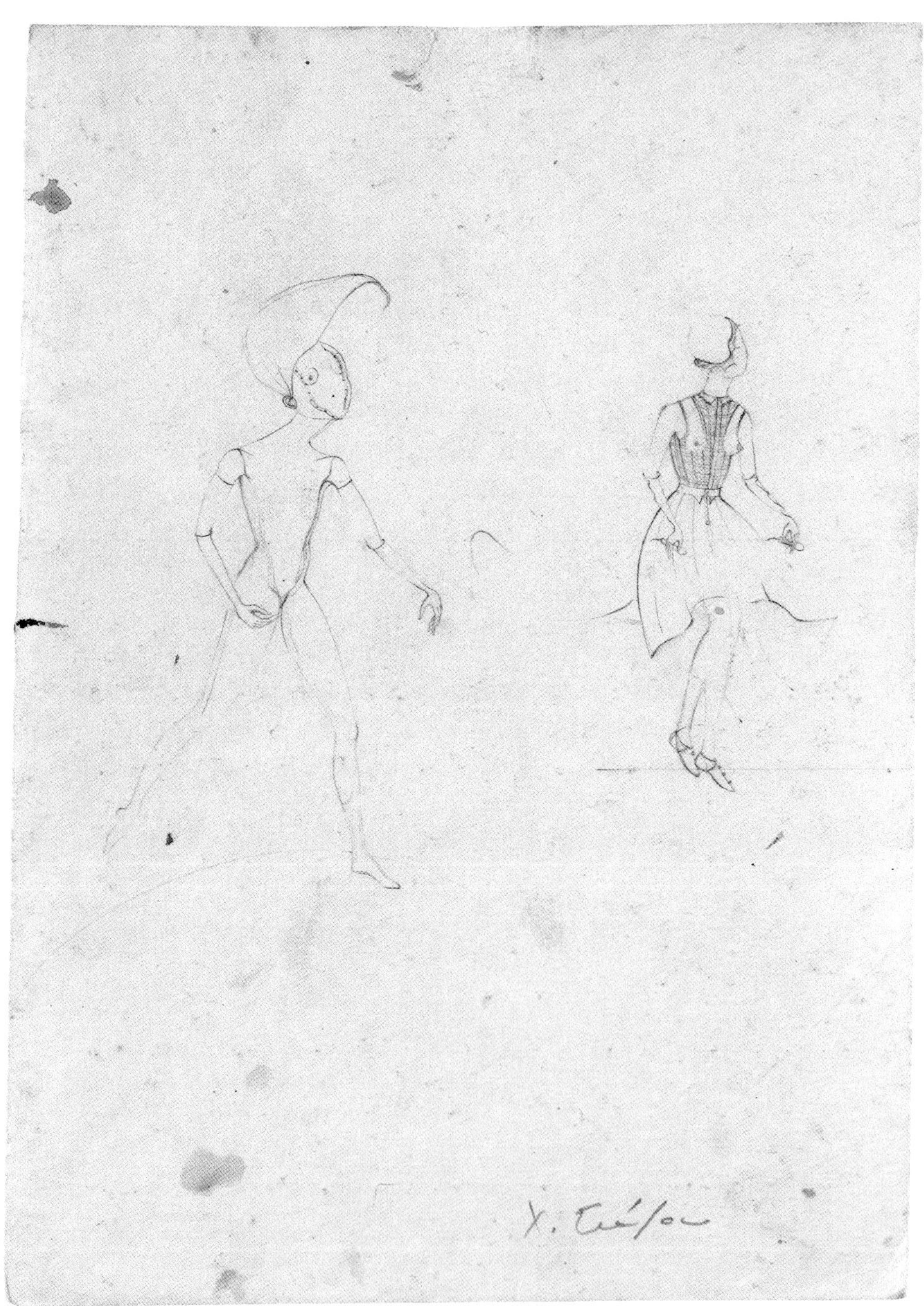

Untitled

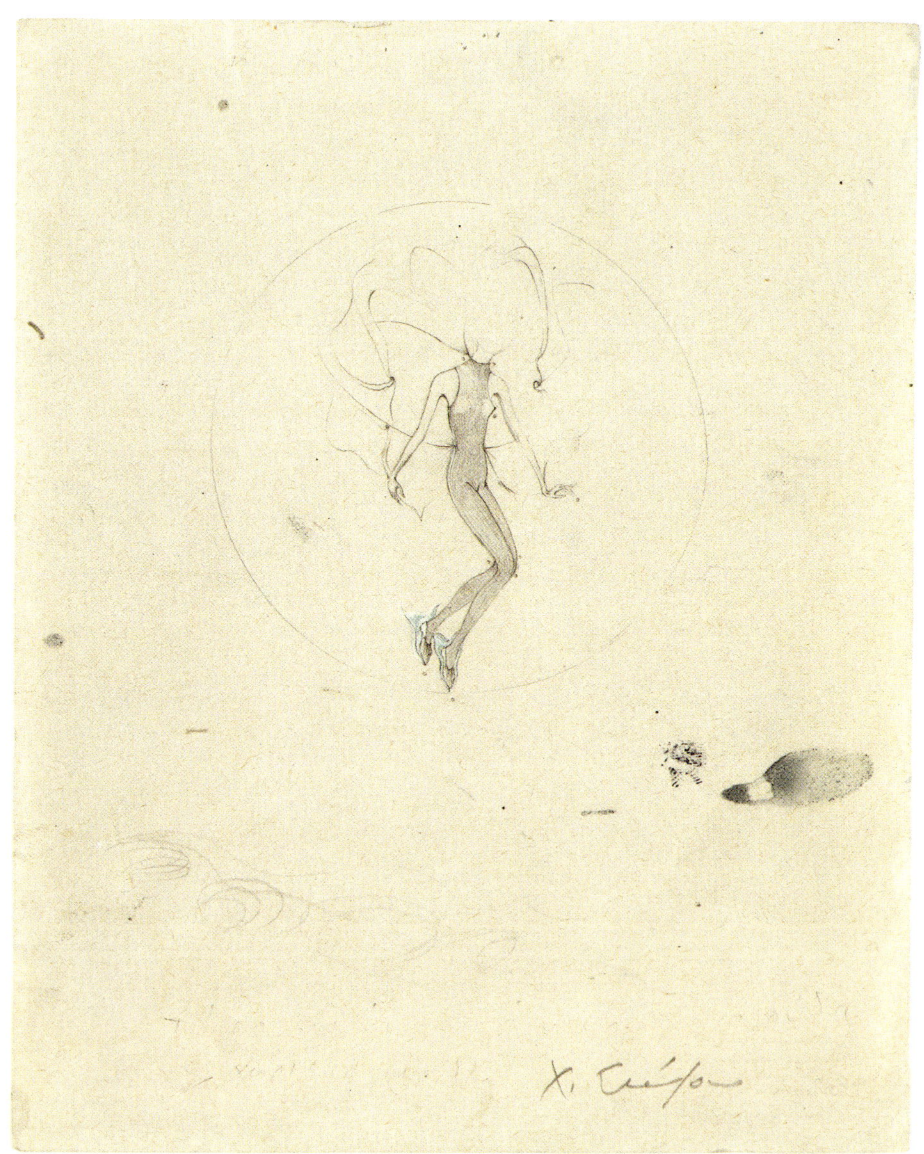

Untitled

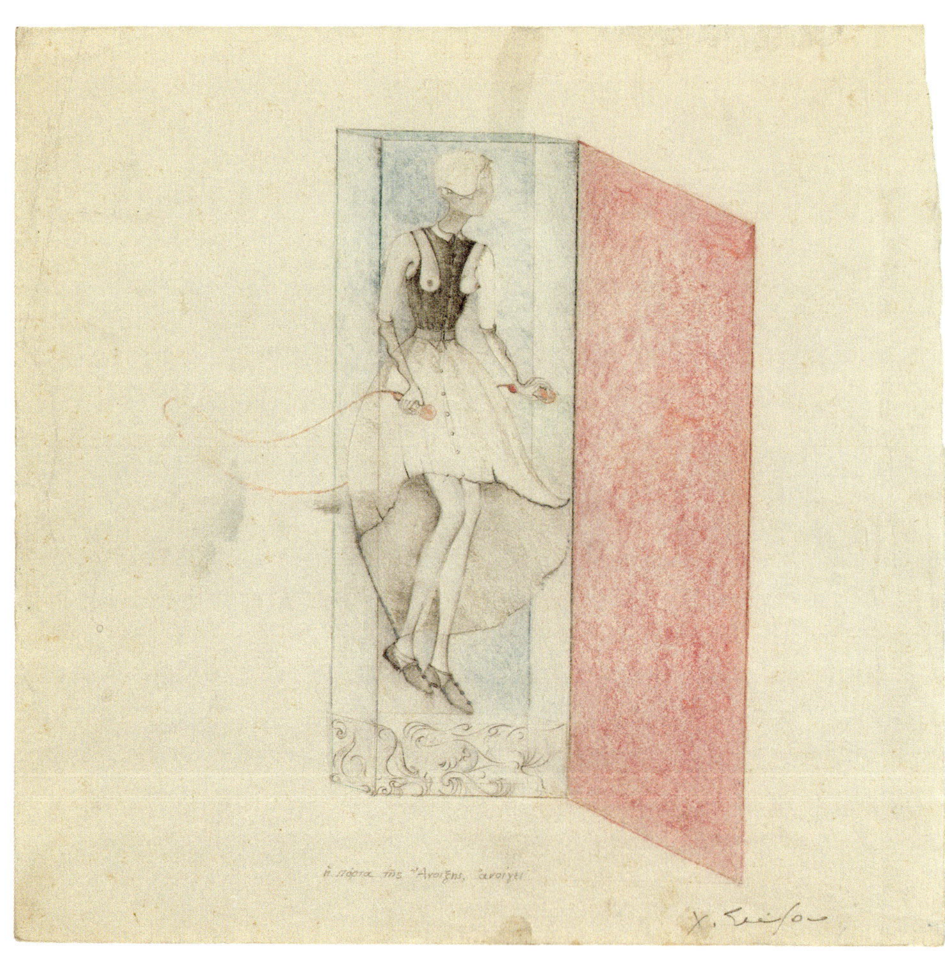

The Spring Doors Open

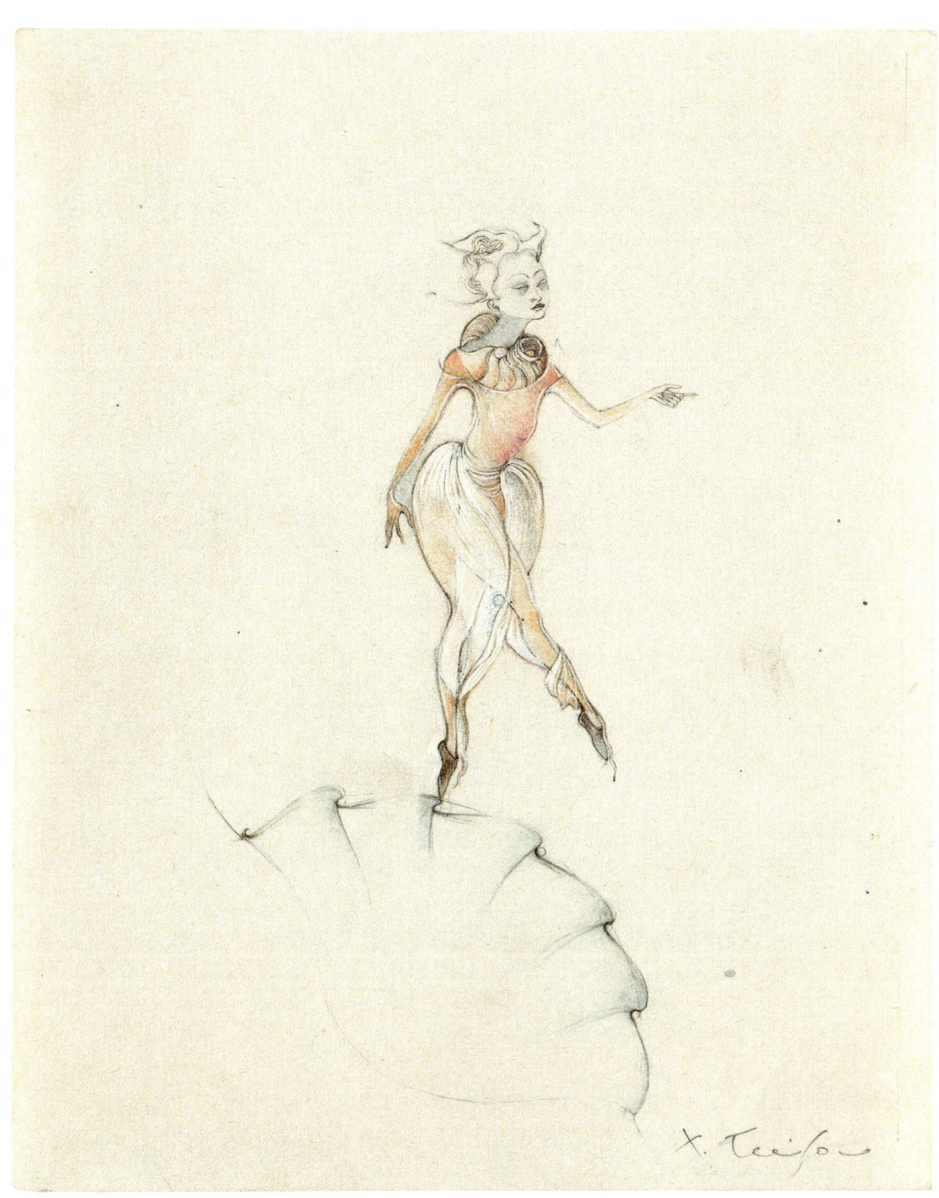

Untitled

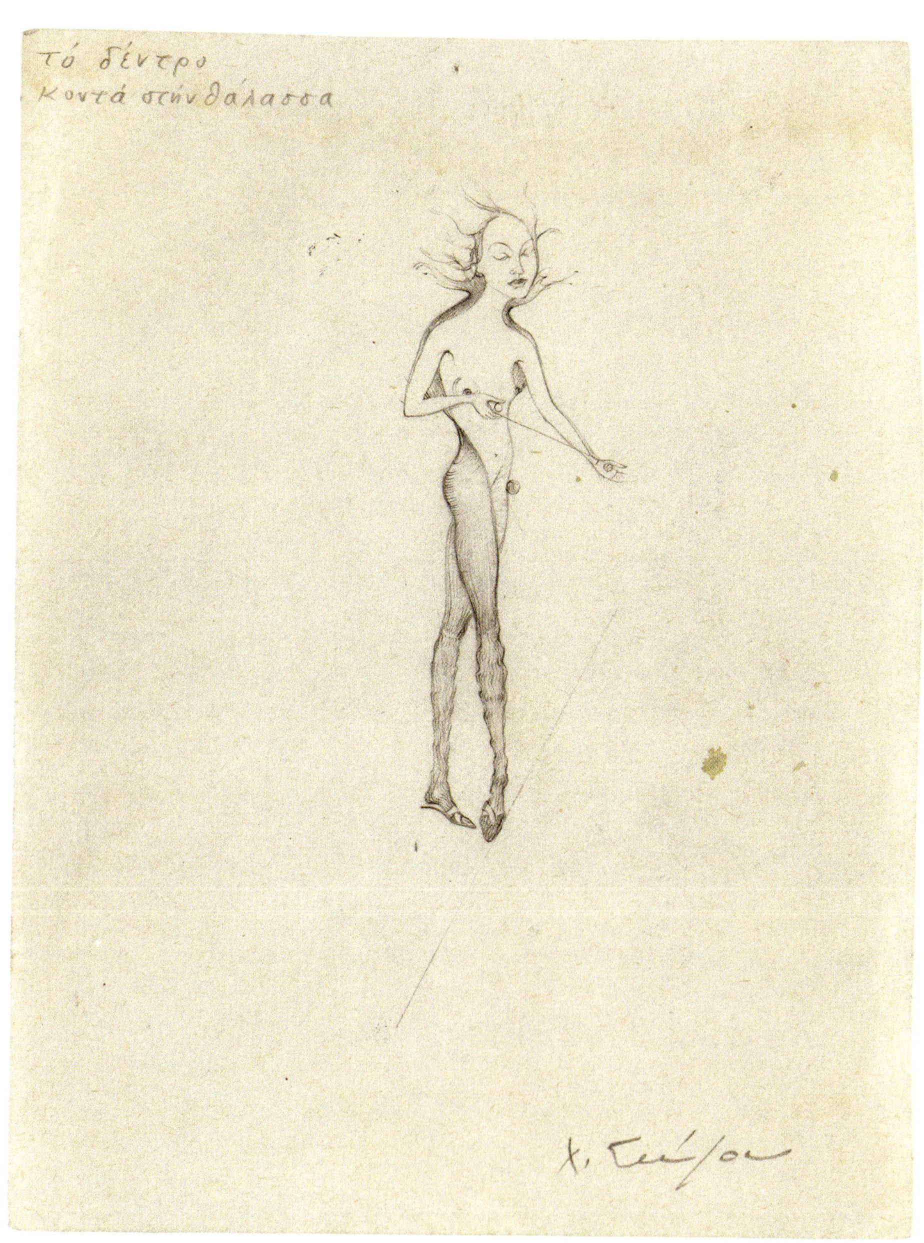

Reference to Lucas Cranach's Venus

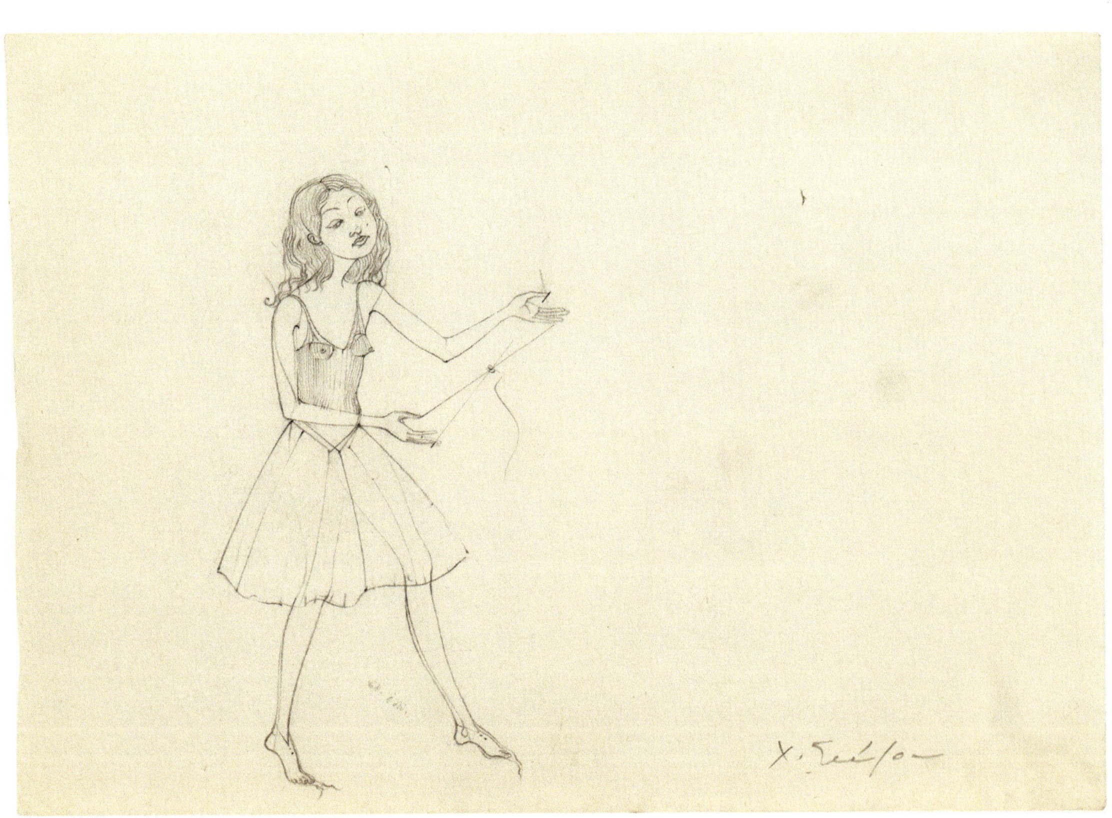

Untitled

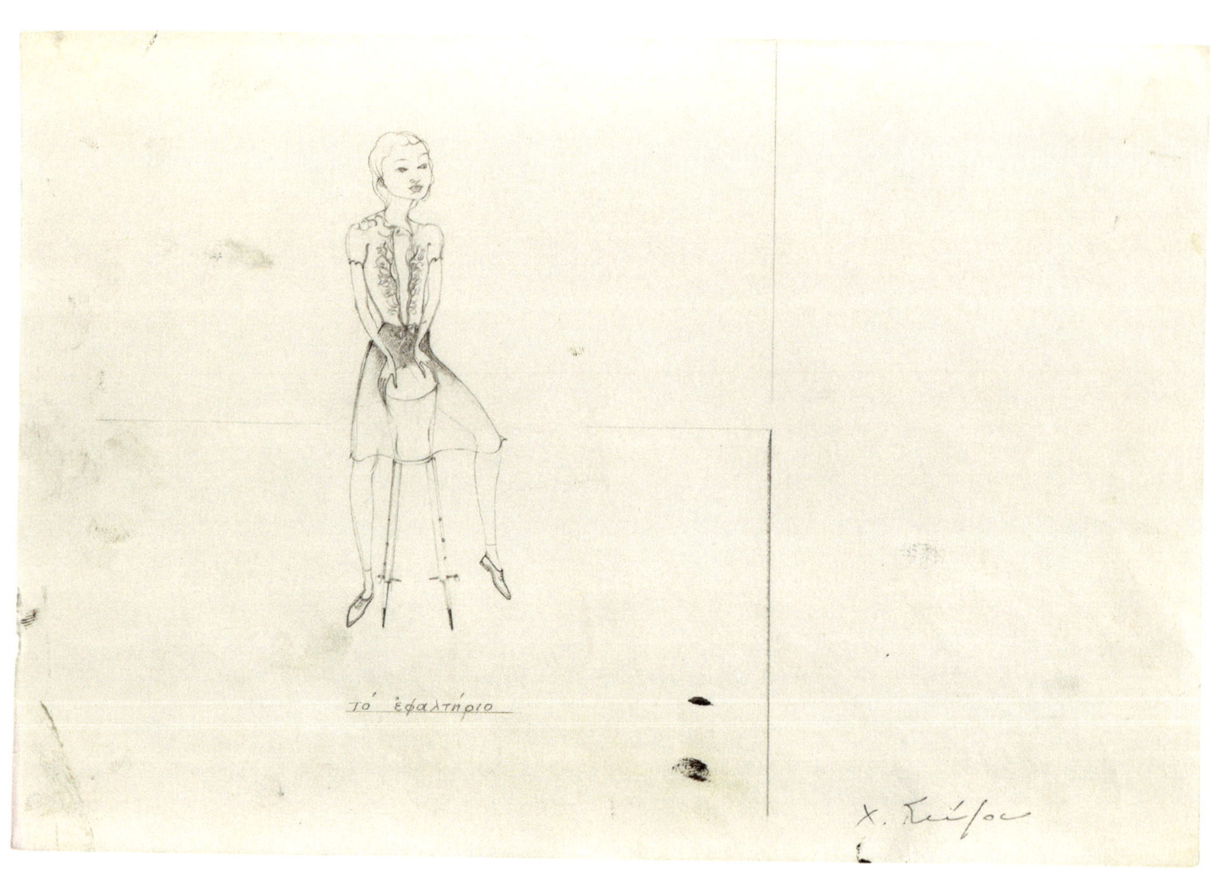

Τό ἐφαλτήριο

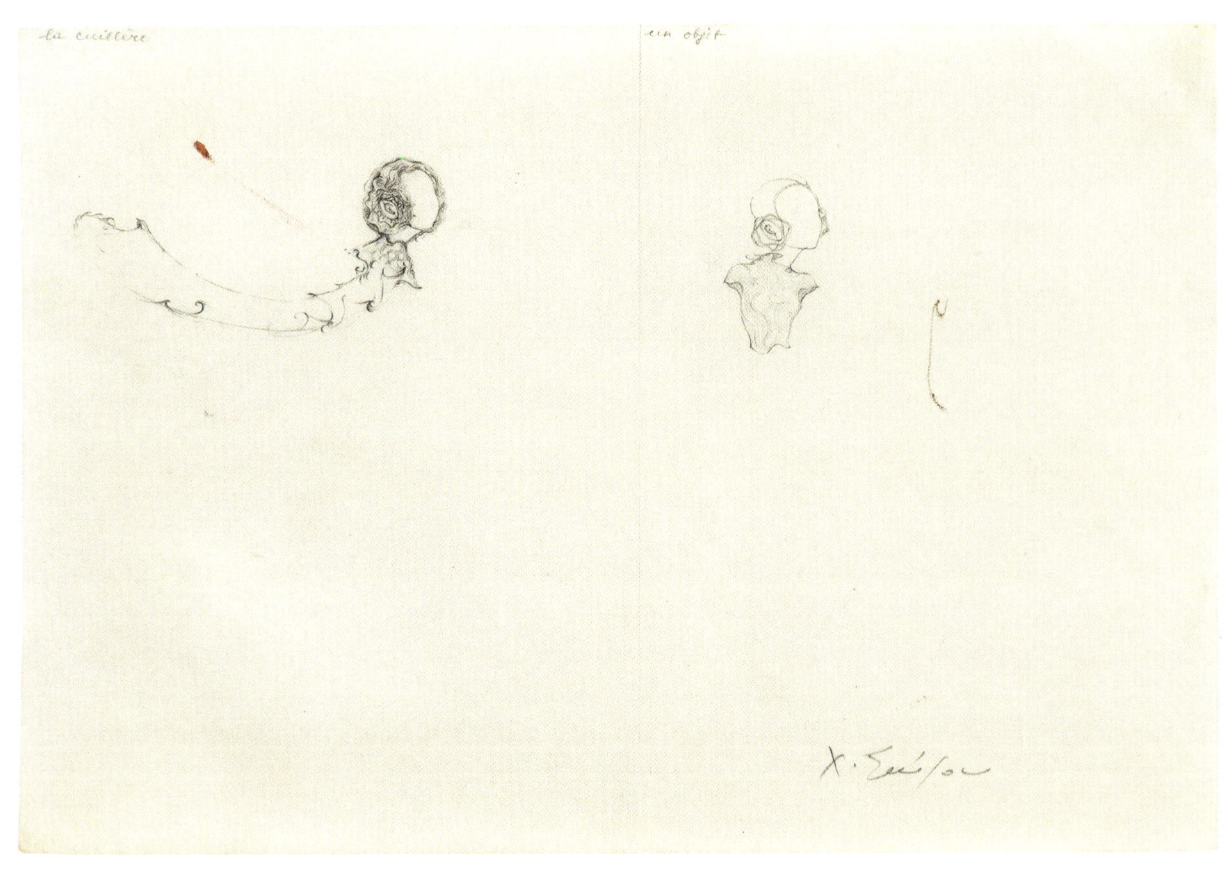

The Spoon, an Object

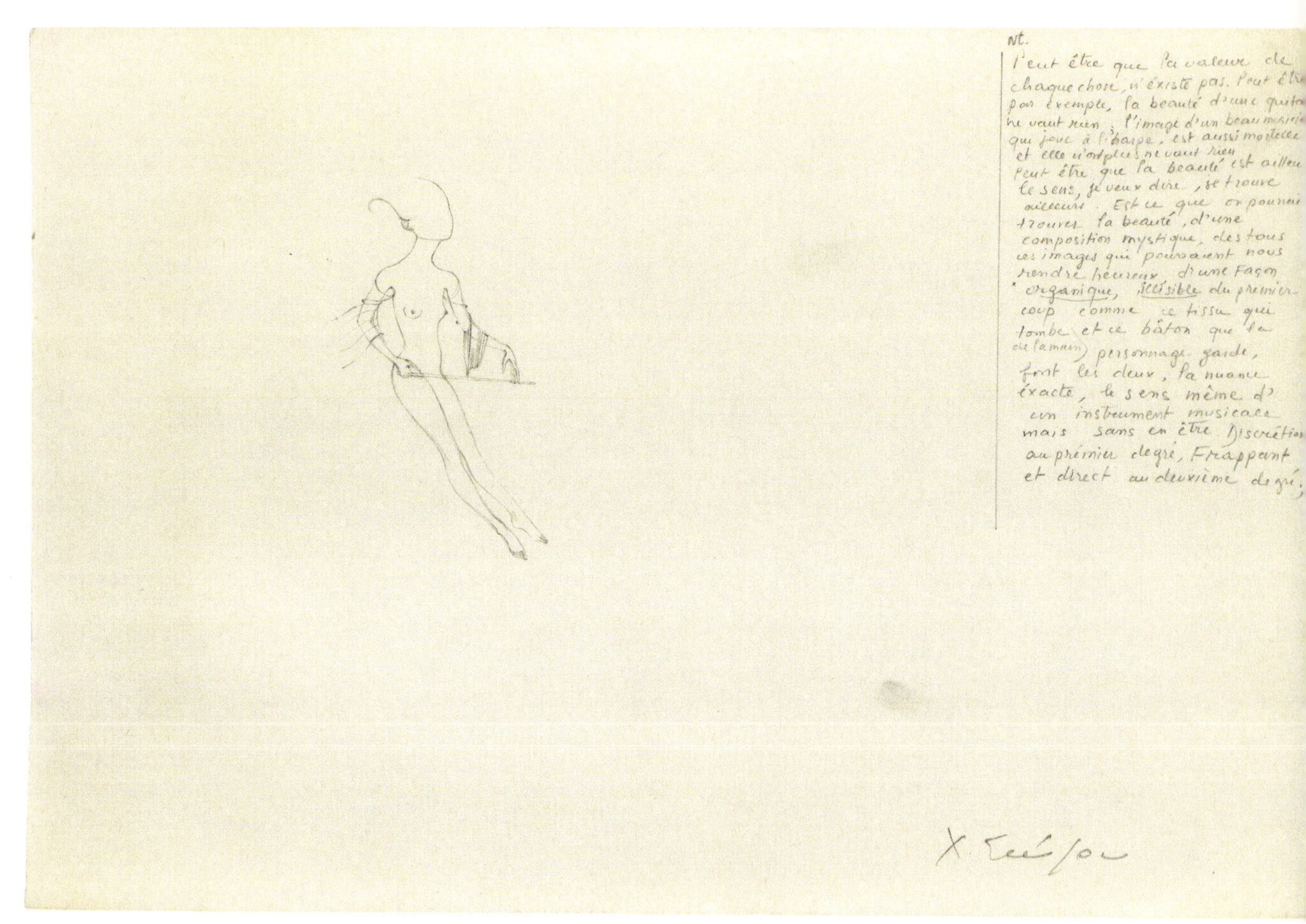

Nt.
Peut être que la valeur de
chaque chose, n'existe pas. Peut être
par exemple, la beauté d'une guitare
ne vaut rien, l'image d'un beau musicien
qui joue à l'harpe, est aussi mortelle
et elle n'ont plus ne vaut rien
peut être que la beauté est ailleurs
le sens, je veux dire, se trouve
ailleurs. Est ce que on pourrait
trouver la beauté, d'une
composition mystique, de tous
ces images qui pourraient nous
rendre heureux, d'une façon
organique, illisible du premier
coup comme ce tissu qui
tombe et ce bâton que la
(de la main) personnage garde,
font les deux, la nuance
exacte, le sens même d'
un instrument musical
mais sans en être Discrétion
au premier degré, Frappant
et direct au deuxième degré;

Untitled

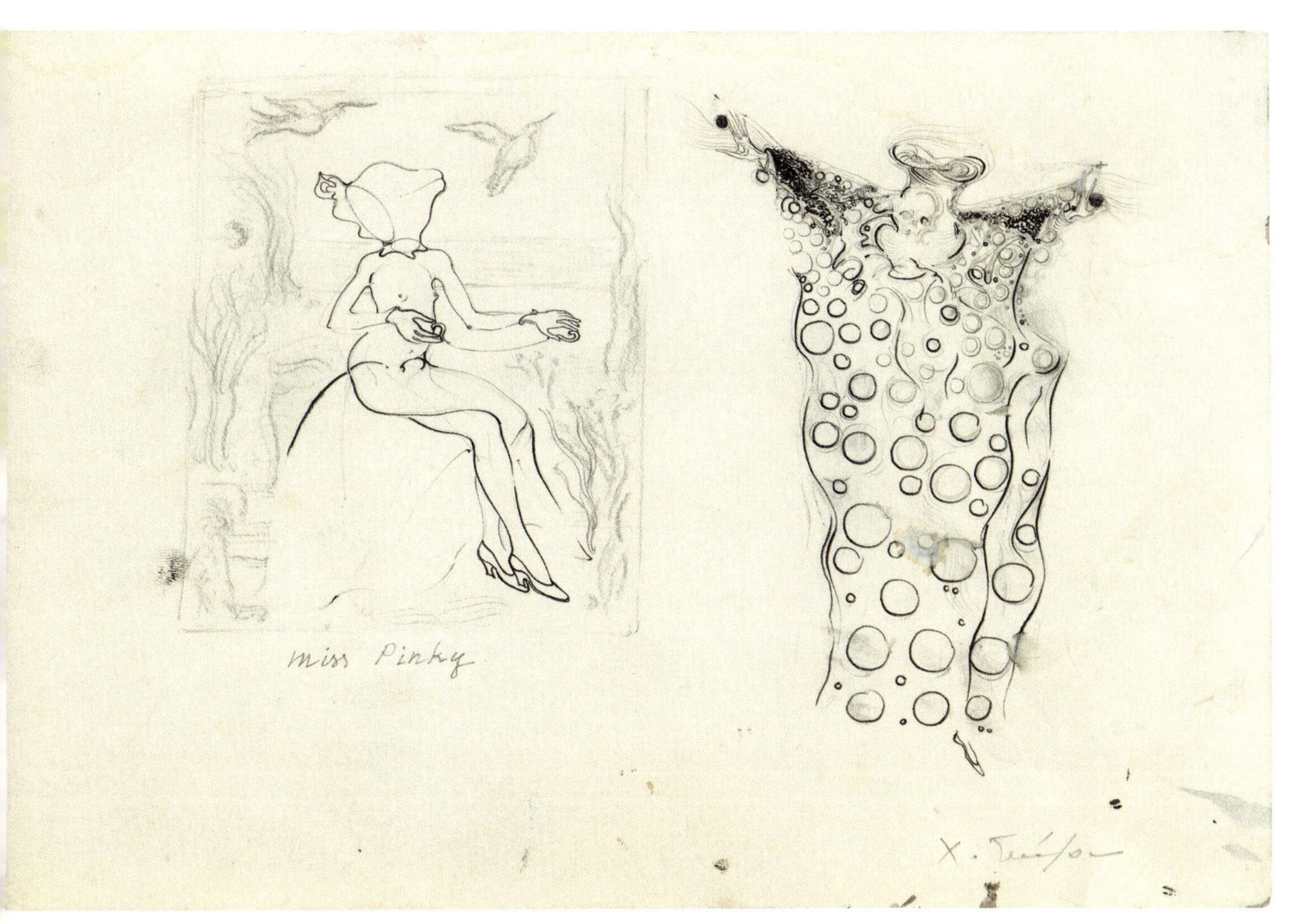

Untitled

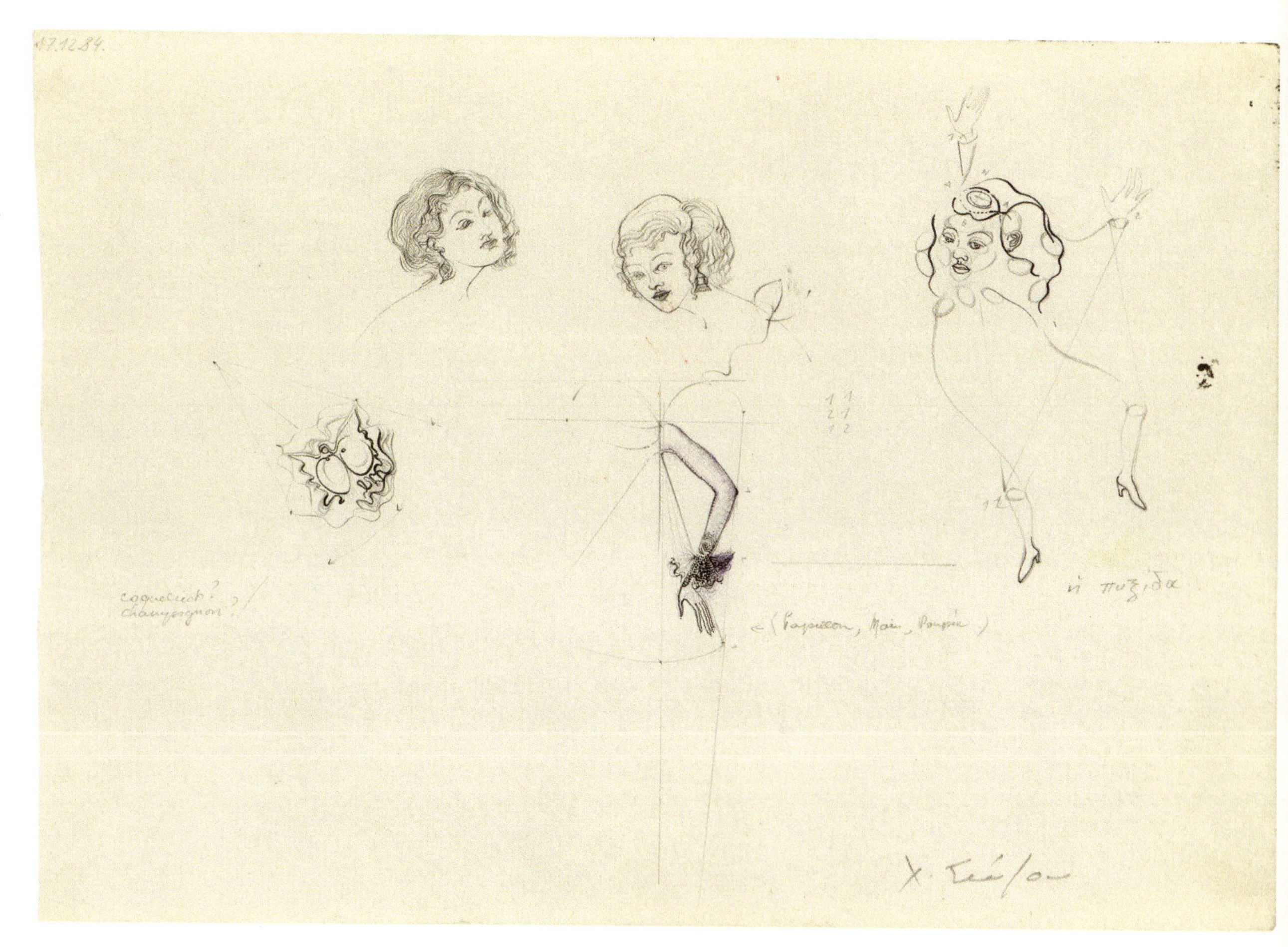

1. Poppy or Mushroom, 2. Butterfly, Hand, Doll, 3. Compass

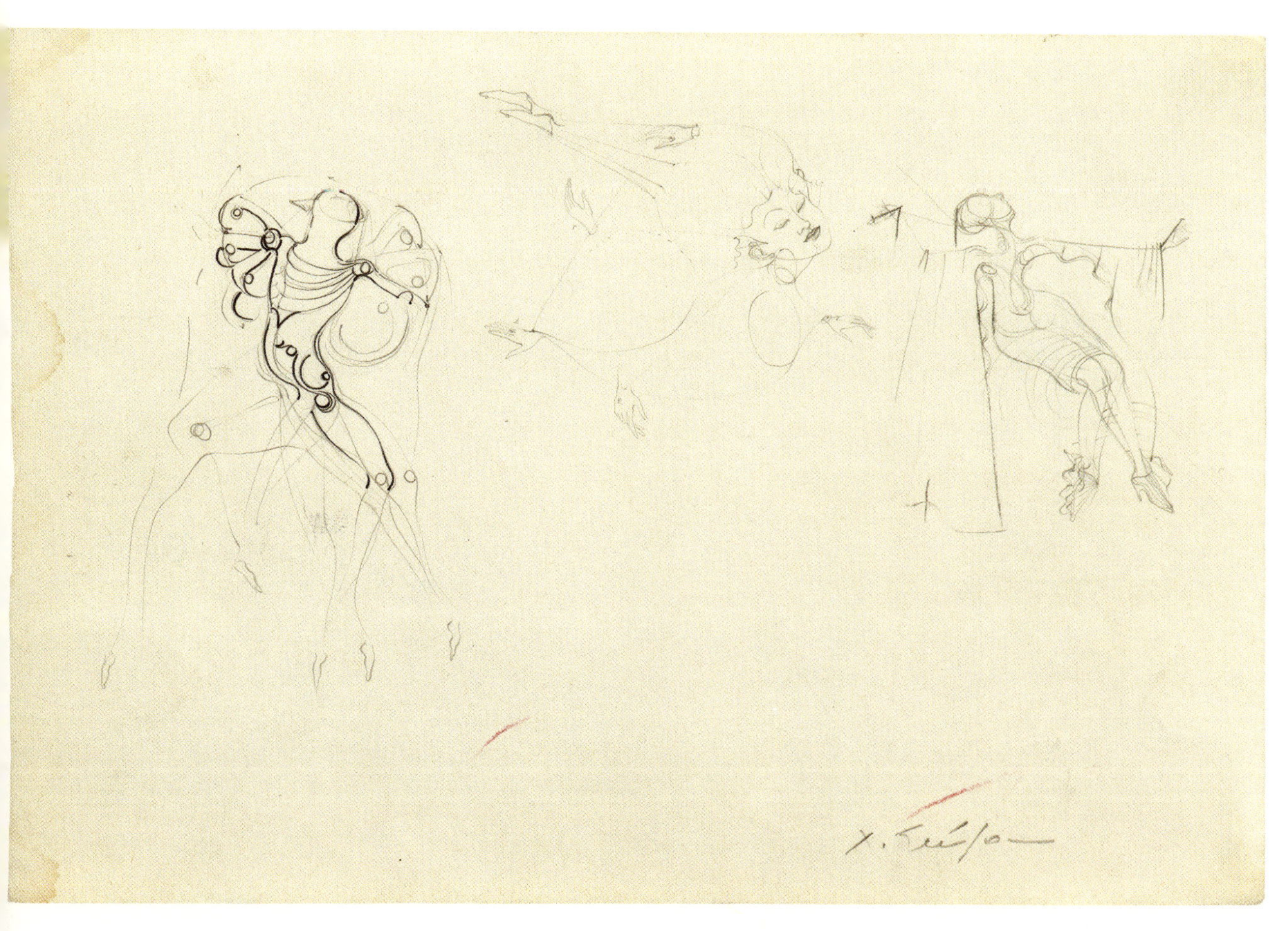

Untitled

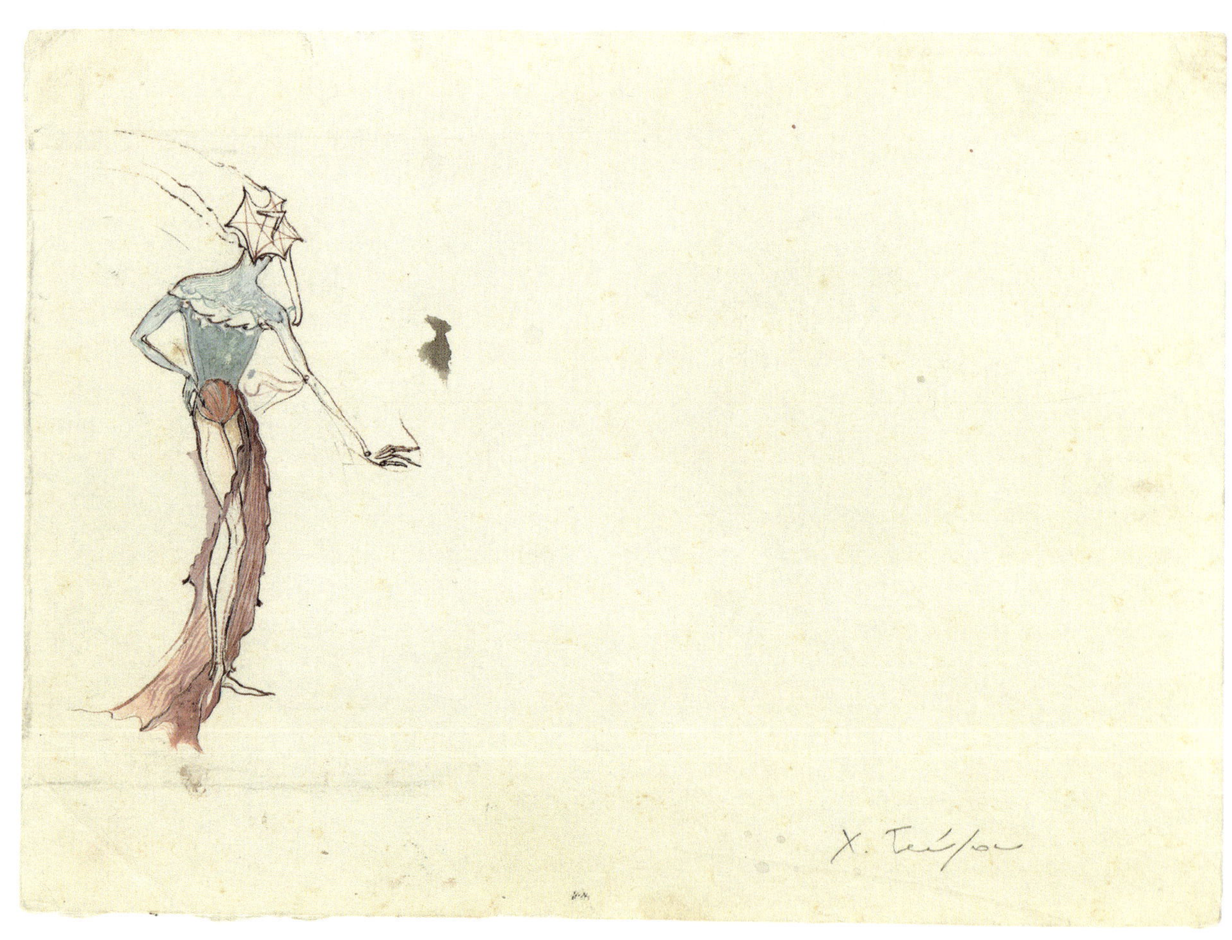

Untitled

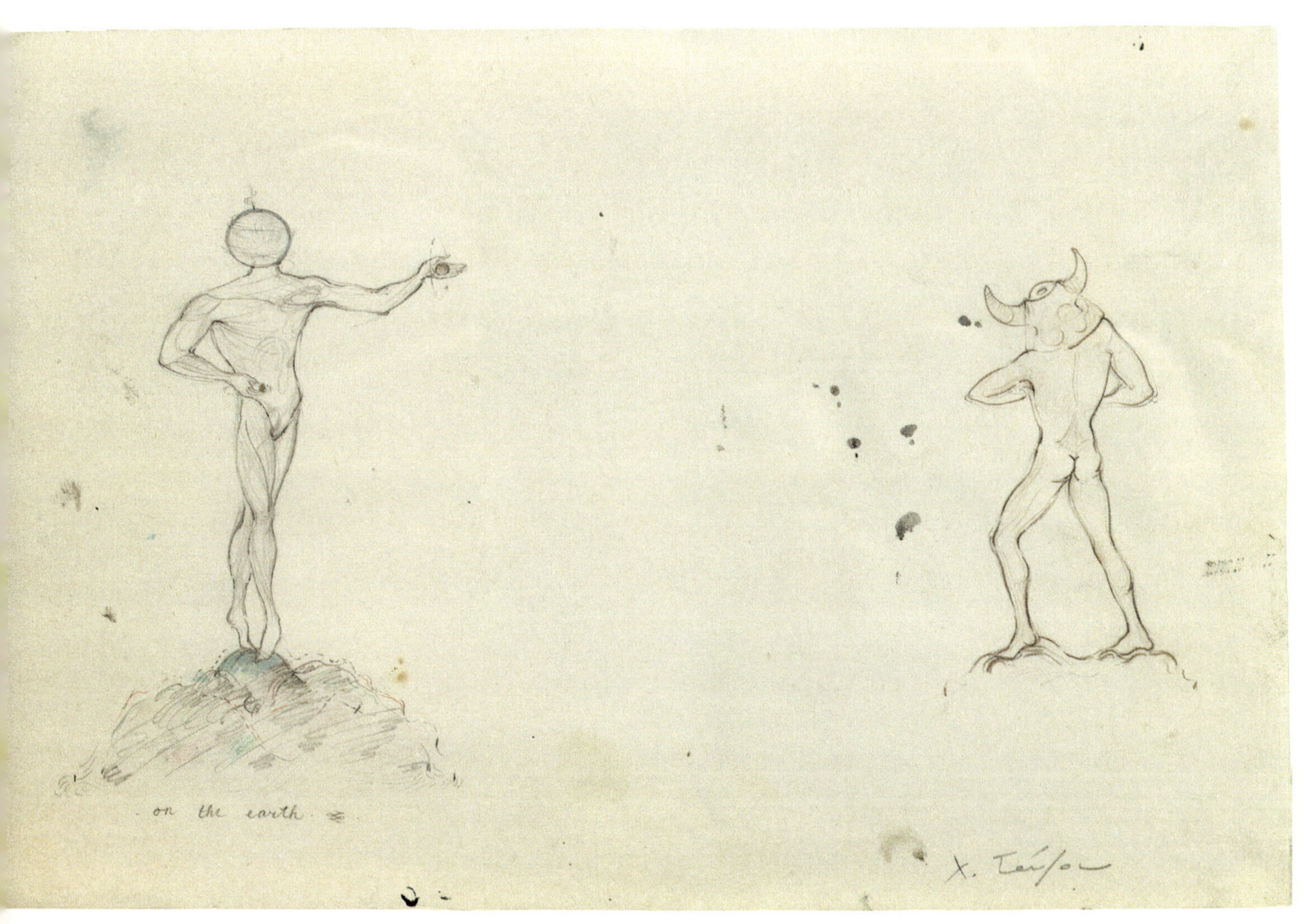

Untitled

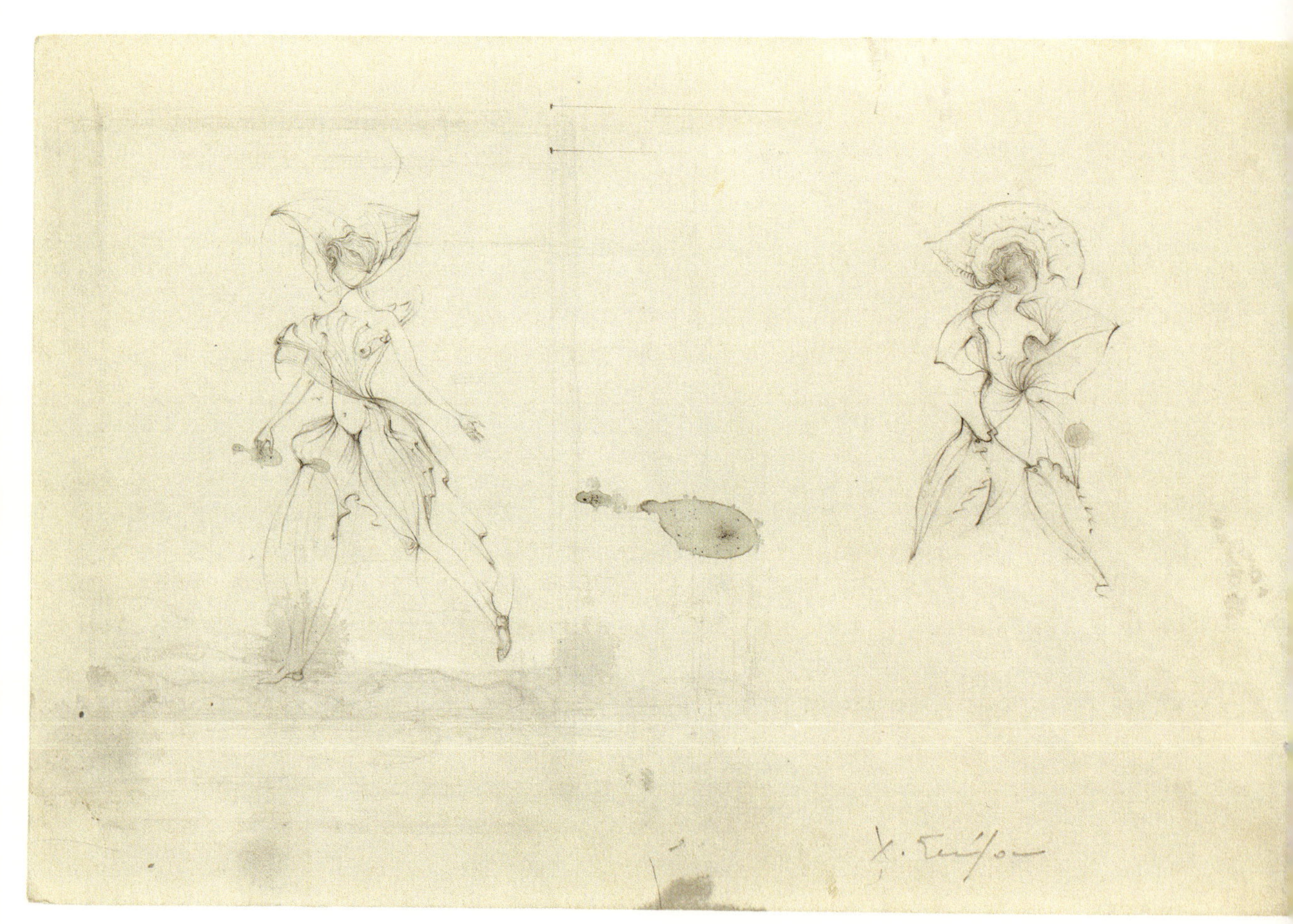

Untitled

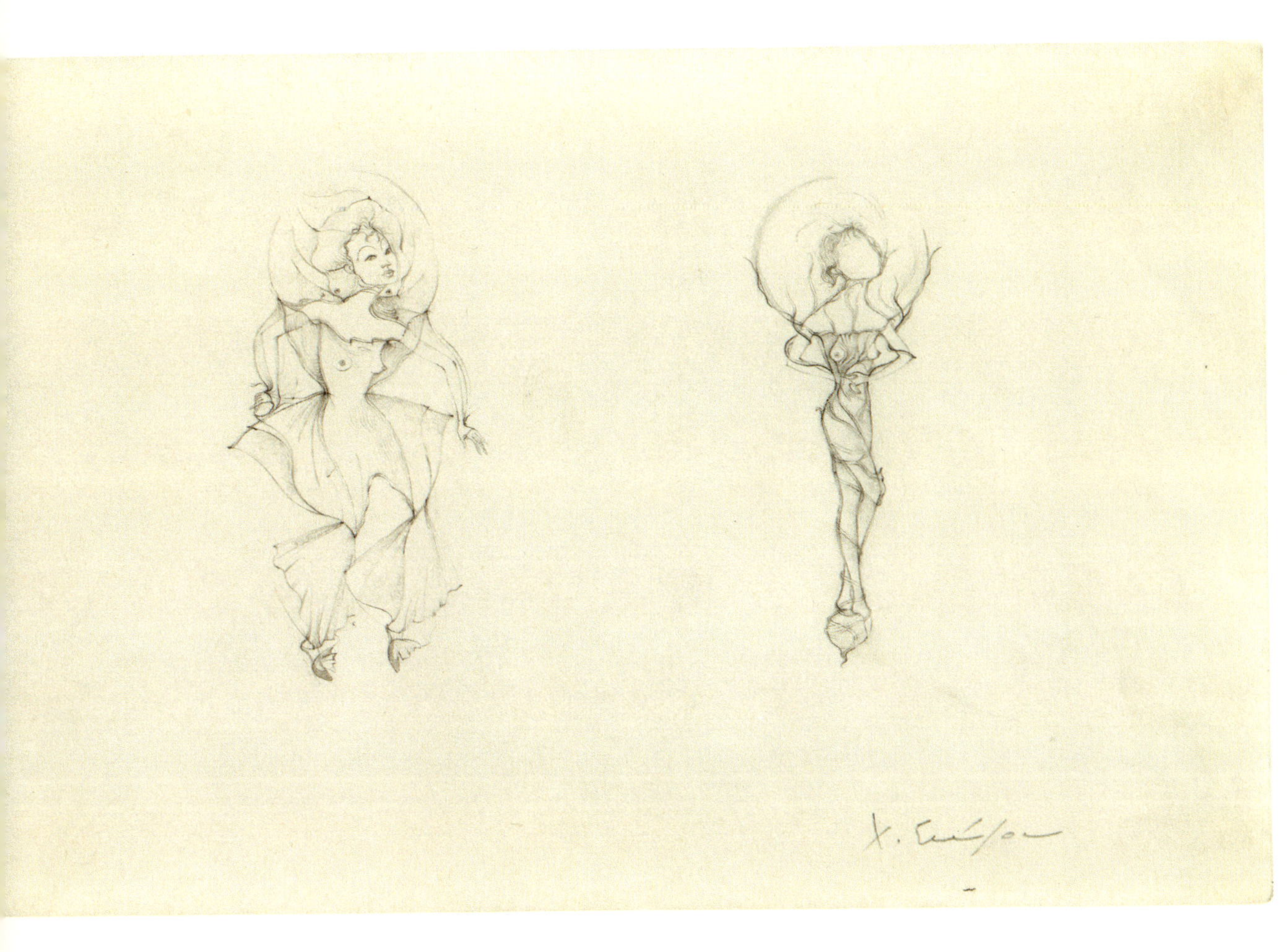

Untitled

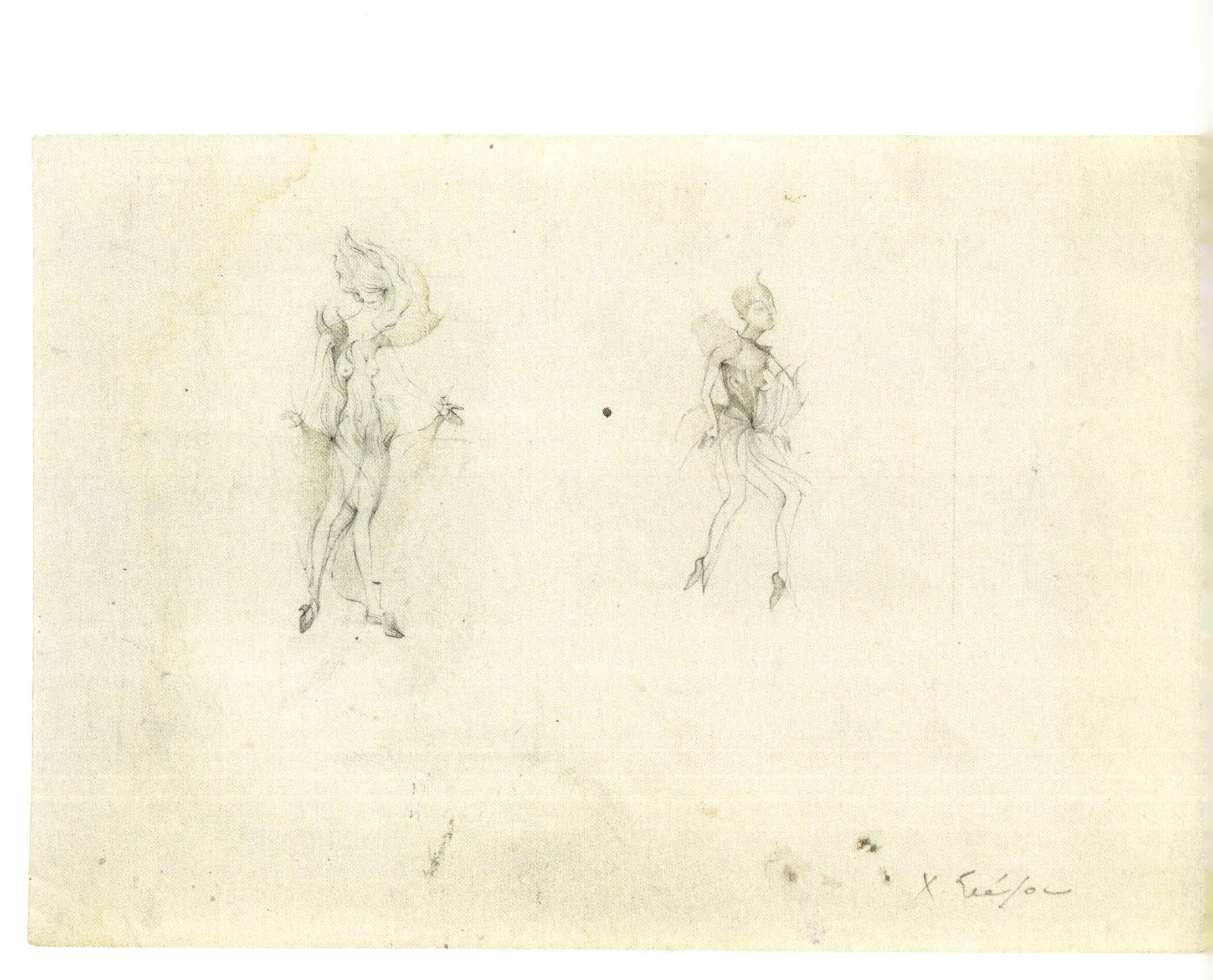

Untitled

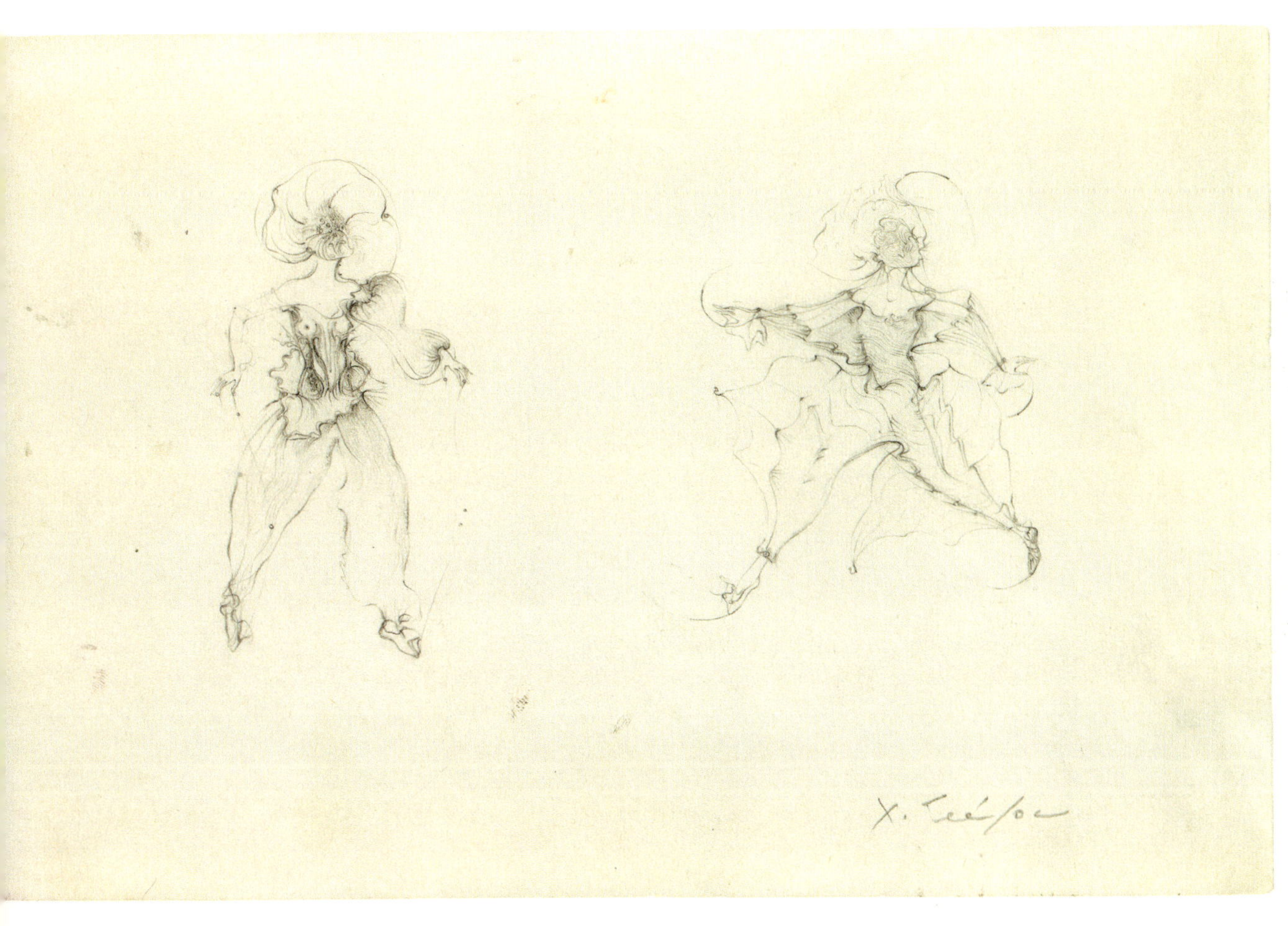

Untitled

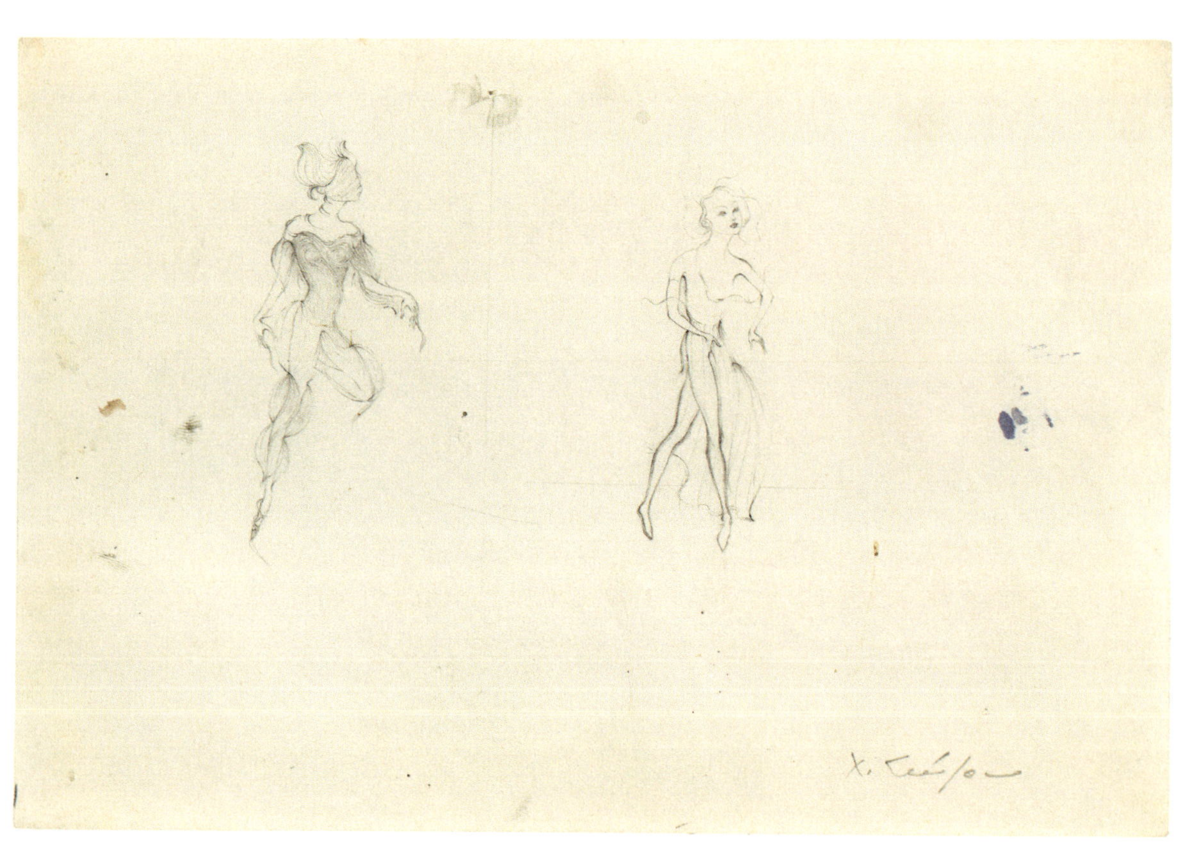

Untitled

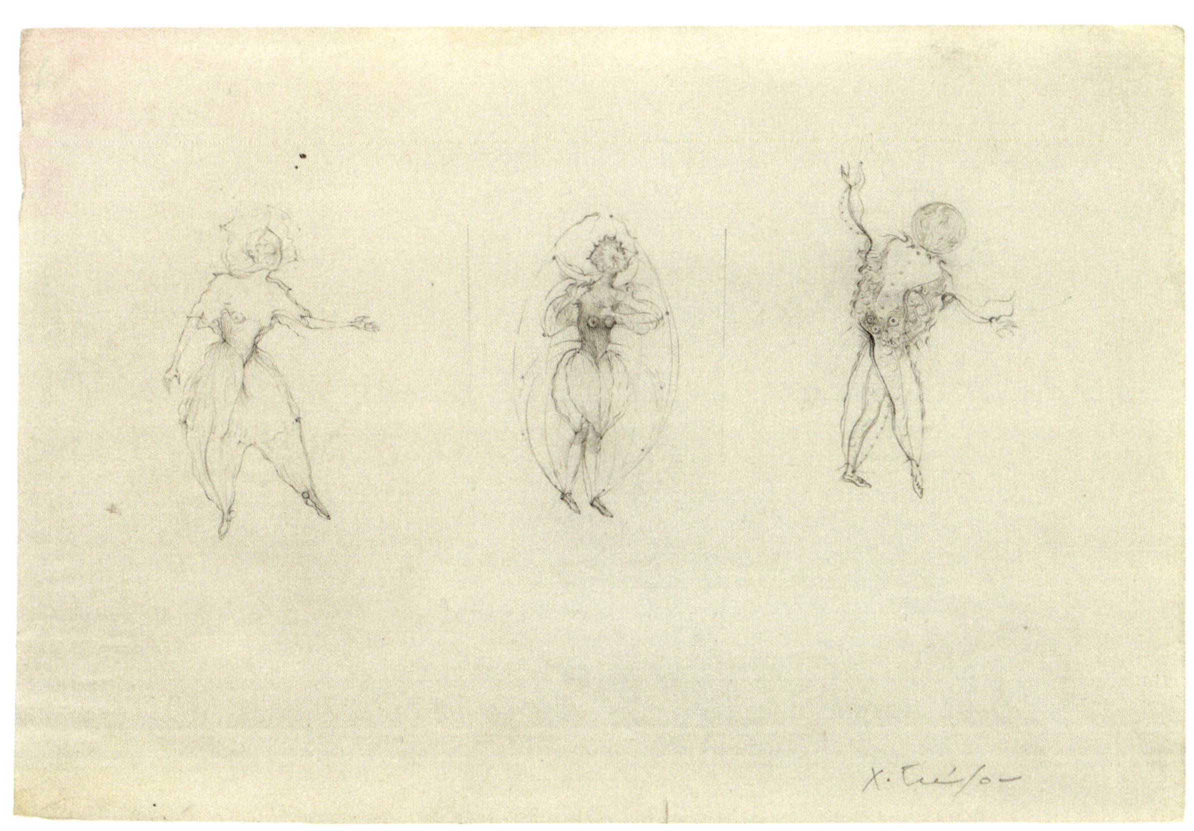

Untitled

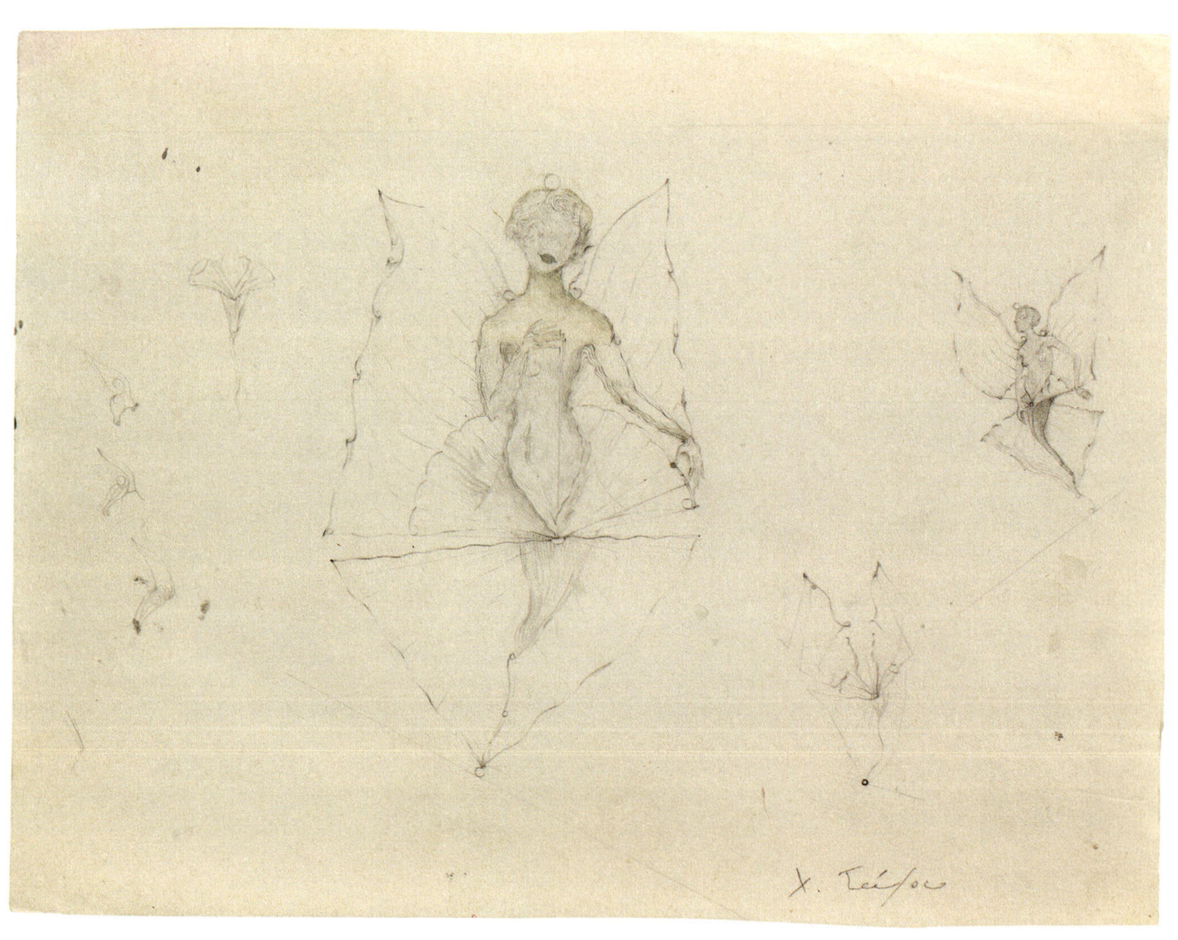

Untitled

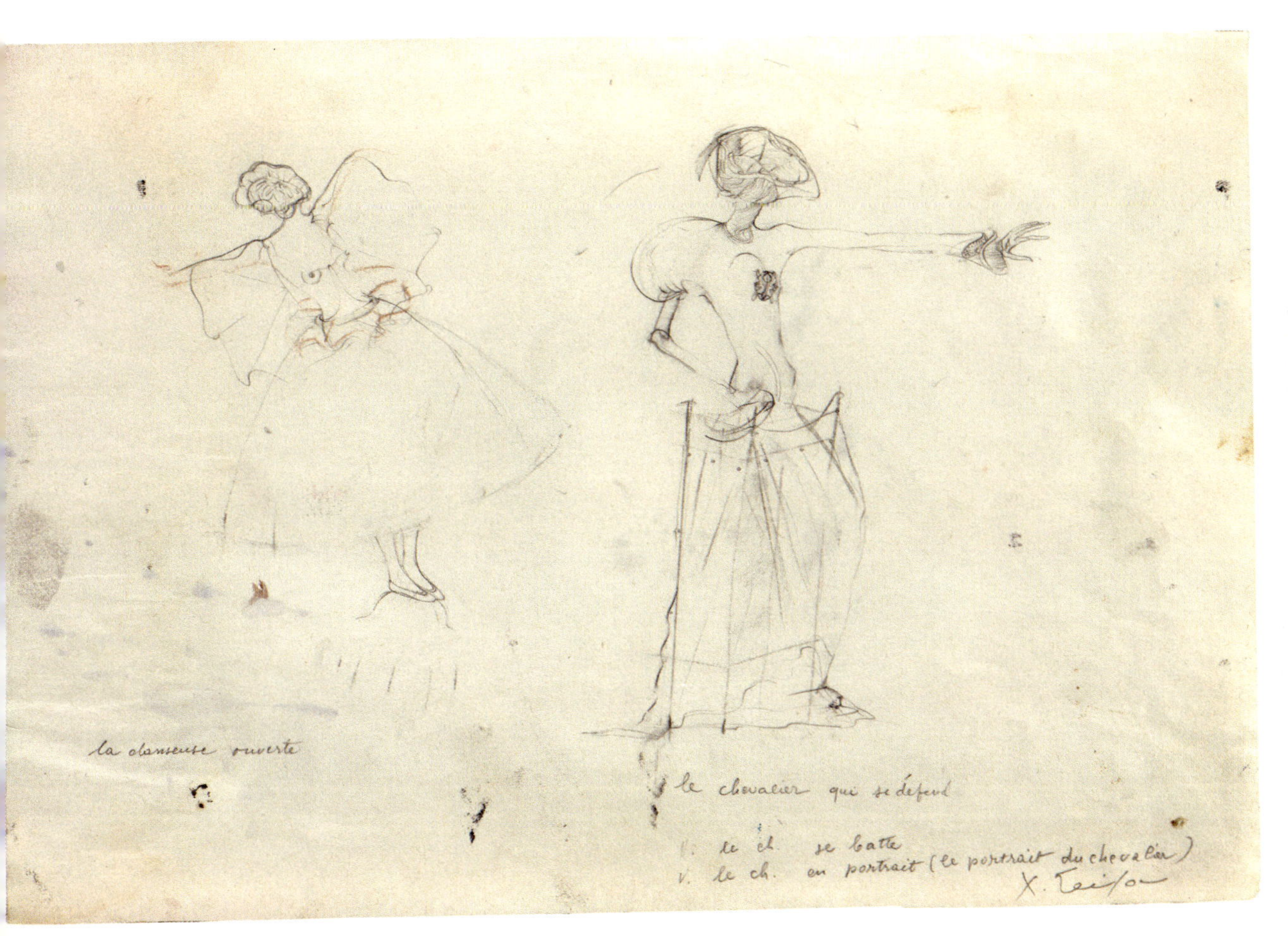

The Open Dancer, the Knight

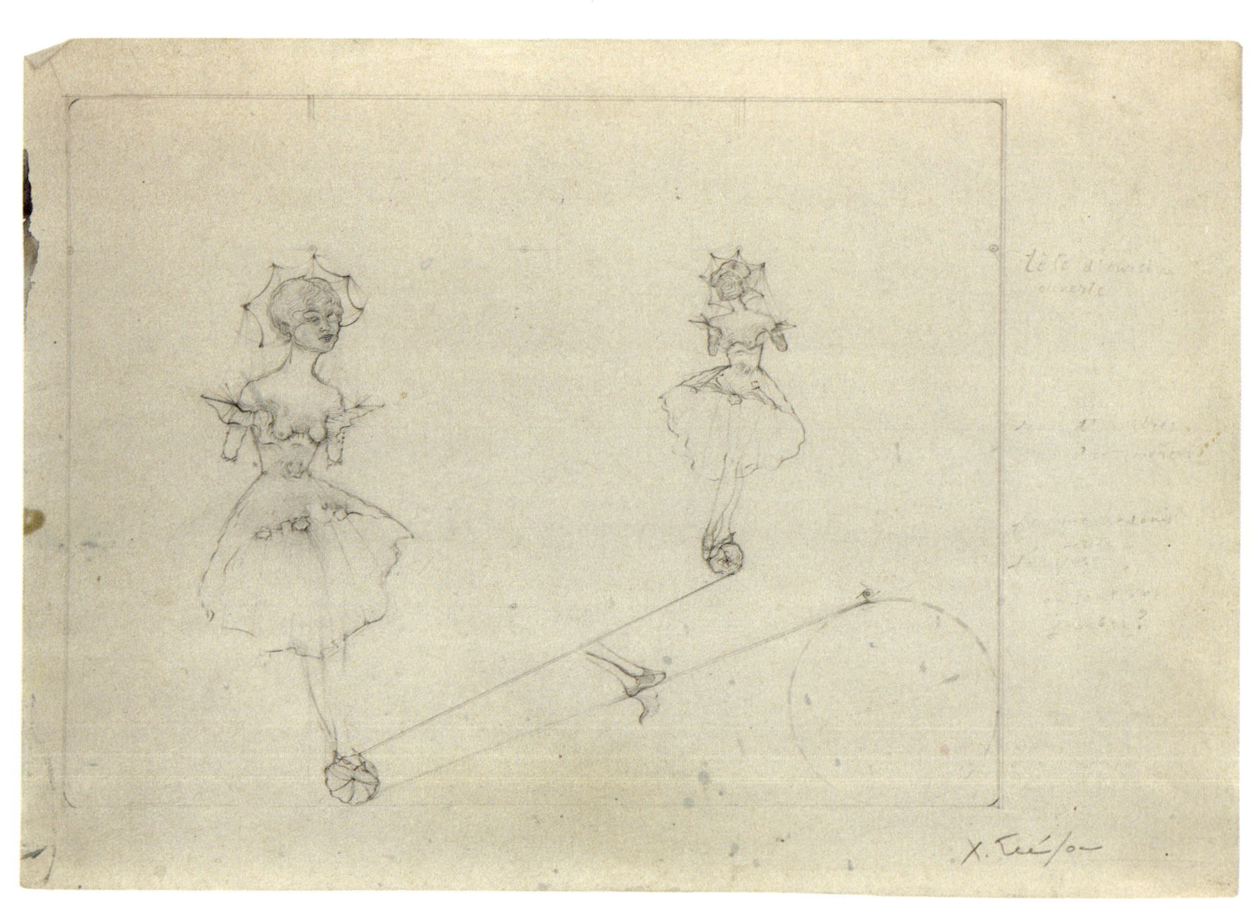

Gorgo (Gargoyle Mermaid)

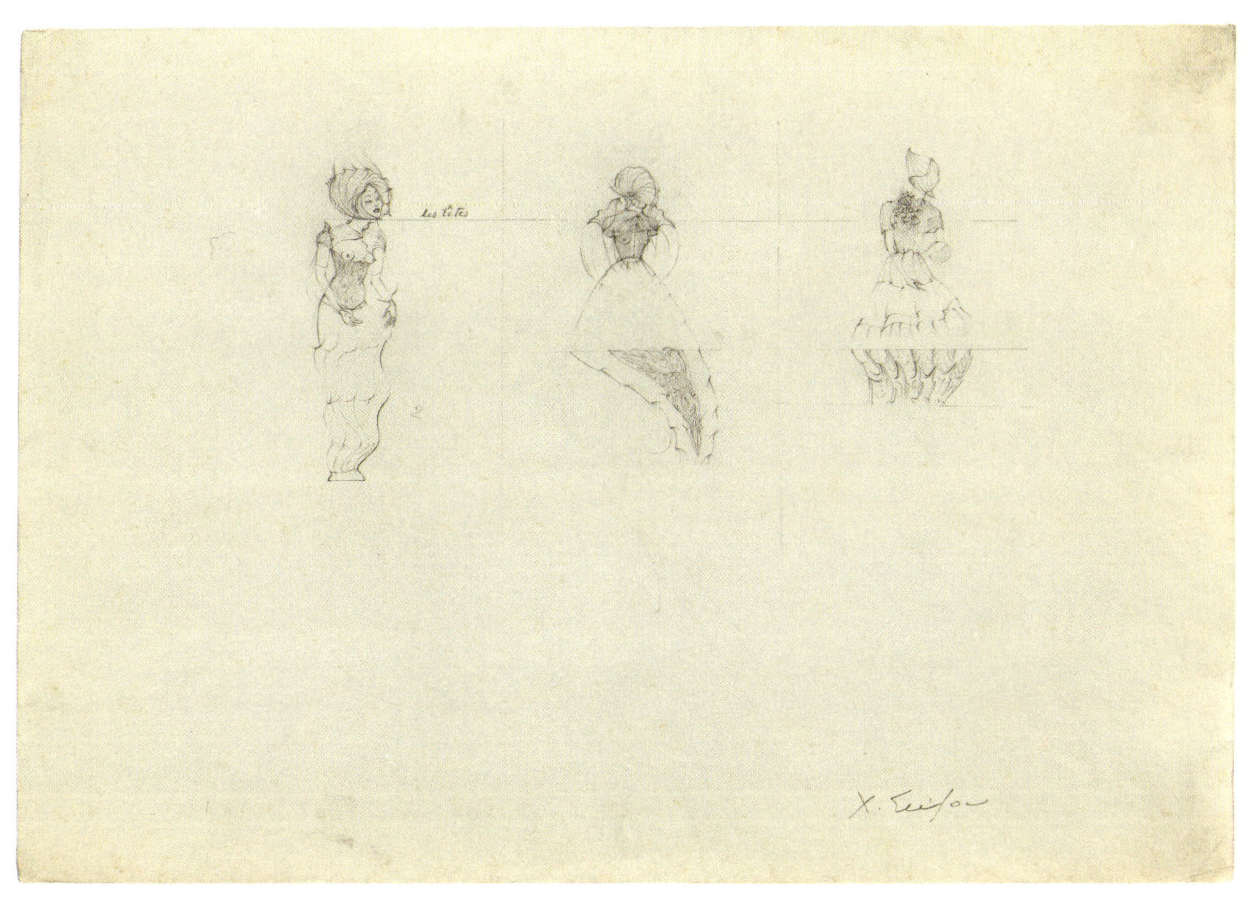

Untitled

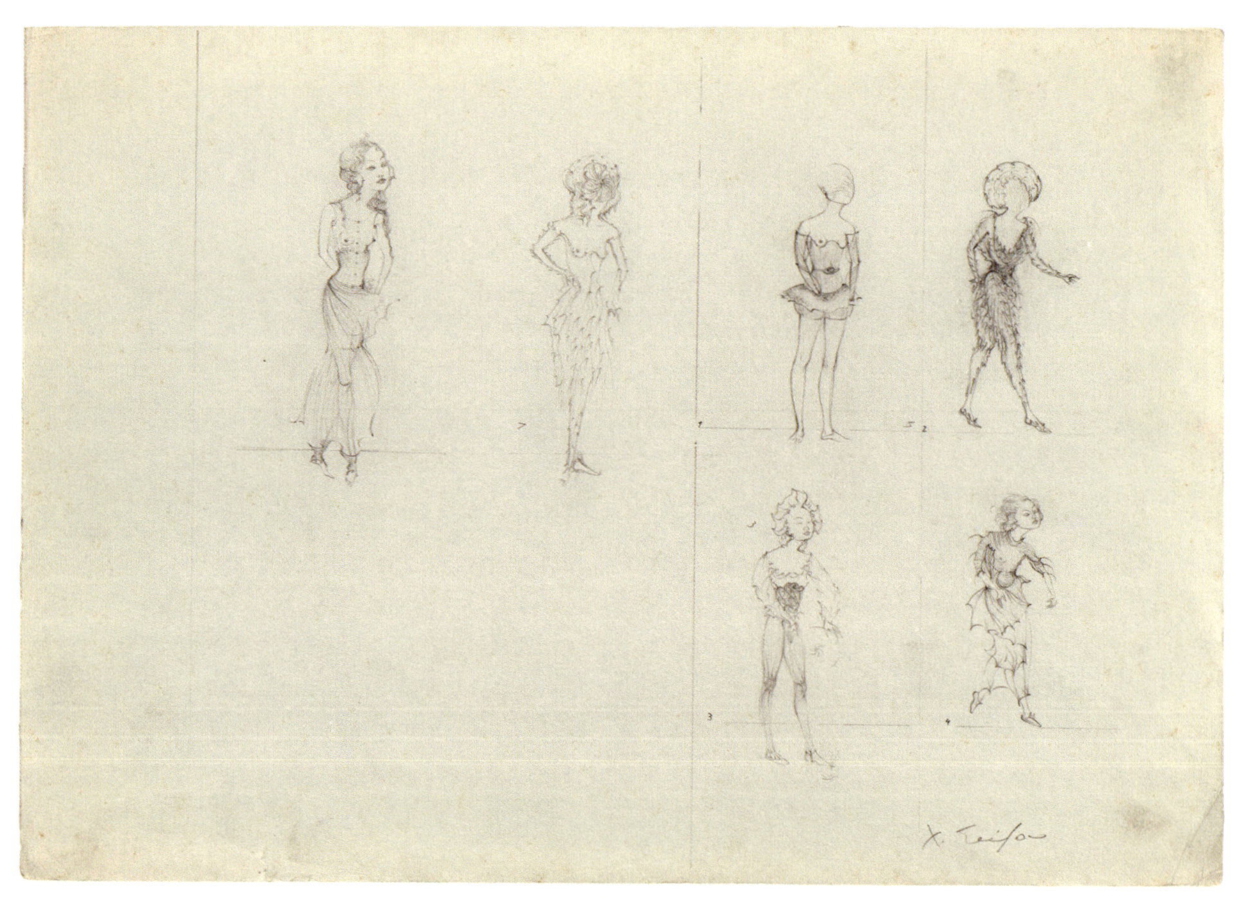

Untitled

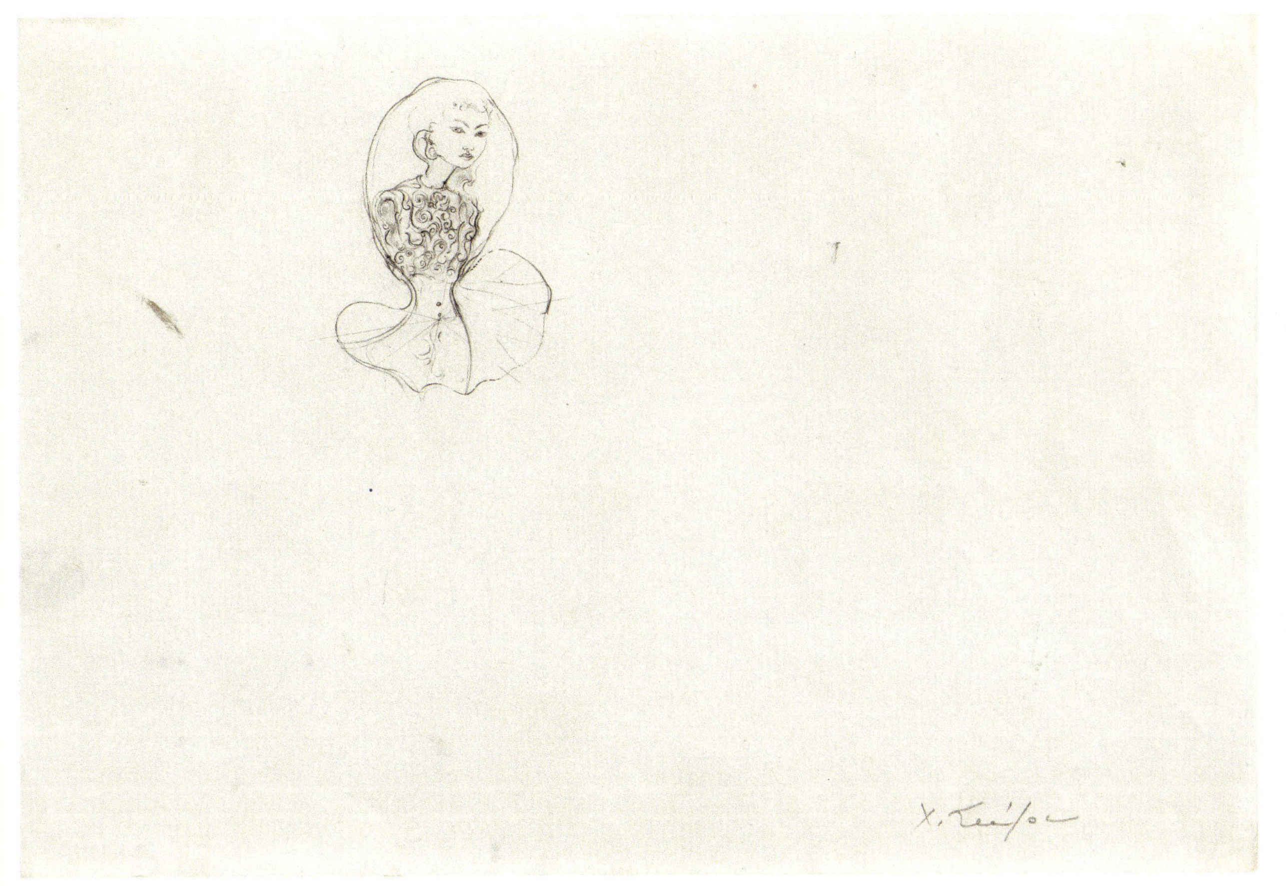

Untitled

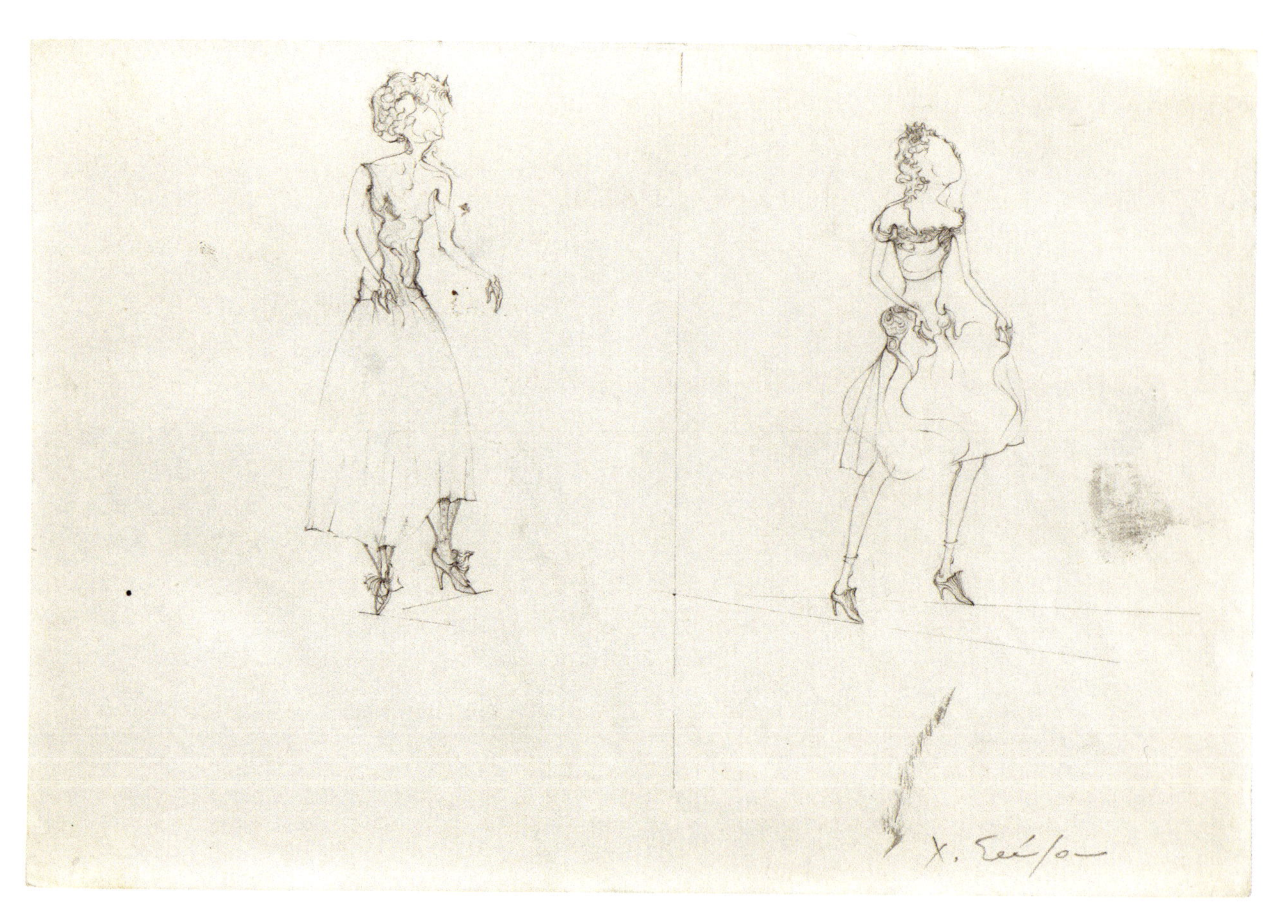

Untitled

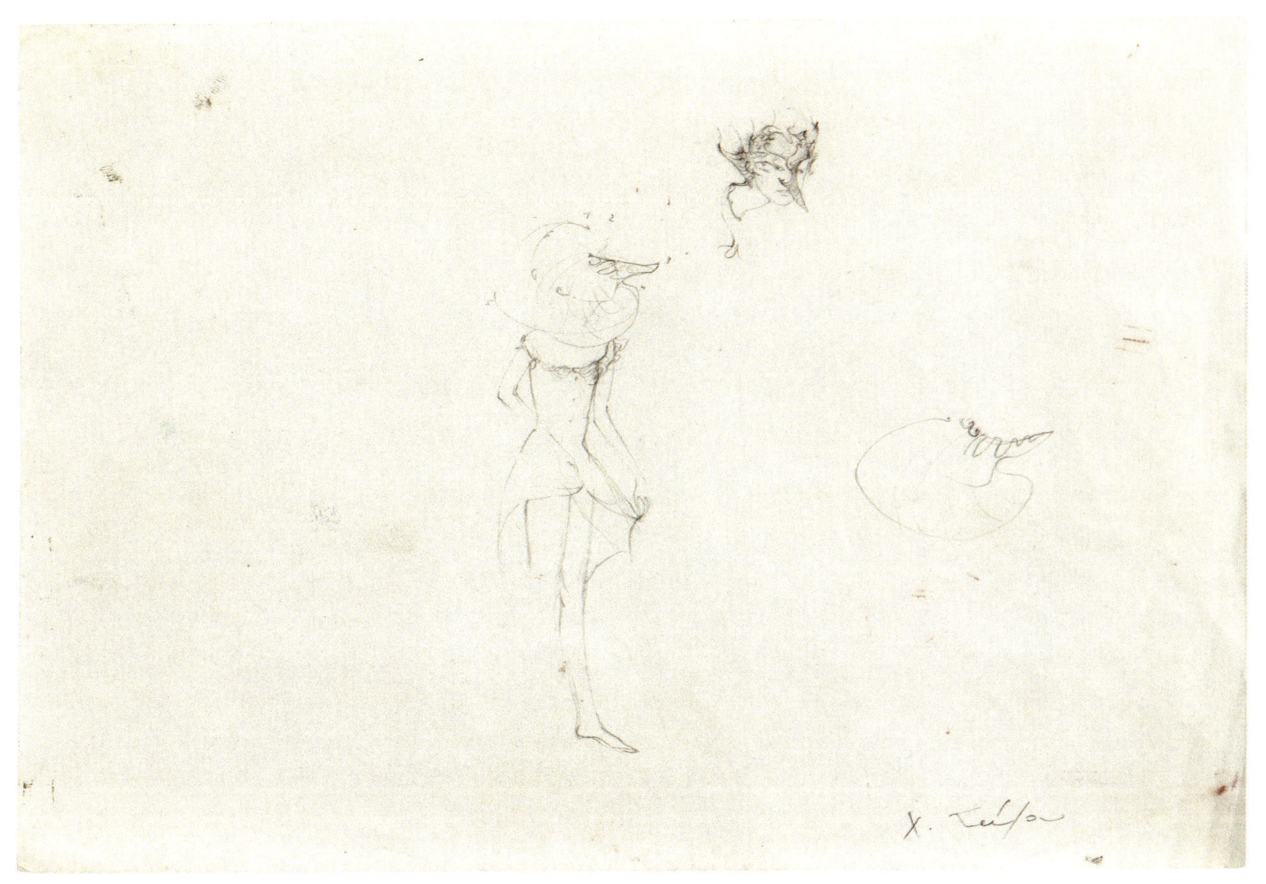

Untitled

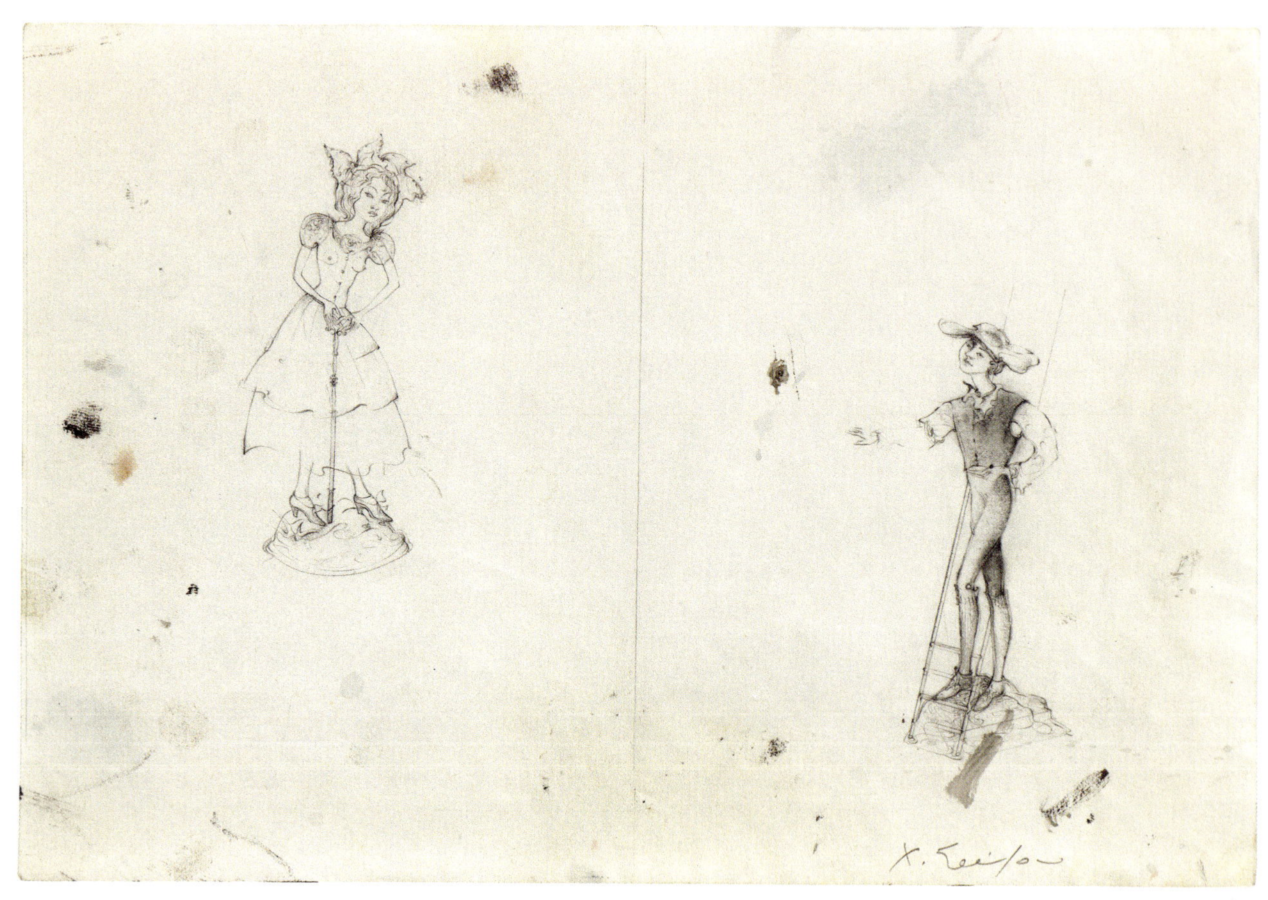

Untitled

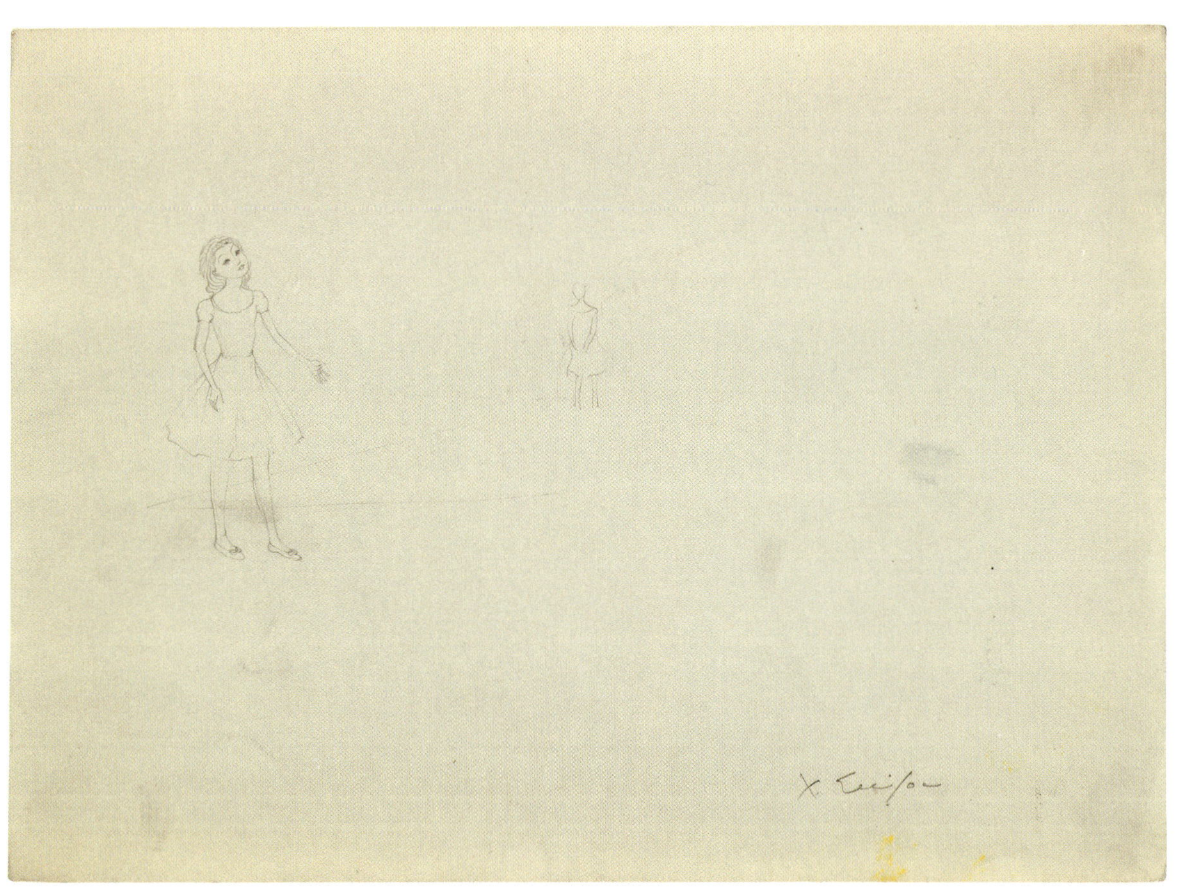

Untitled

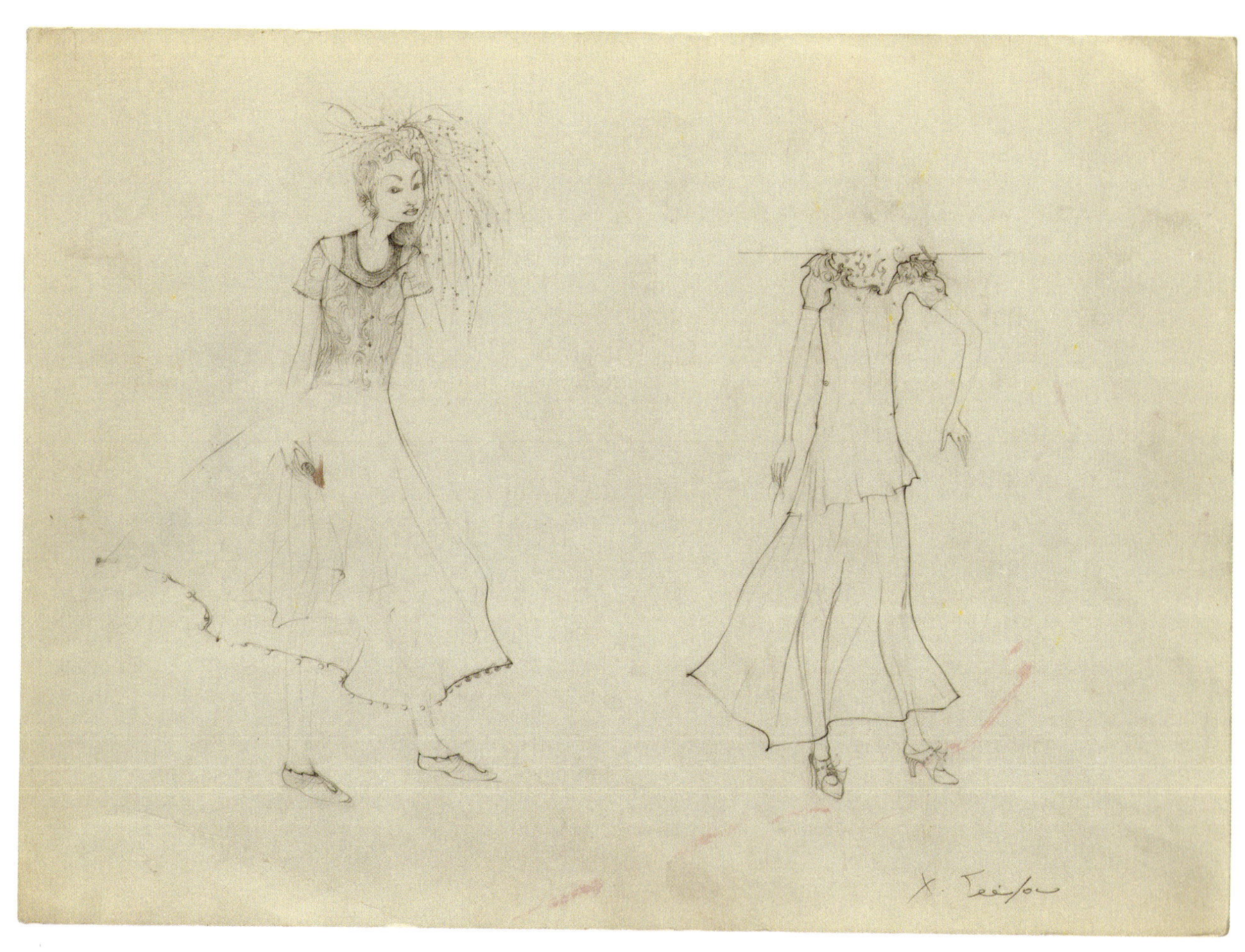

Untitled

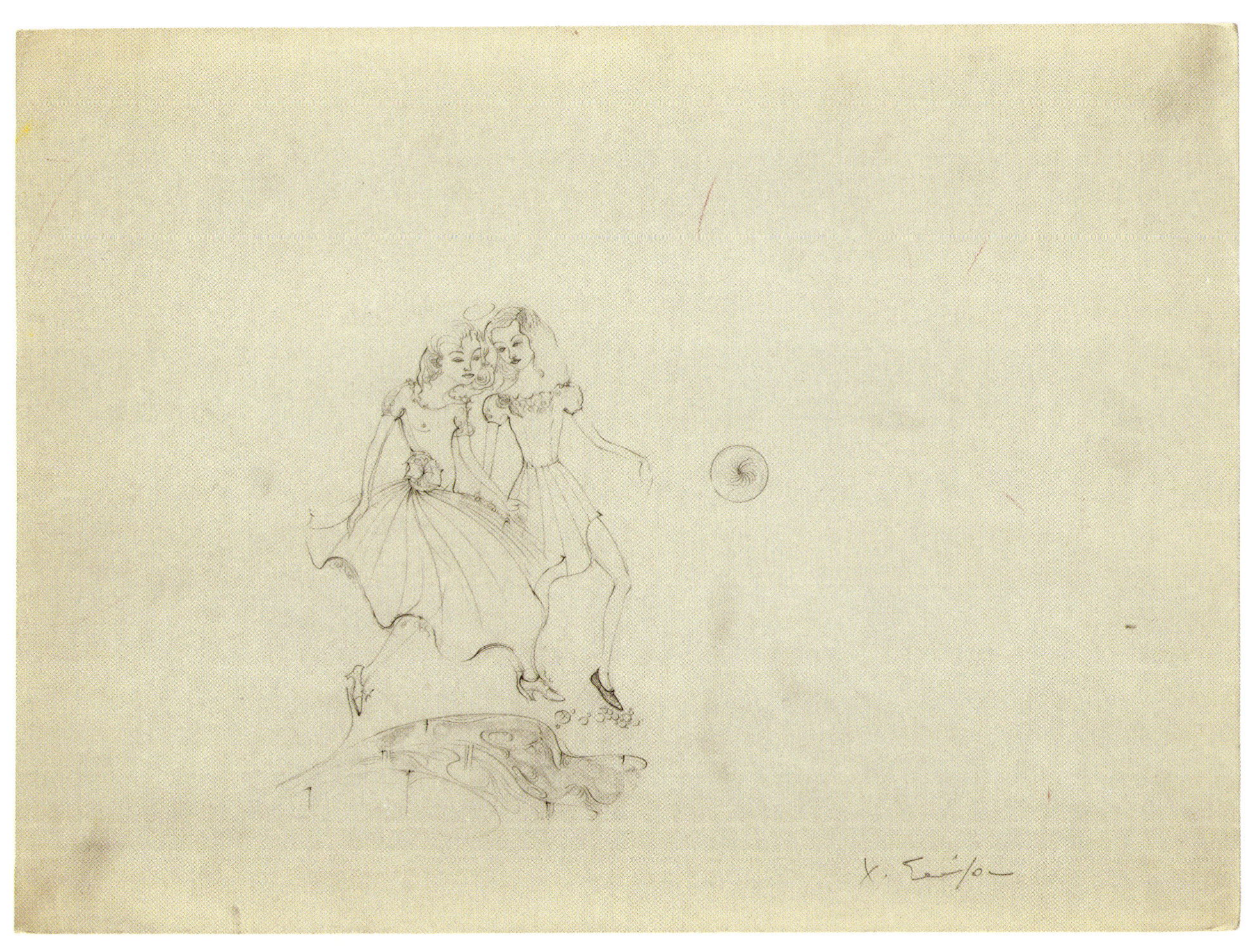

Untitled

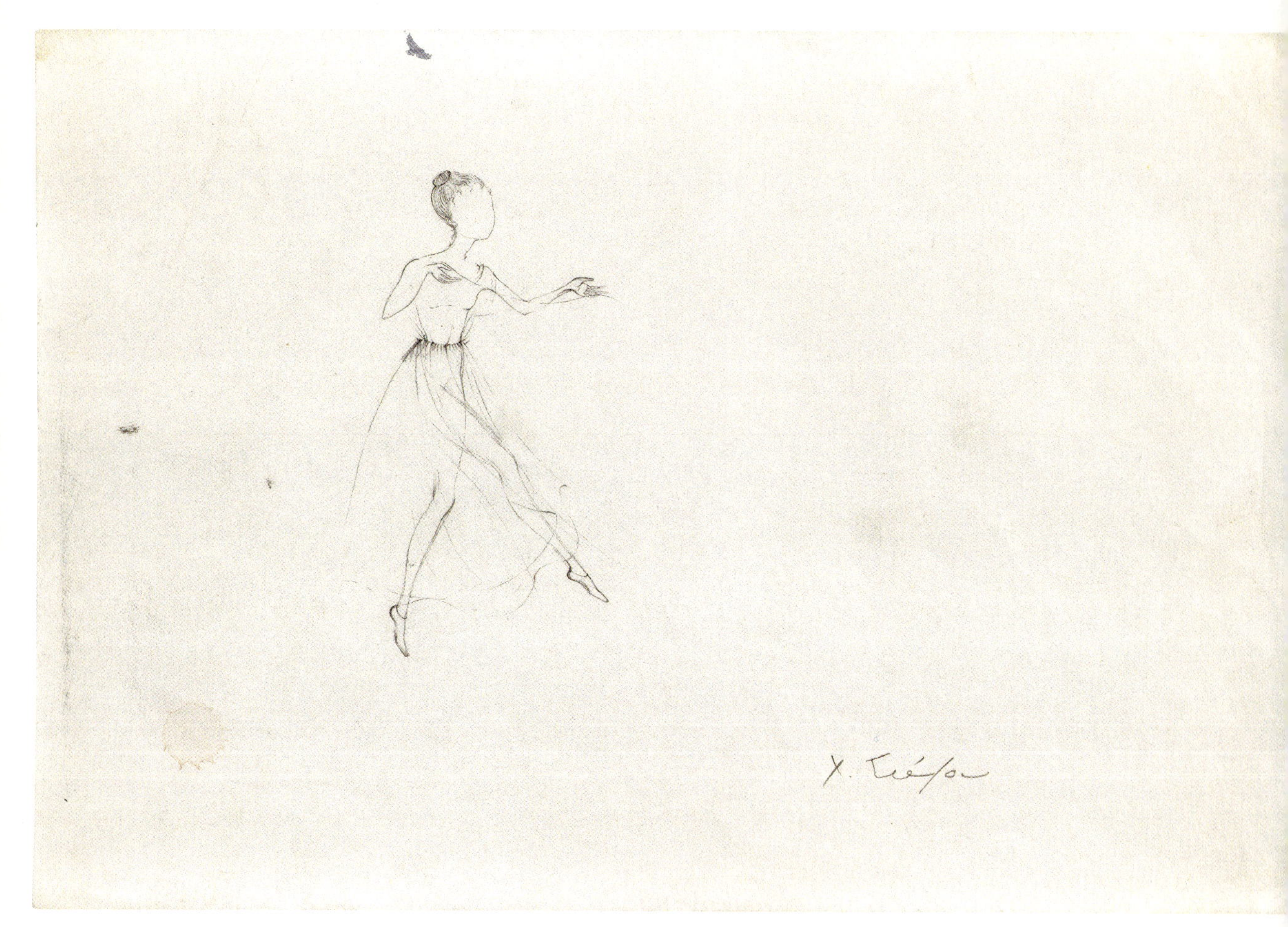

Untitled

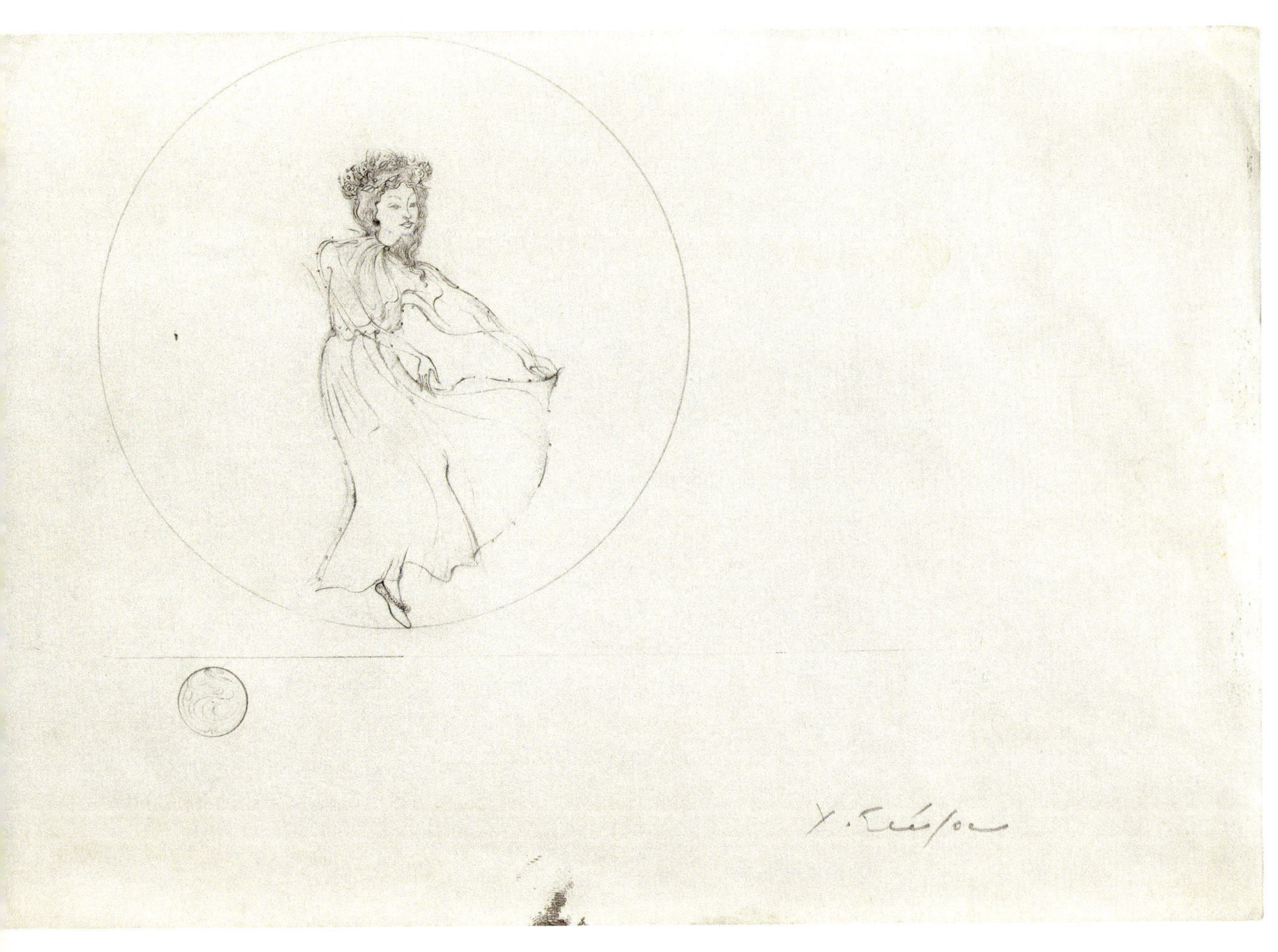

Untitled

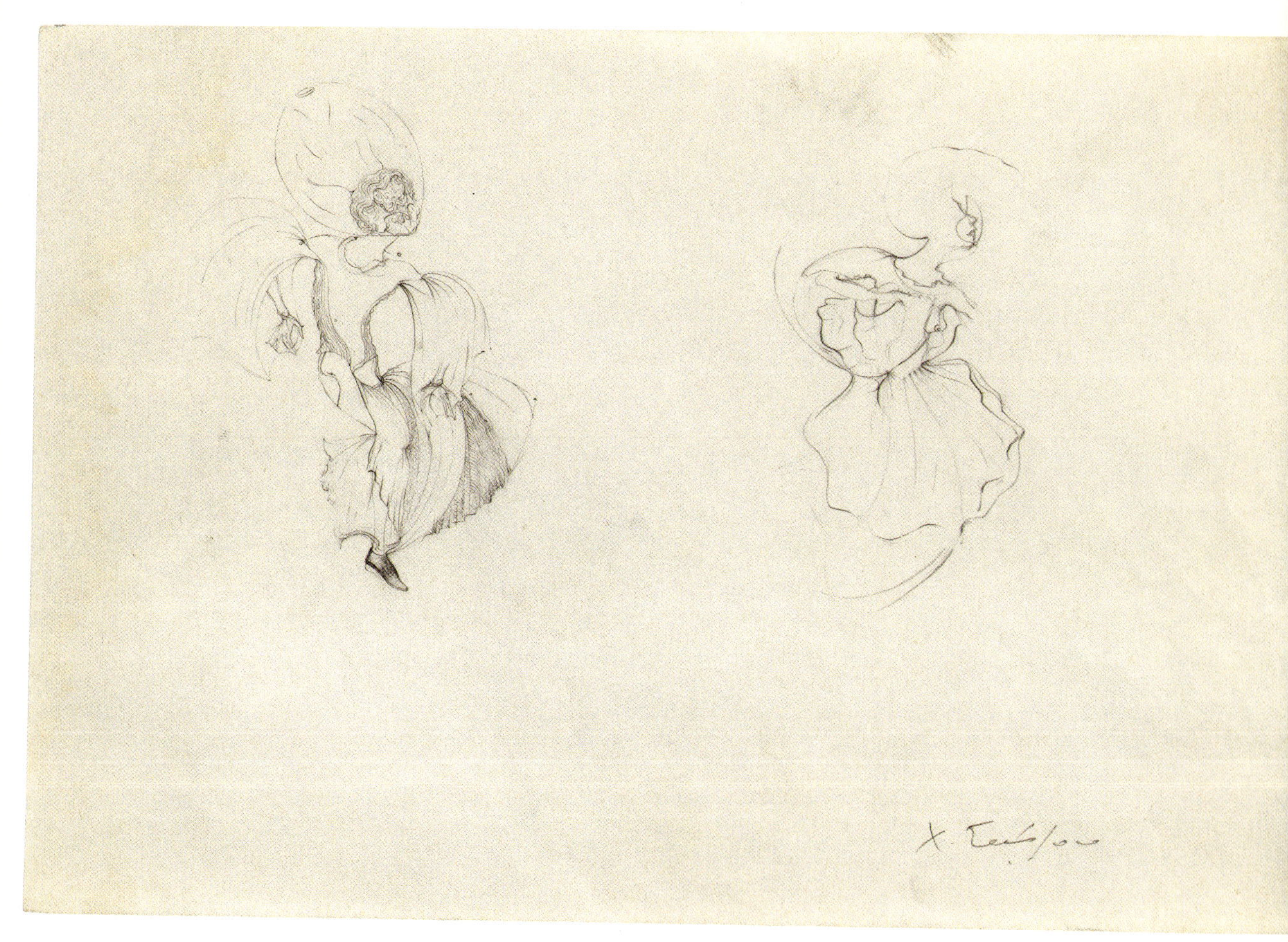

Untitled

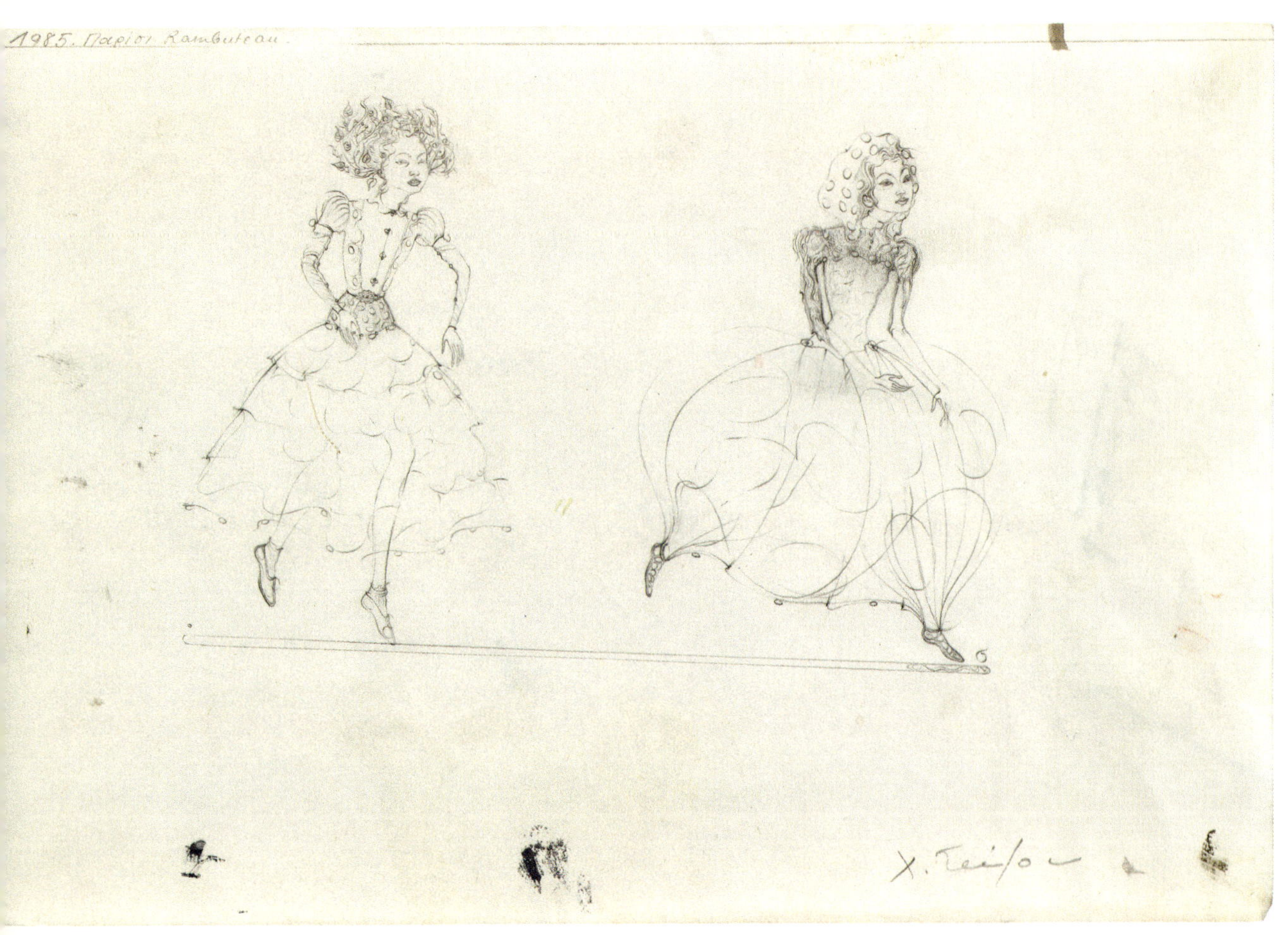

Untitled

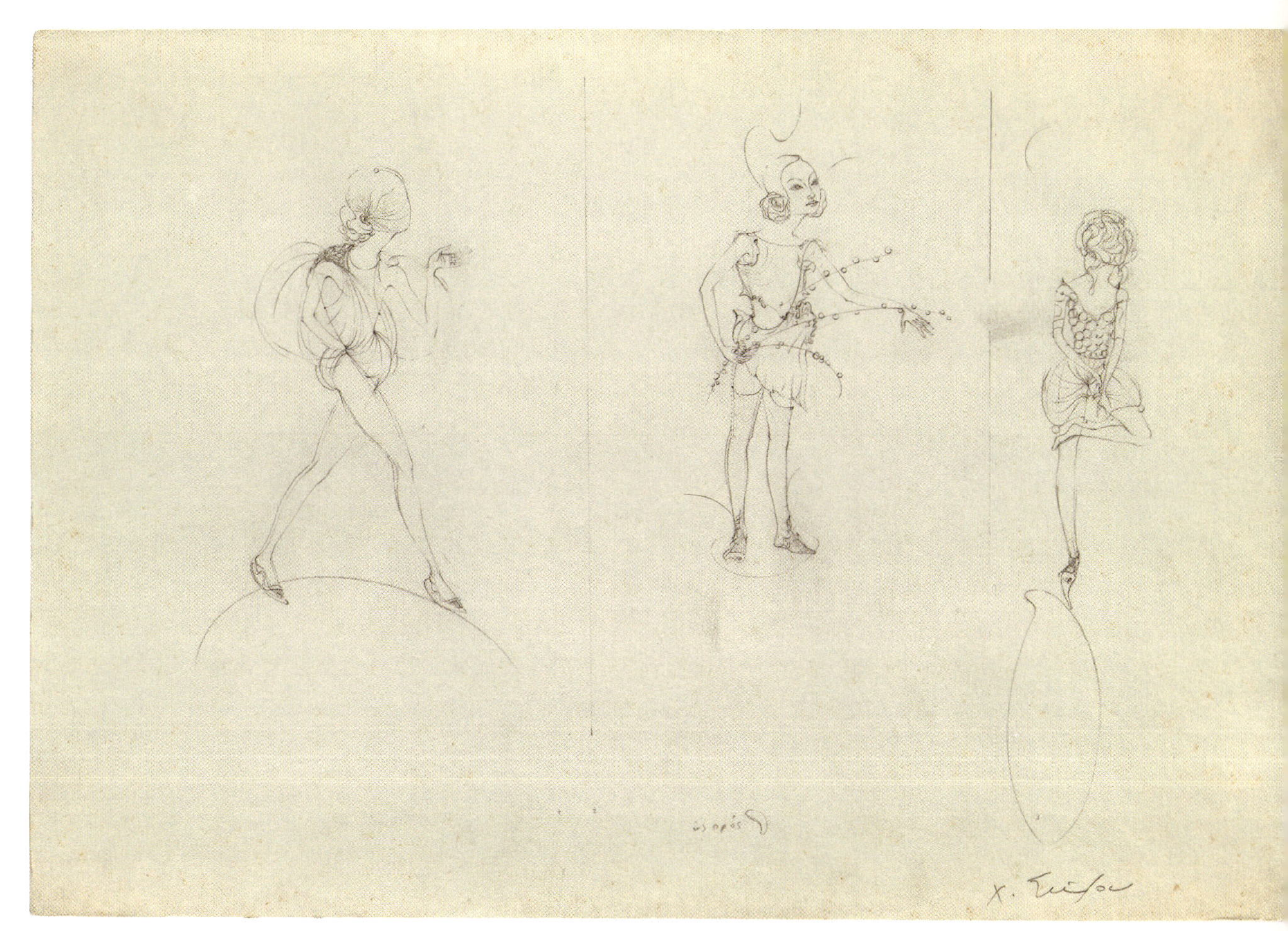

Untitled

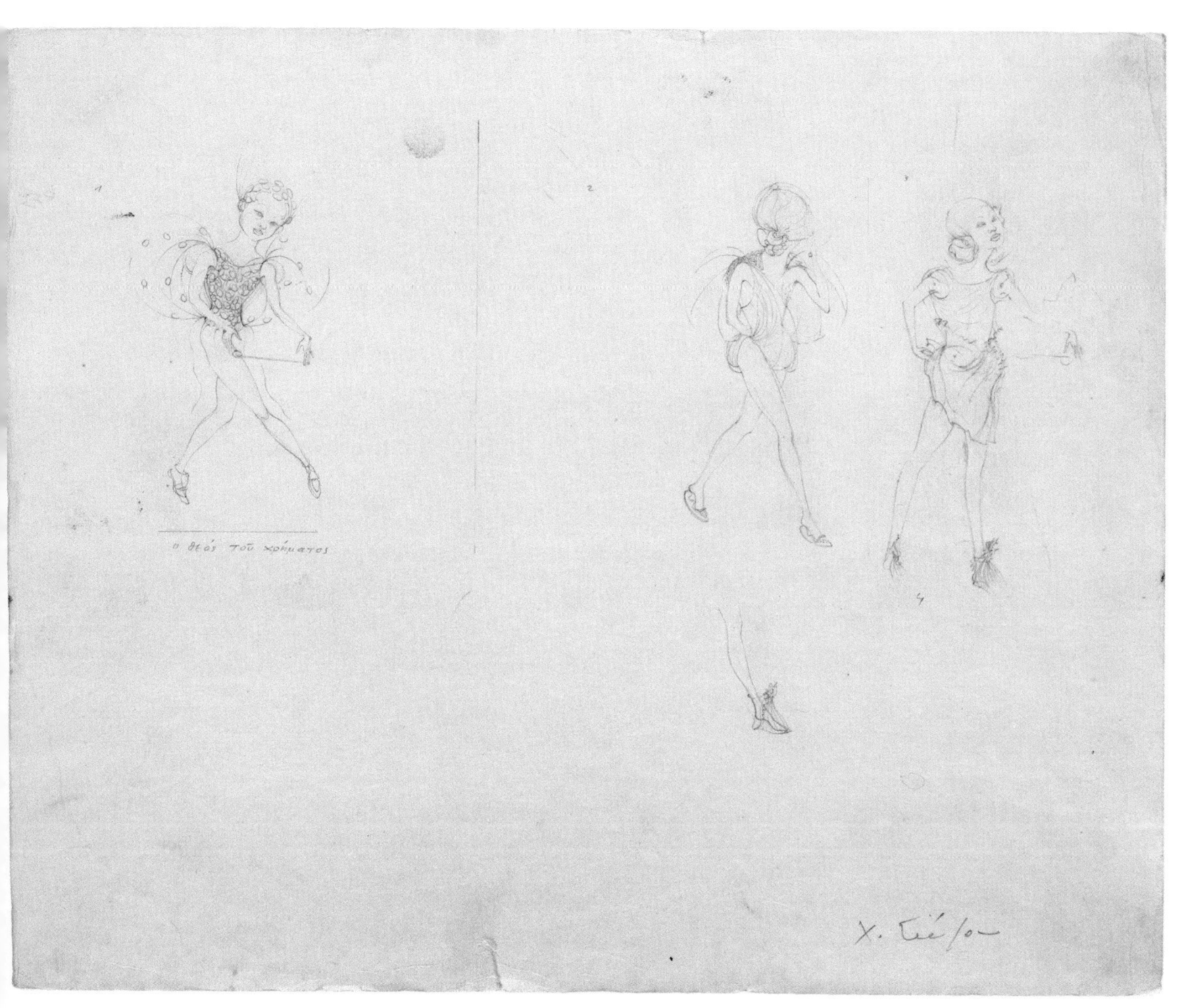

The God of Money

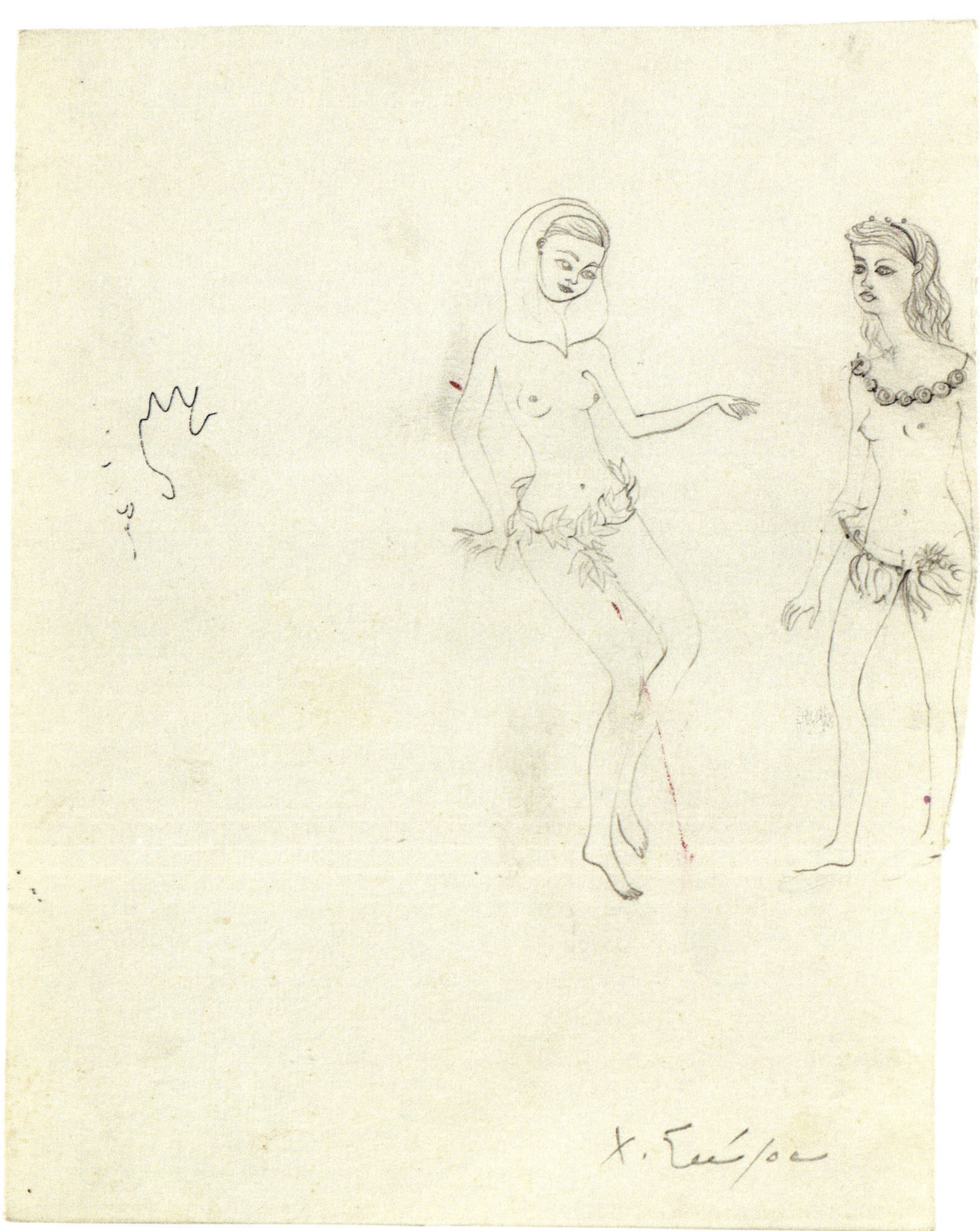

Untitled

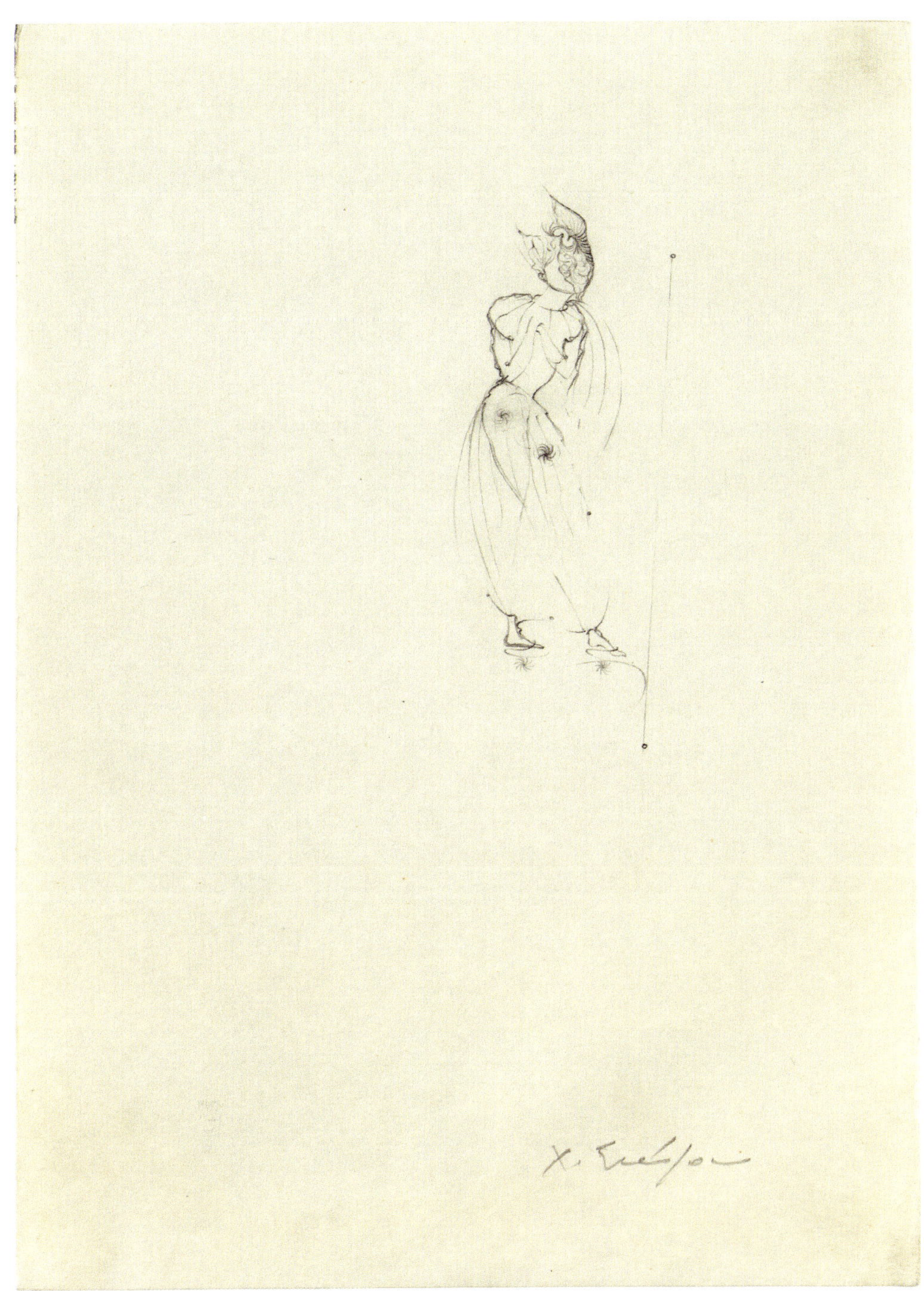

Untitled

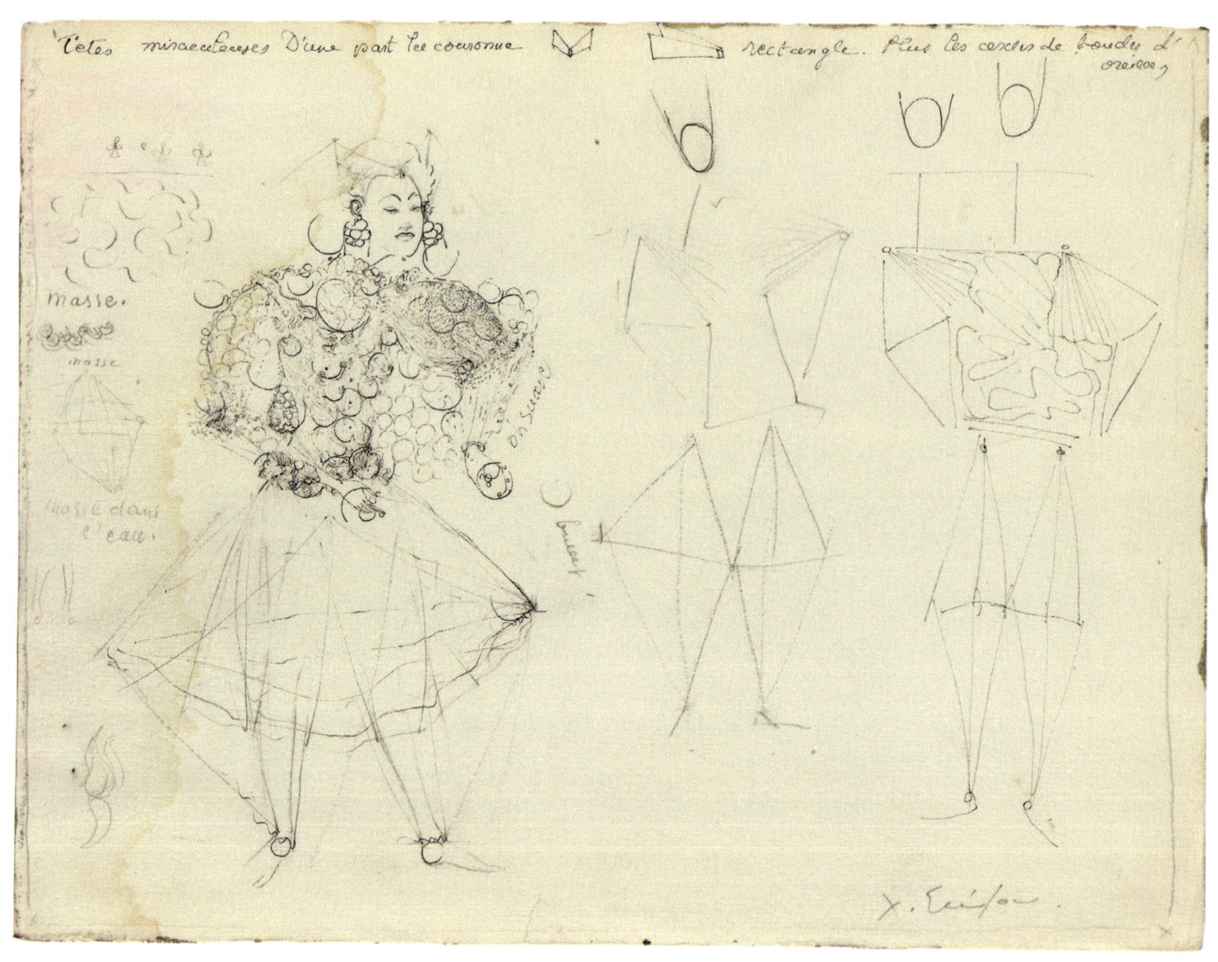

Têtes miraculeuses D'une part la couronne
rectangle. Plus les cercles de boucles d'
oreilles
masse.
masse
masse dans
l'eau.
X. Ensor.

Untitled

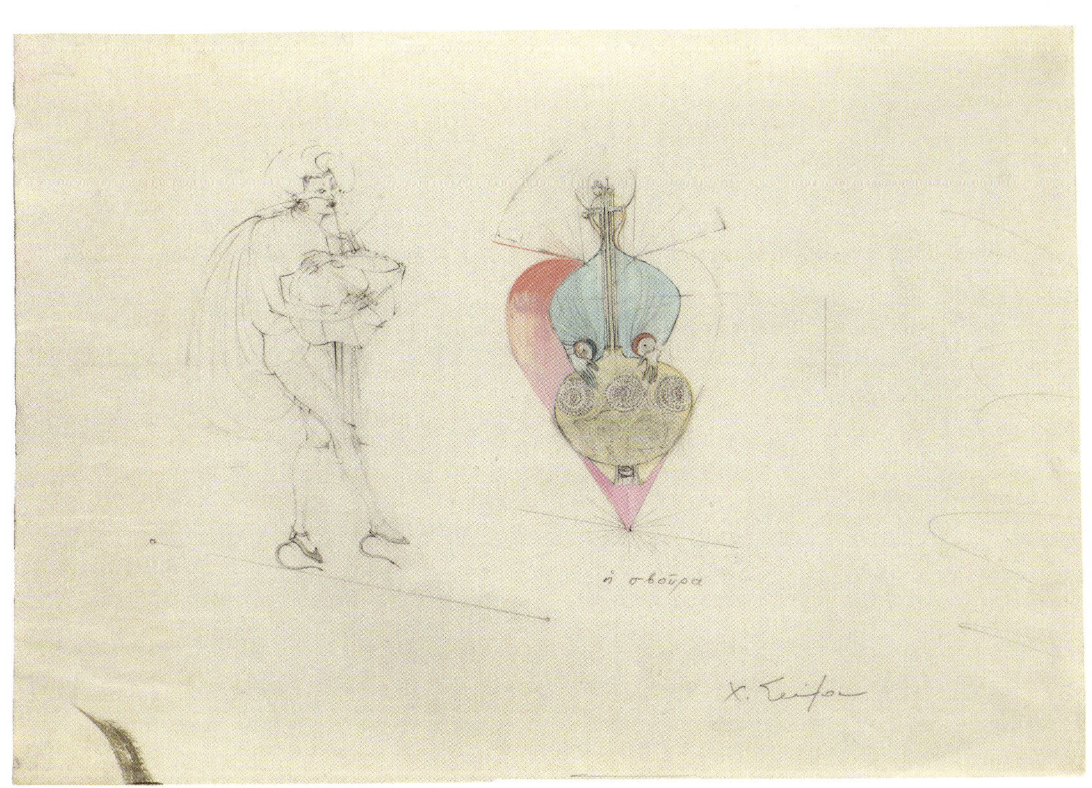

The Spinning Top

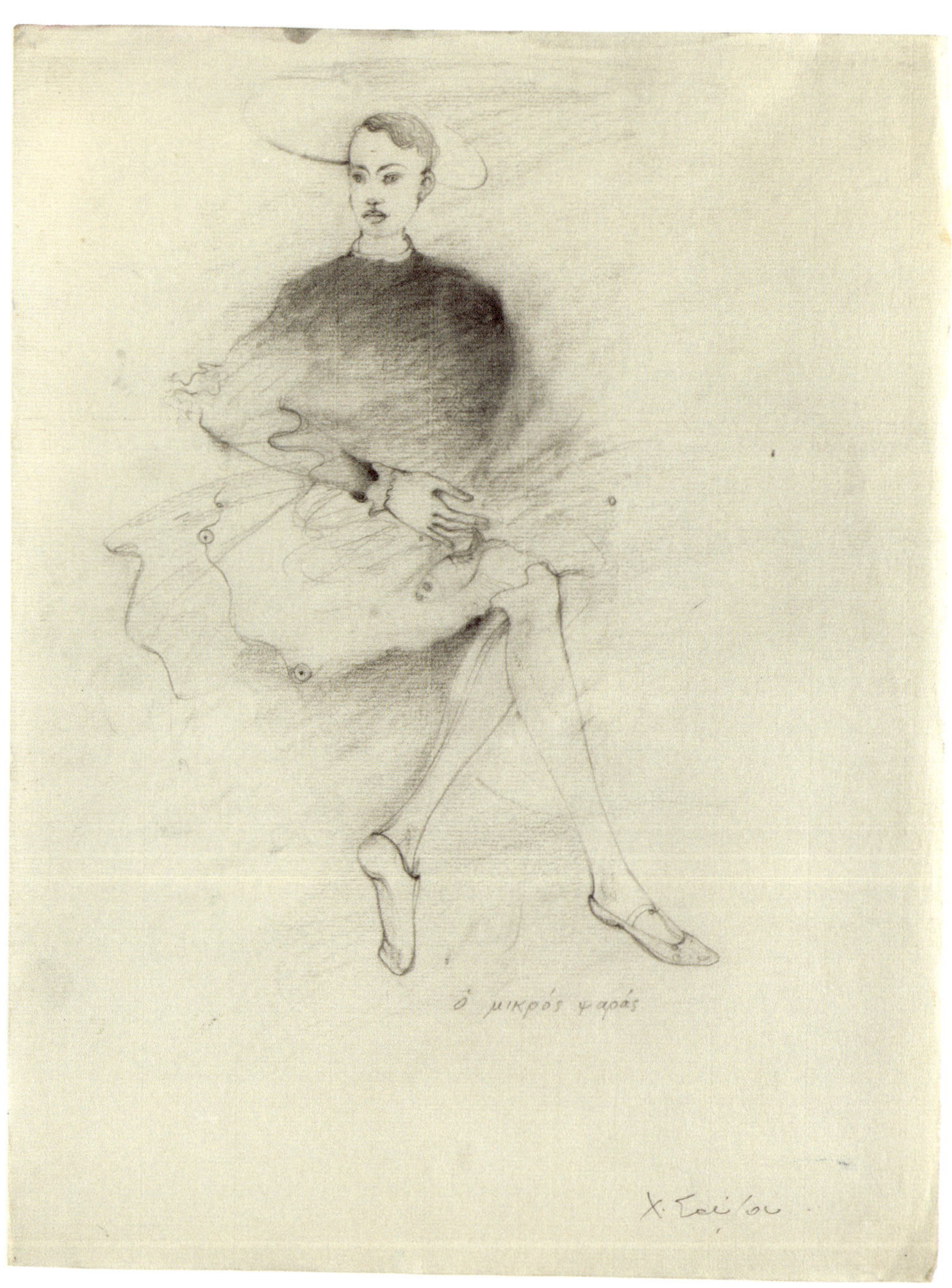

The Little Fisherman

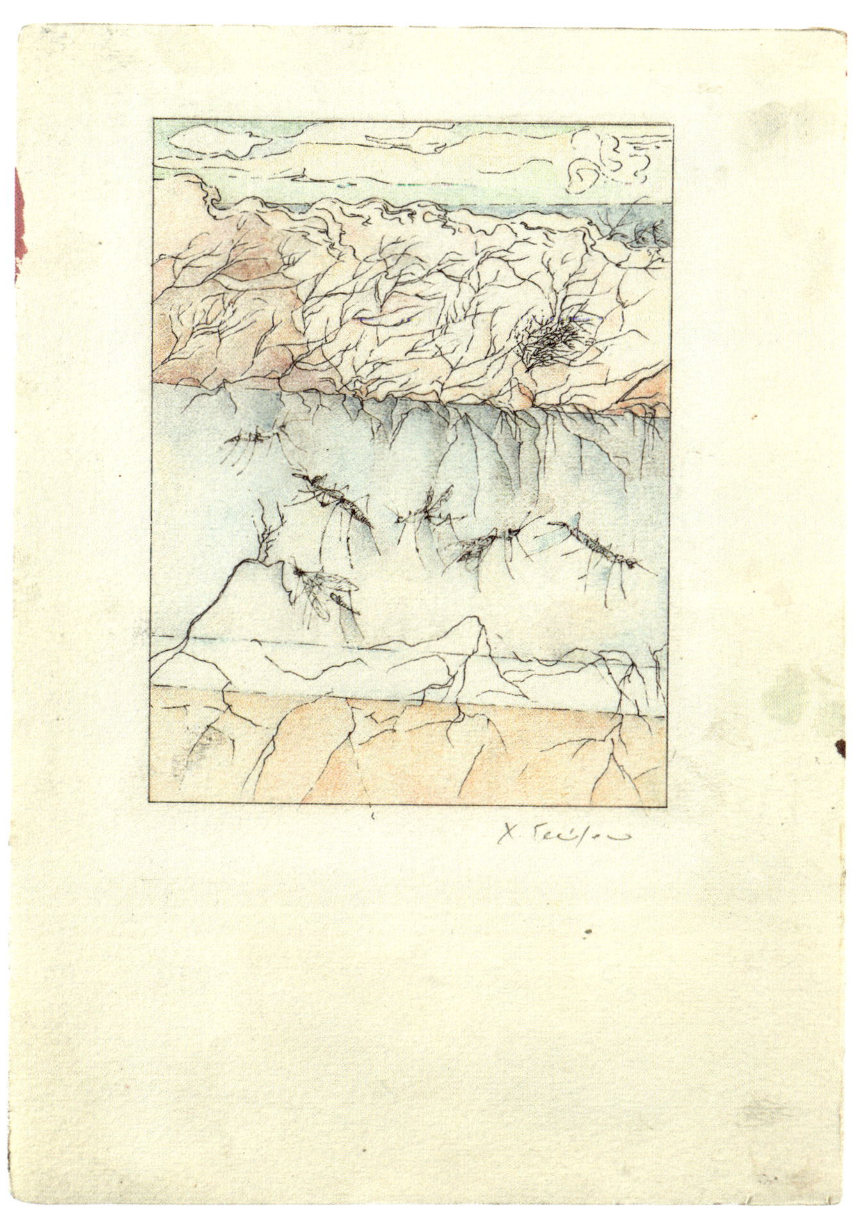

After Yves Bonnefoy's *On the Motion and Immobility of Douve*

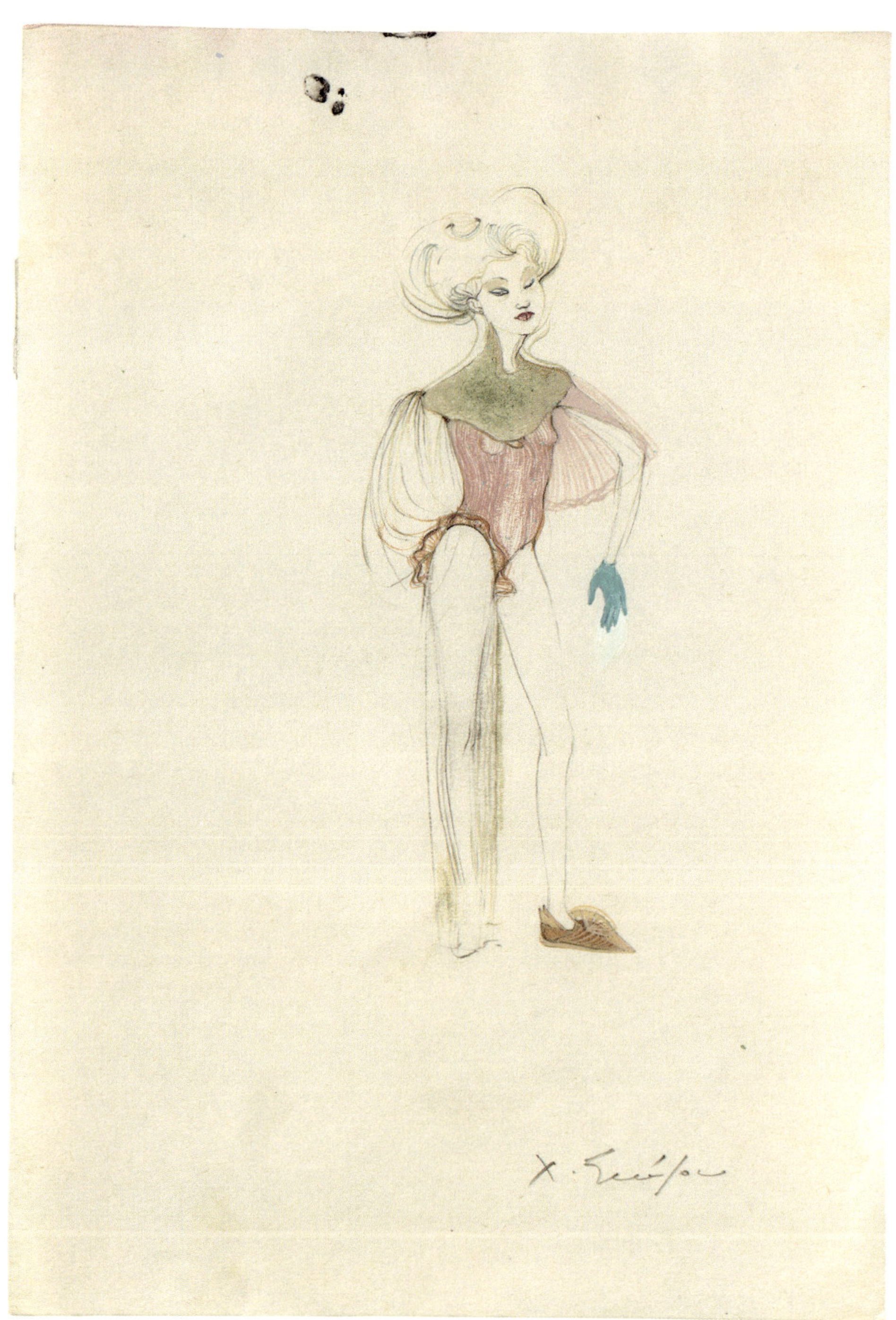

Untitled

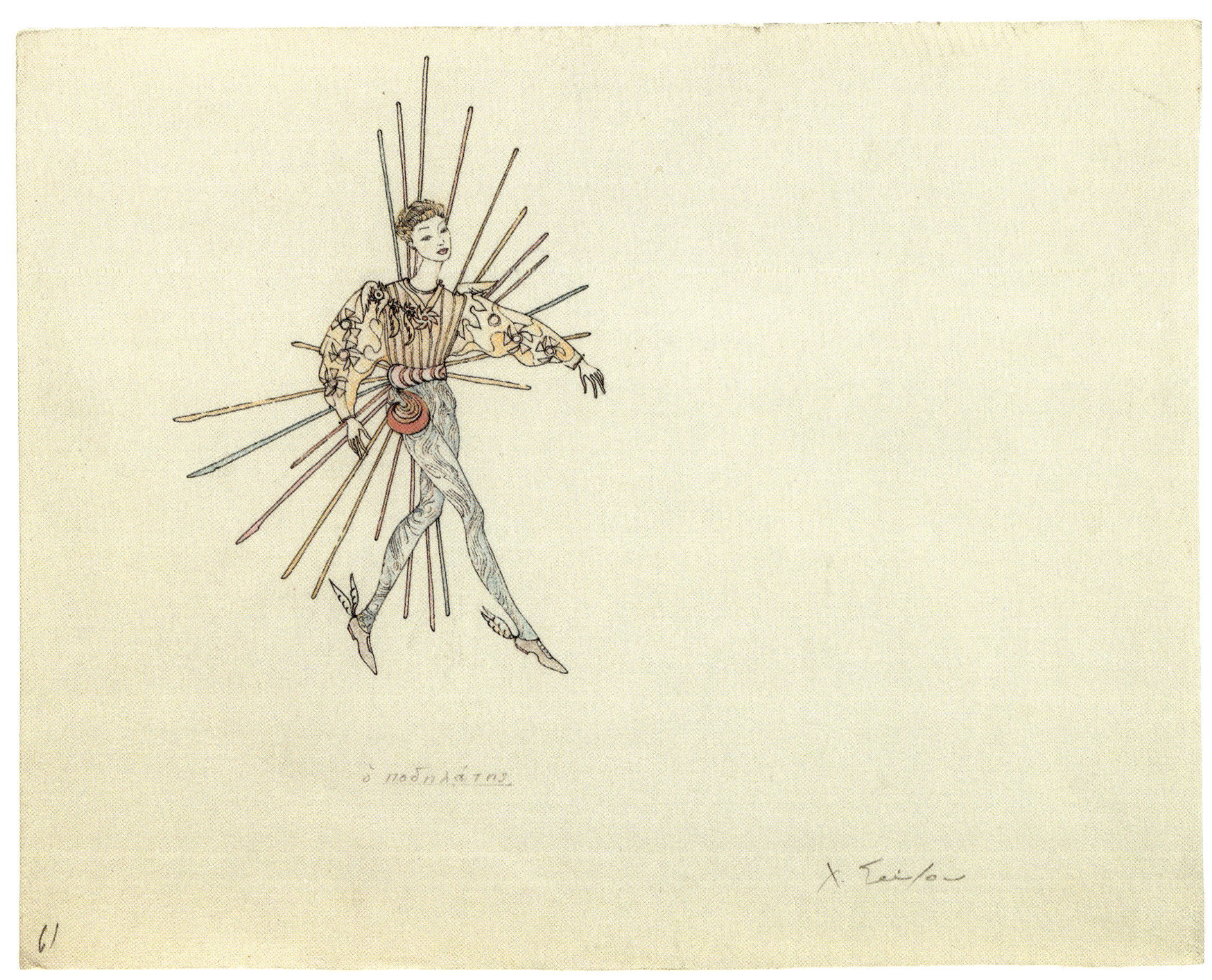

The Cyclist

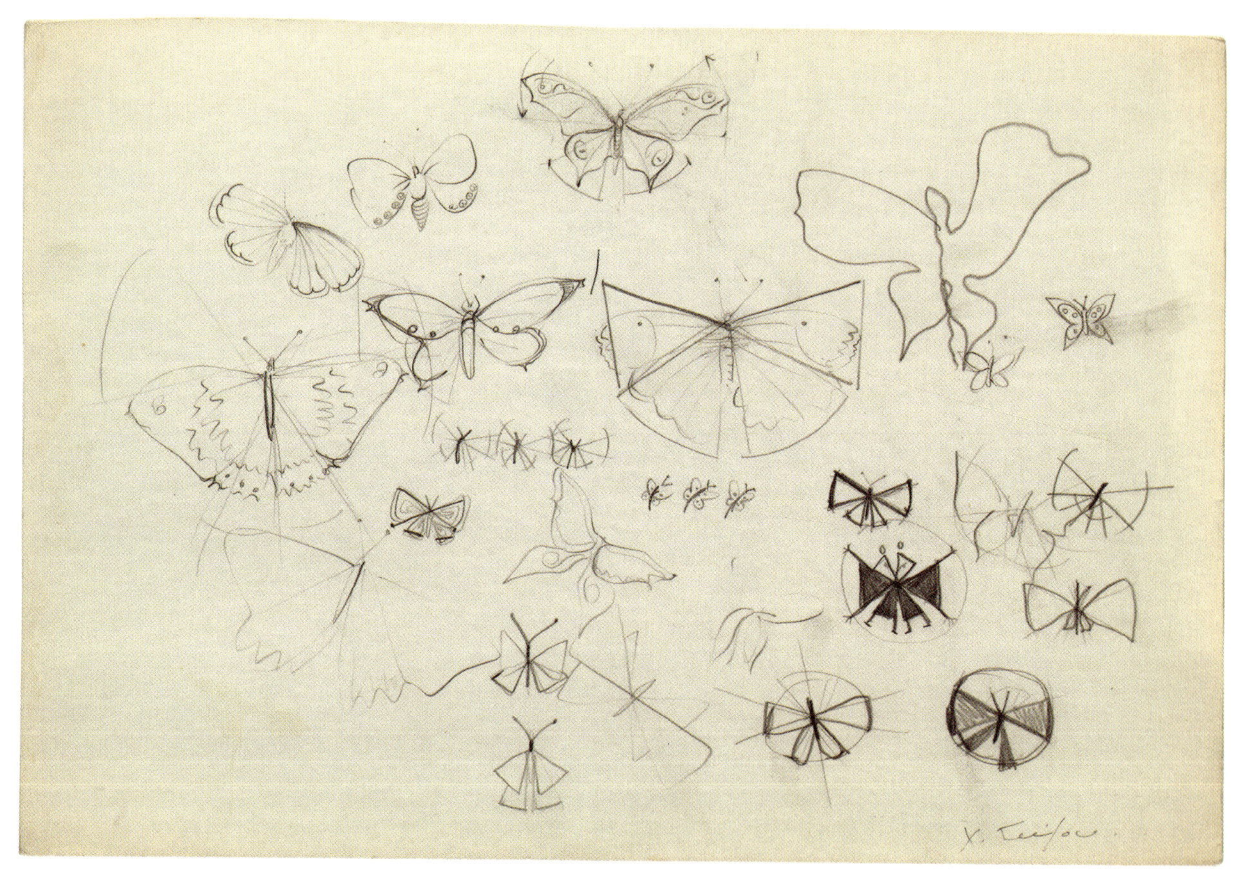

Untitled

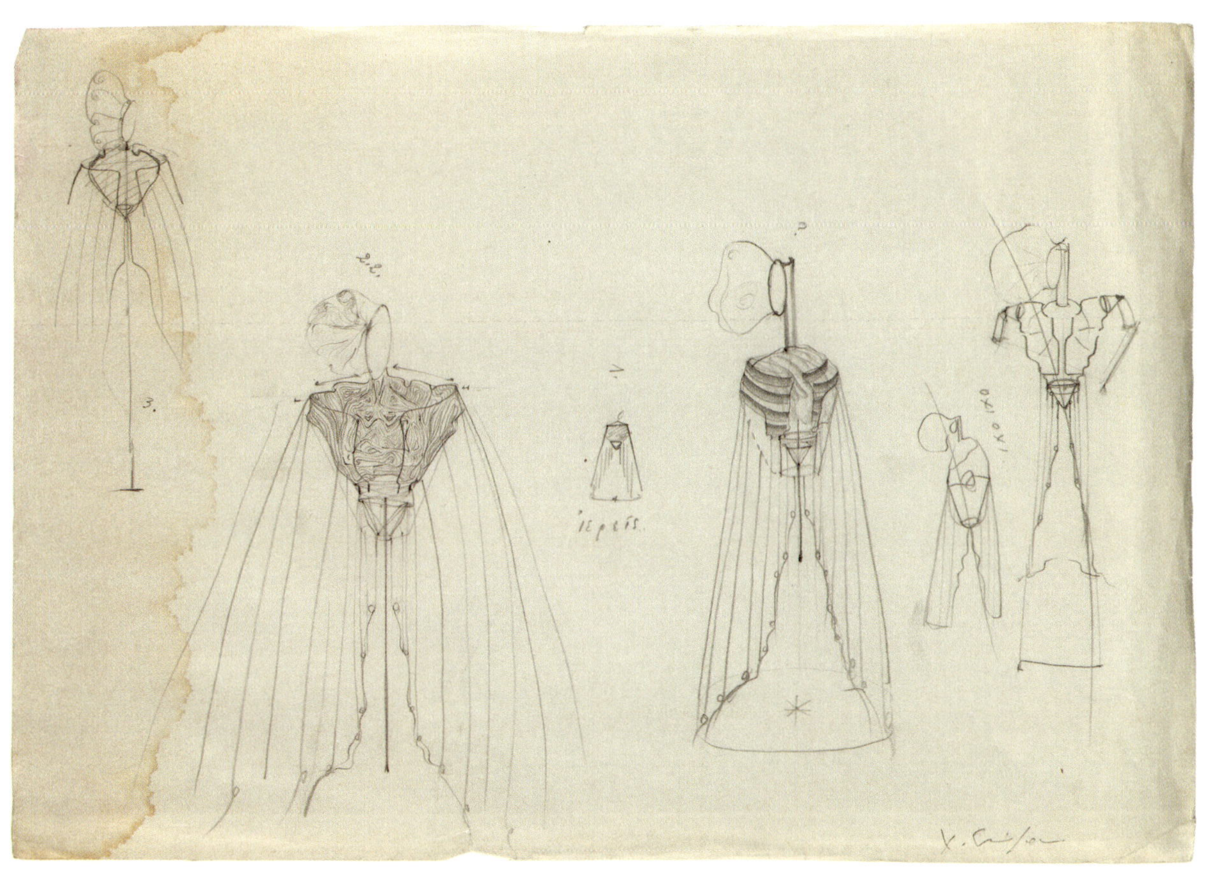

Priests

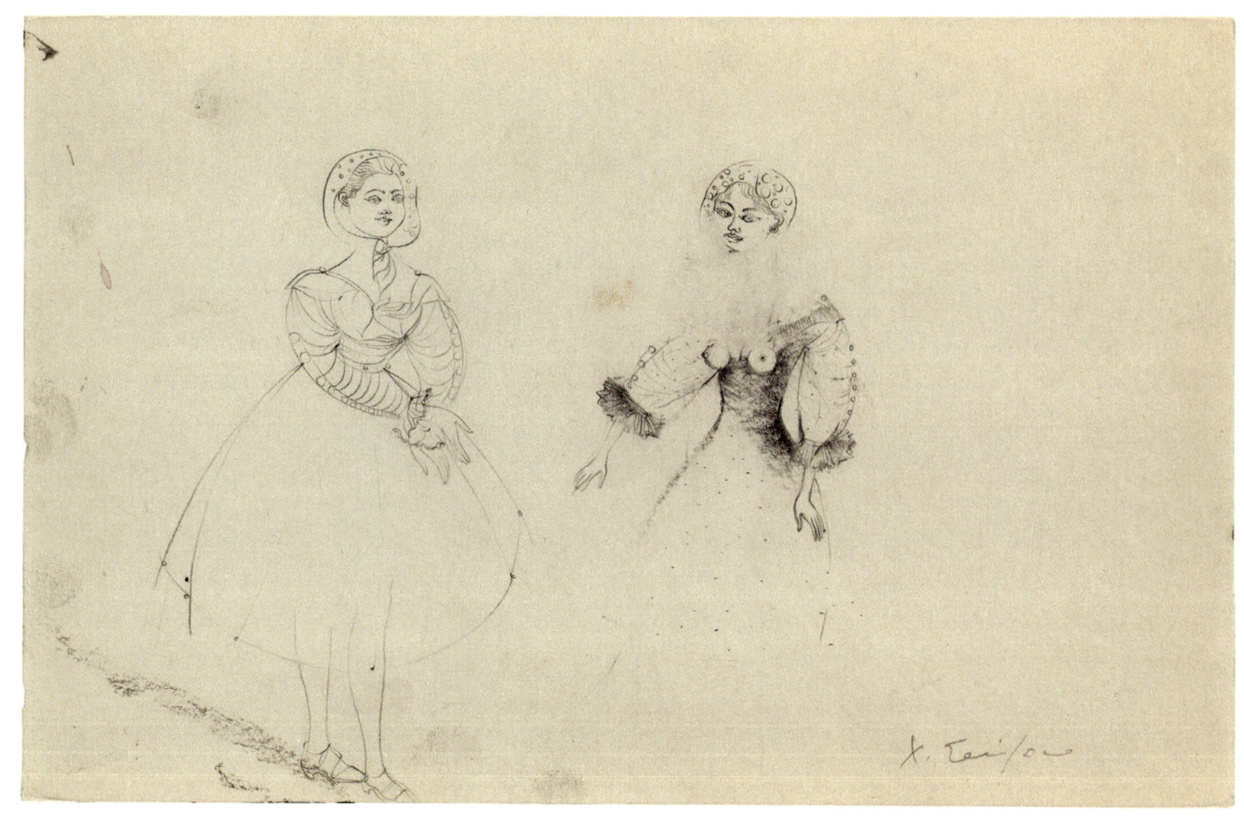

Untitled

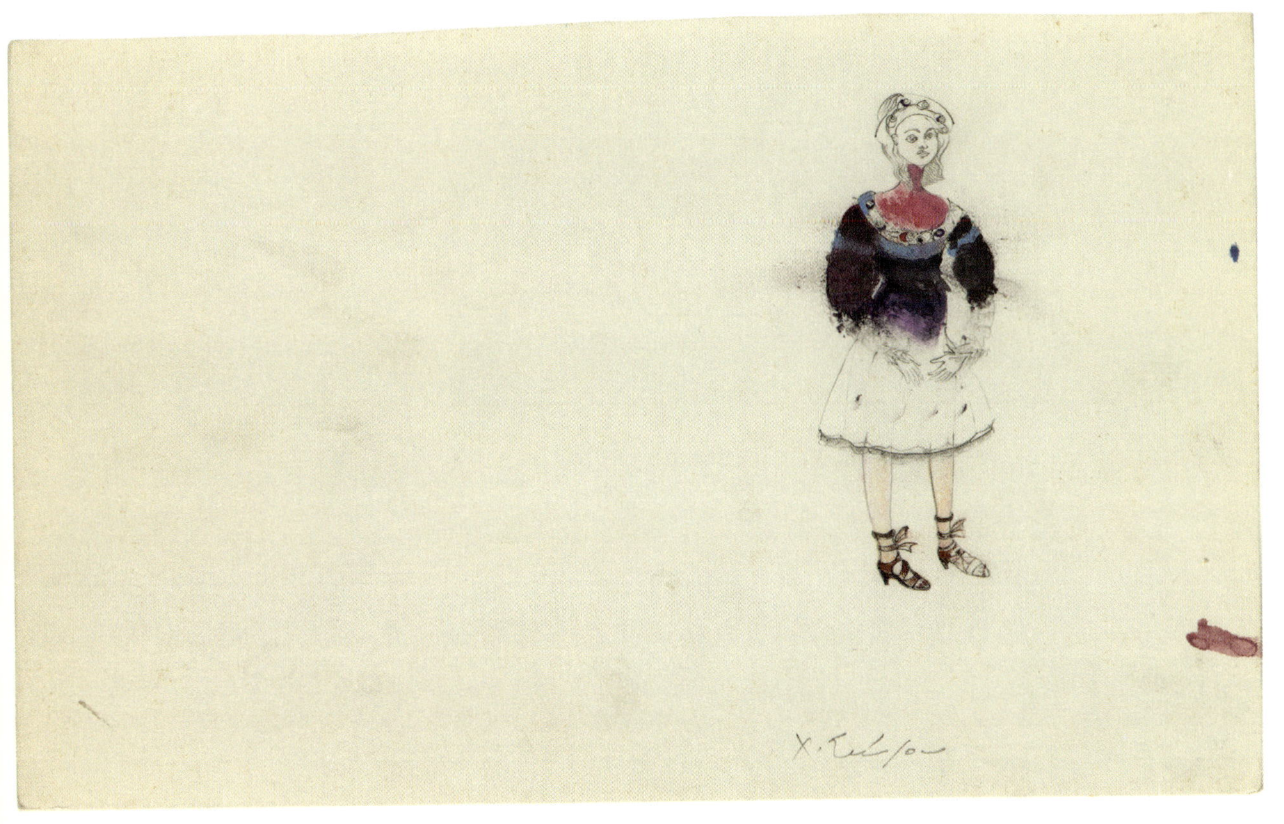

Priests

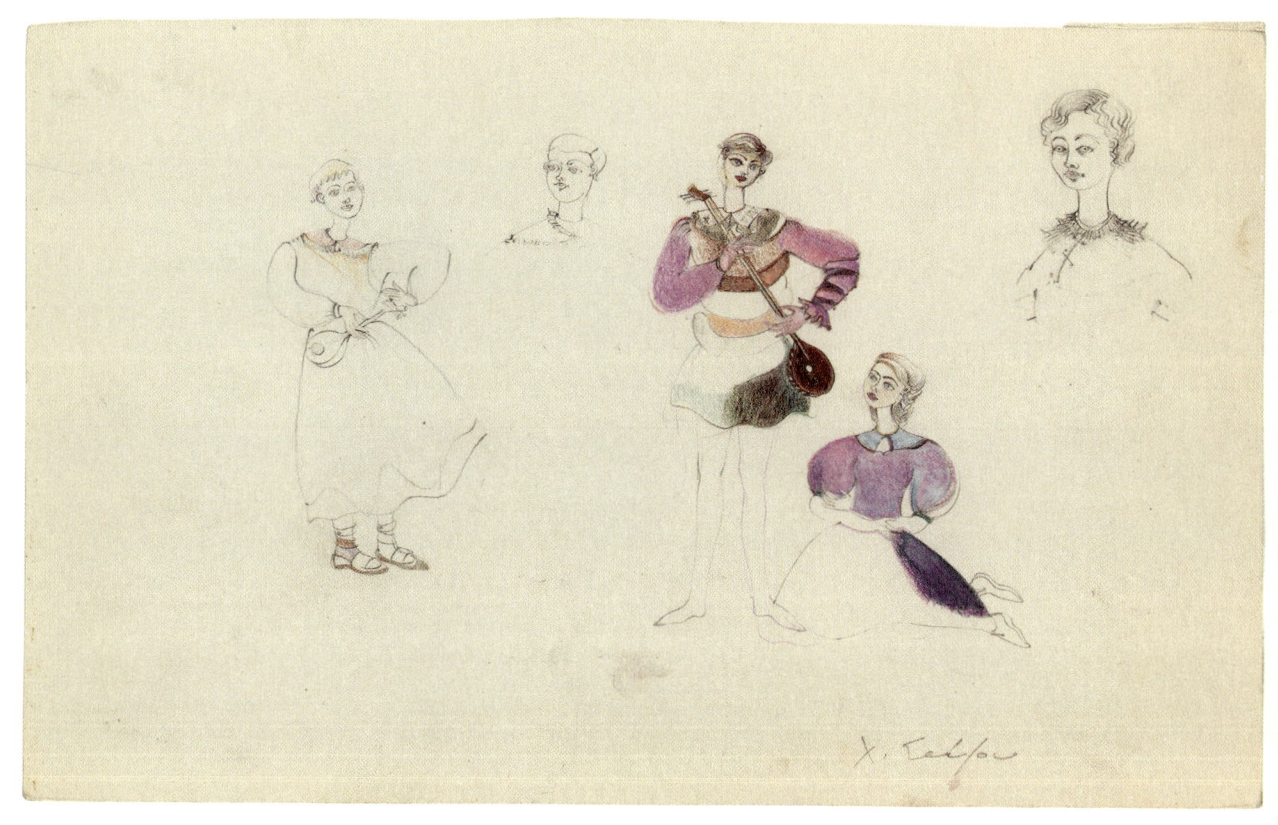

Untitled

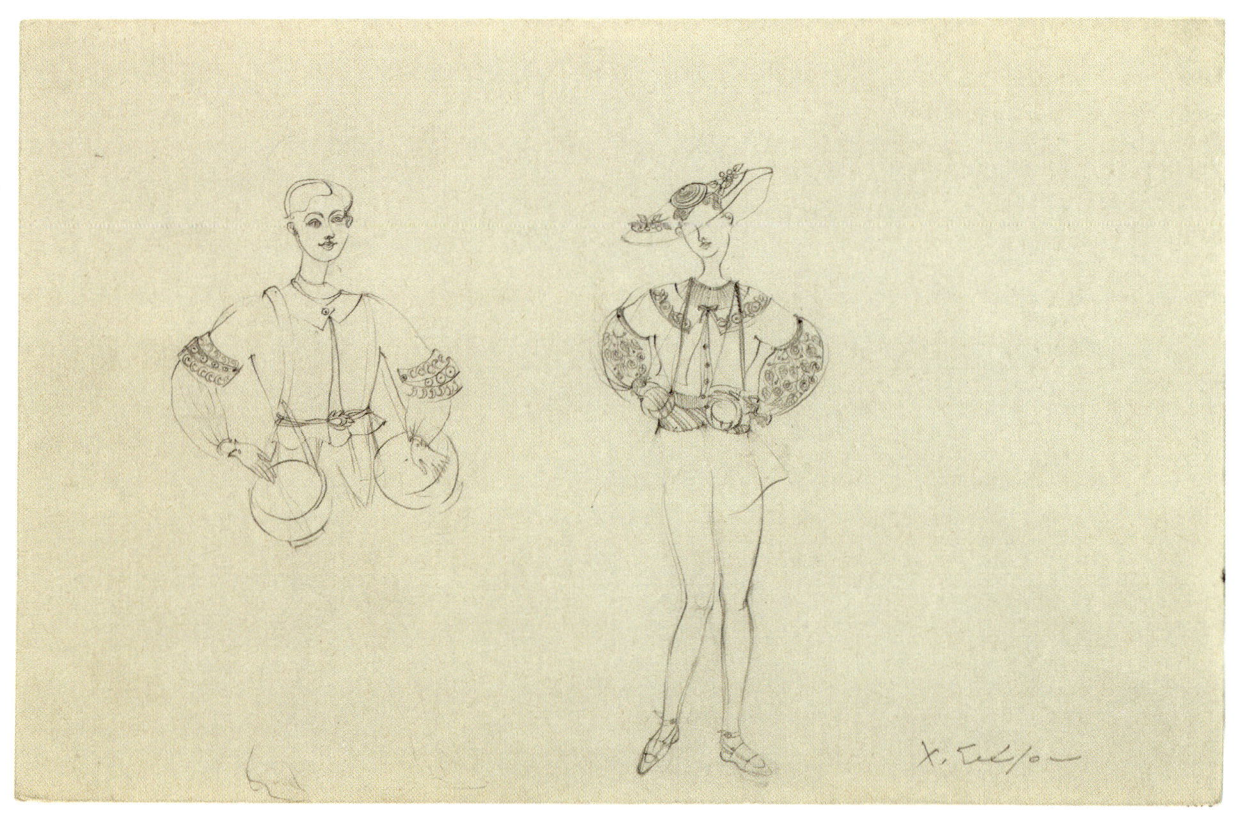

Untitled

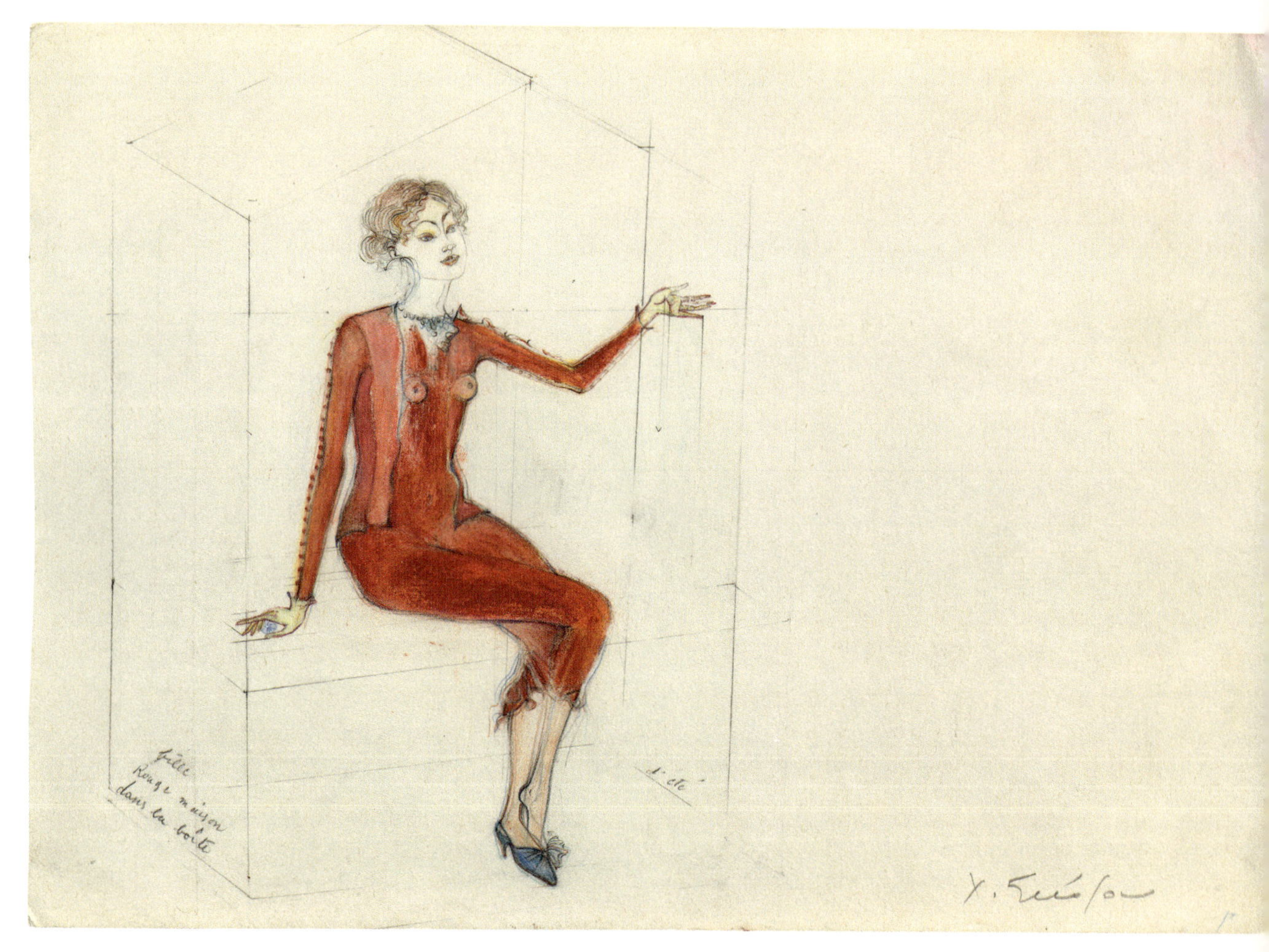

Girl in the Red Box

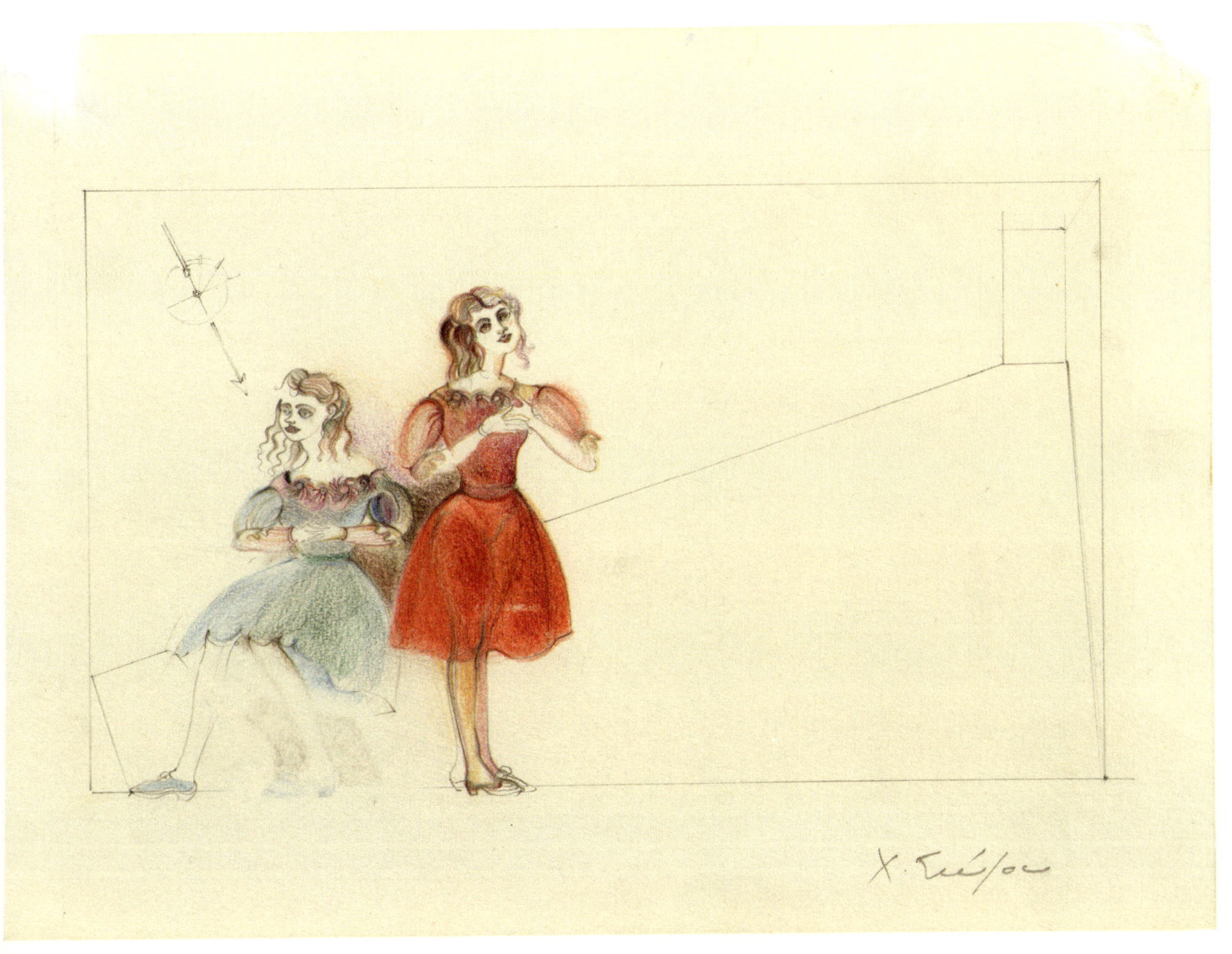

Untitled

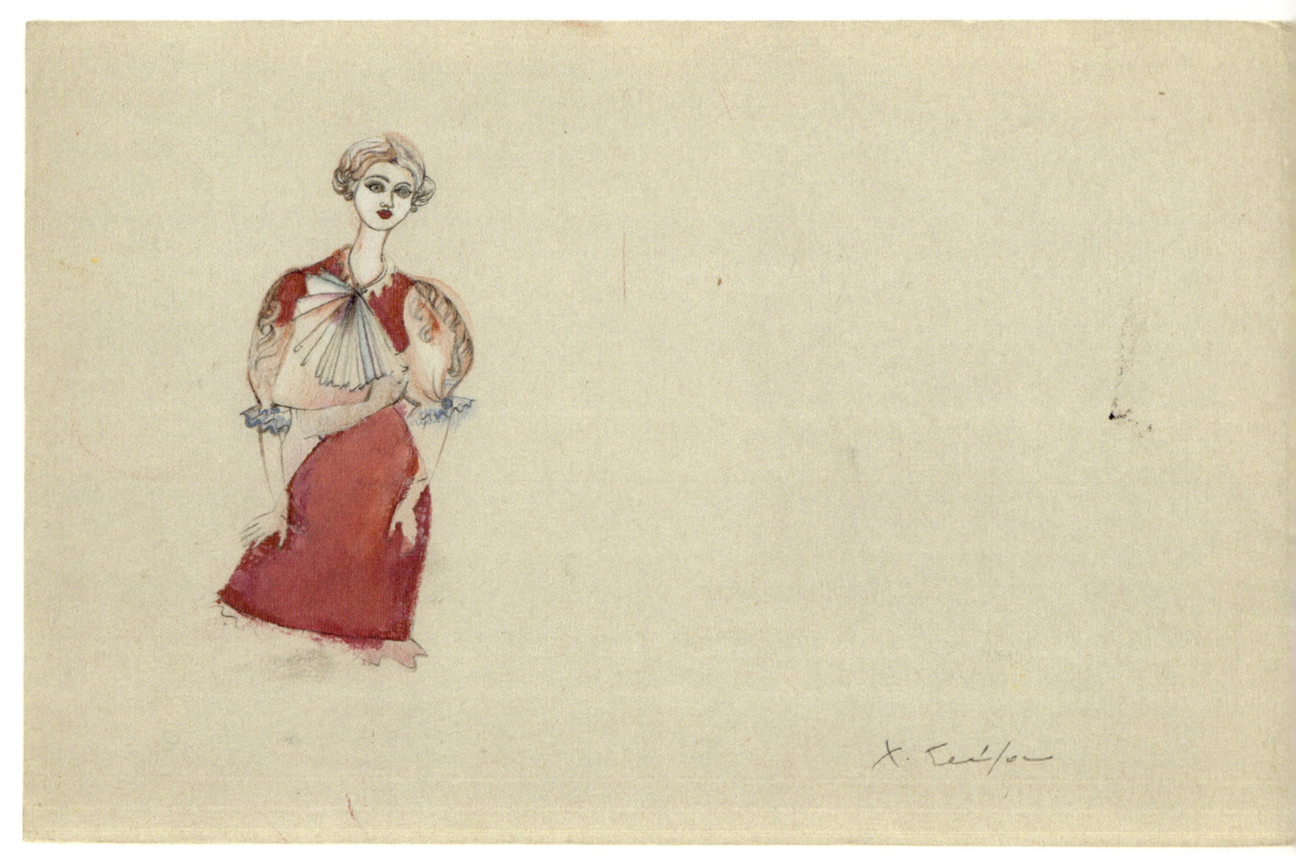

Untitled

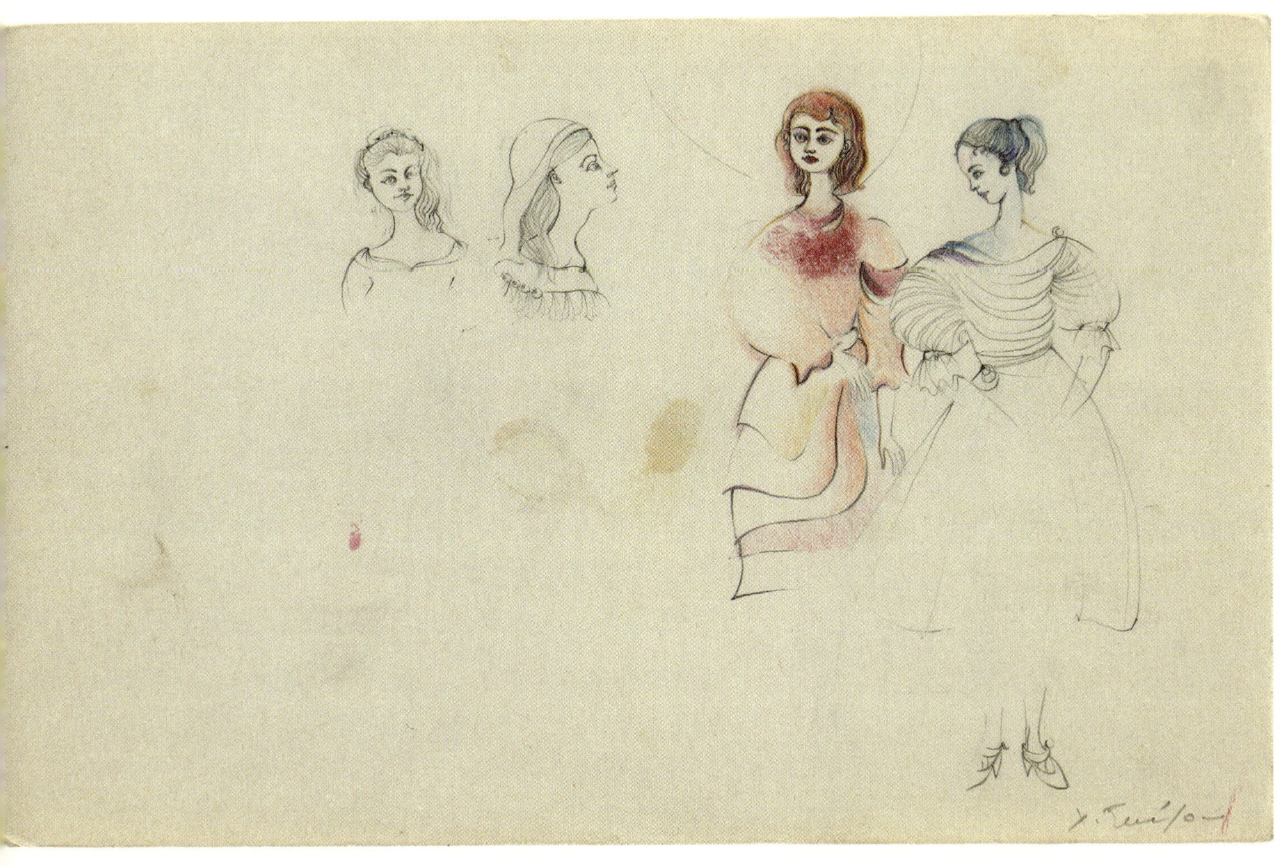

Untitled

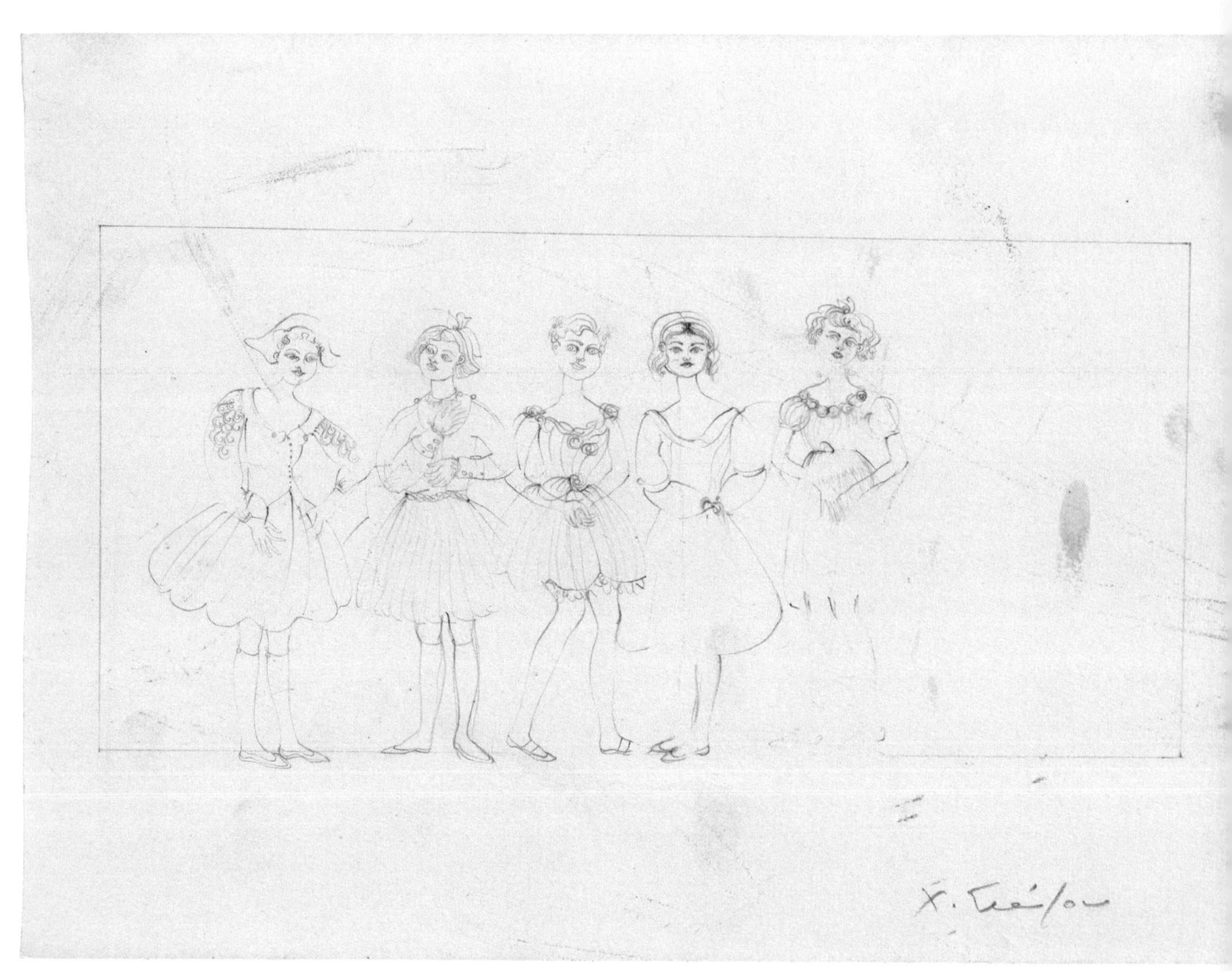

Untitled

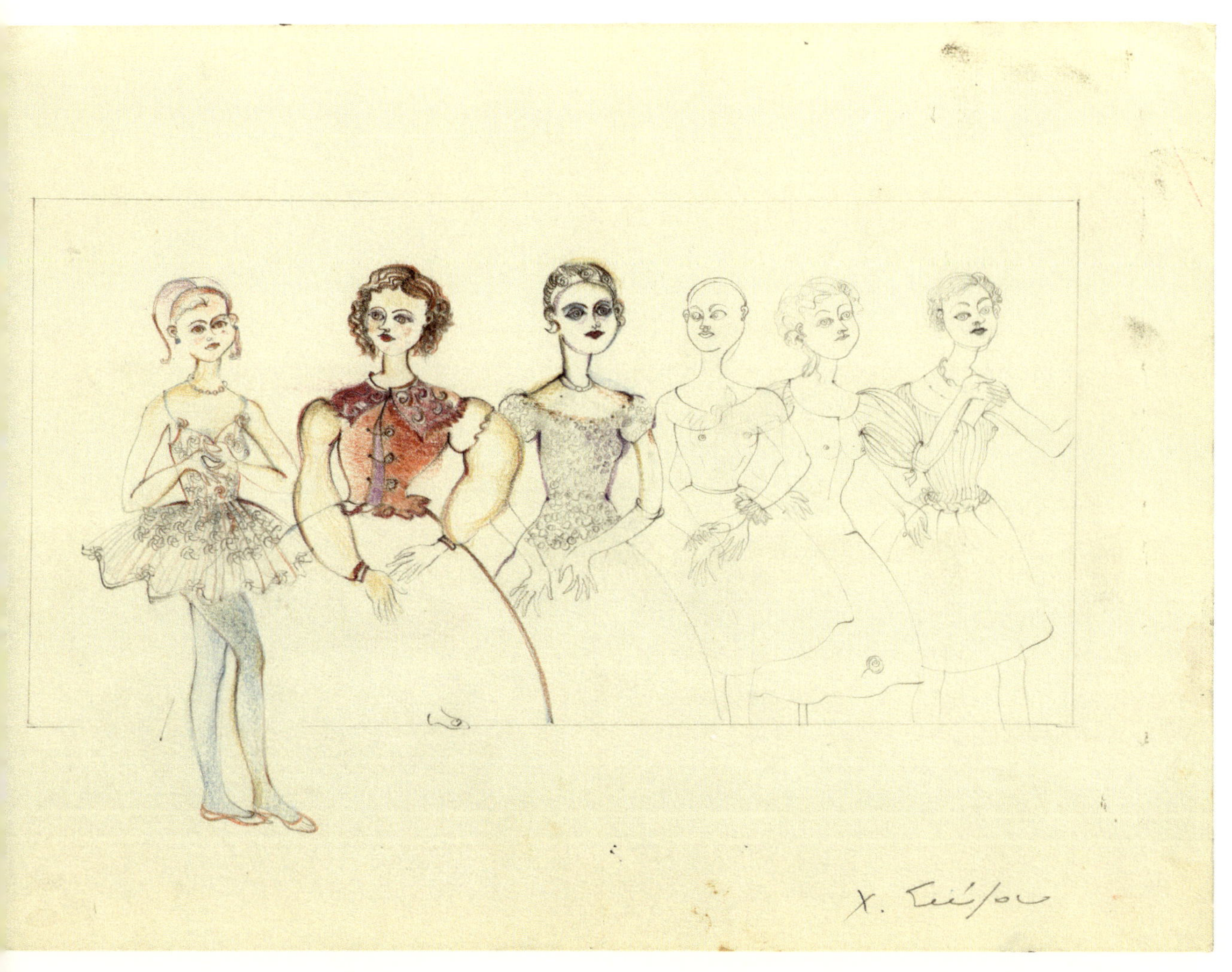

Untitled

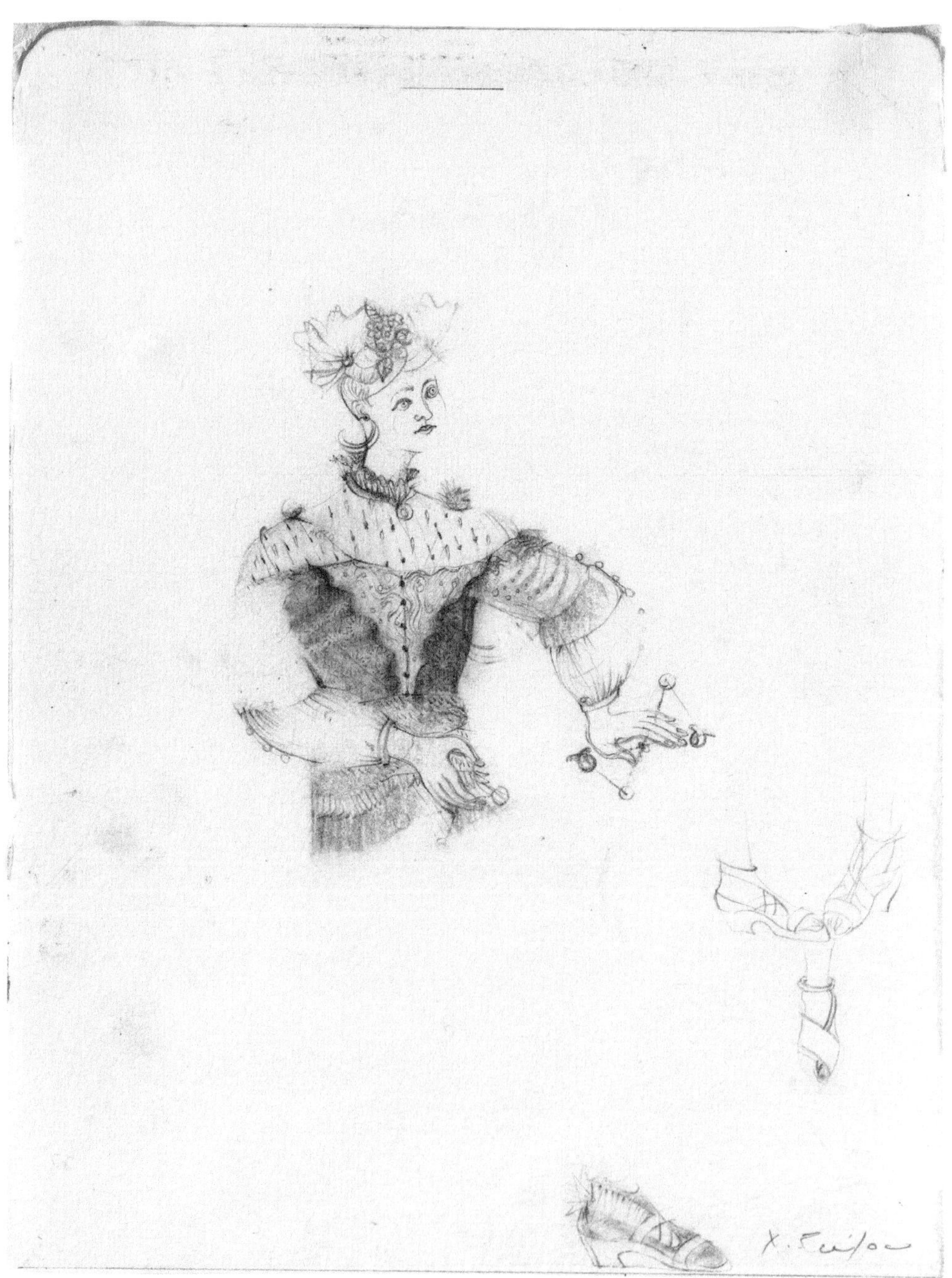

Untitled

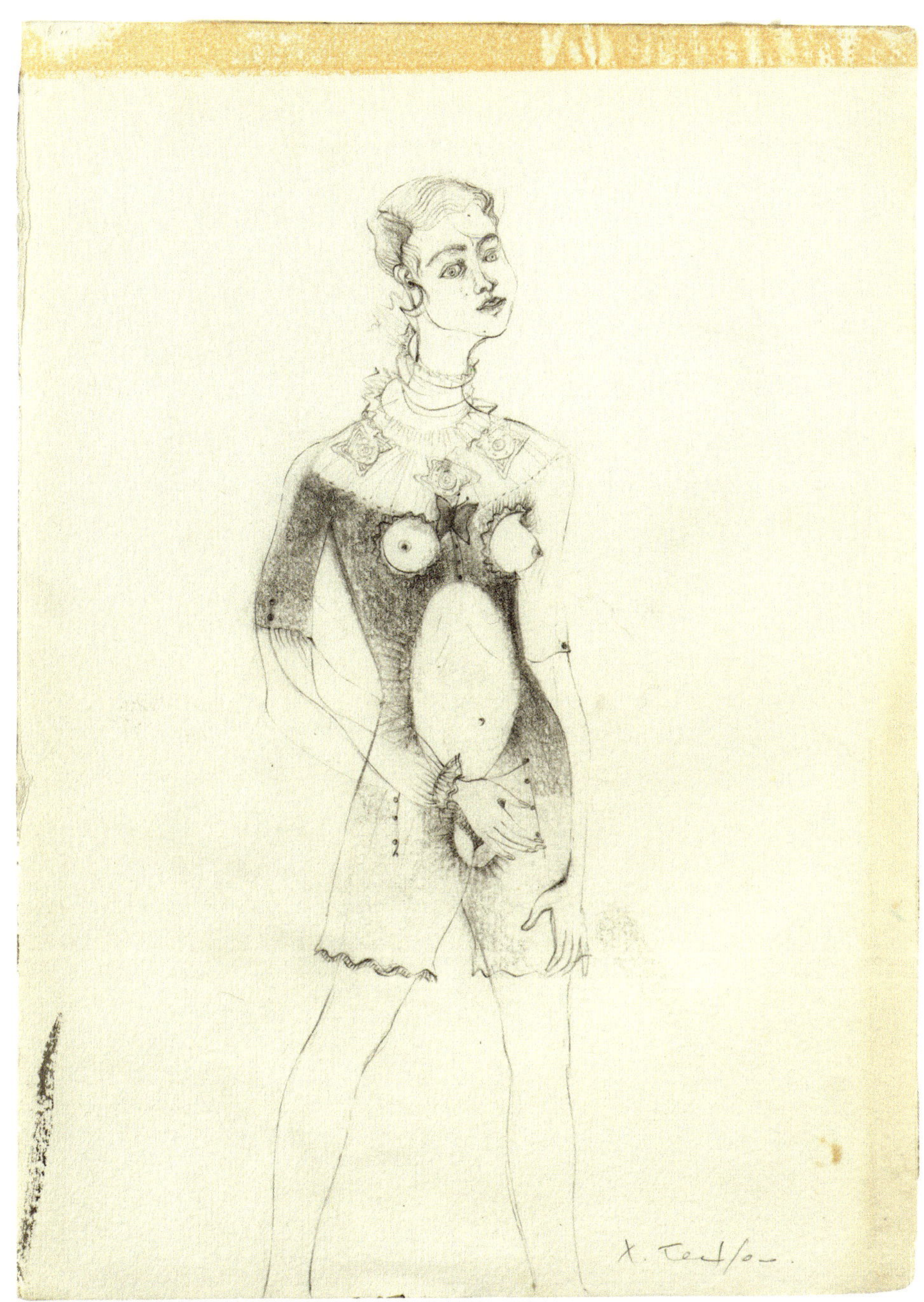

Untitled

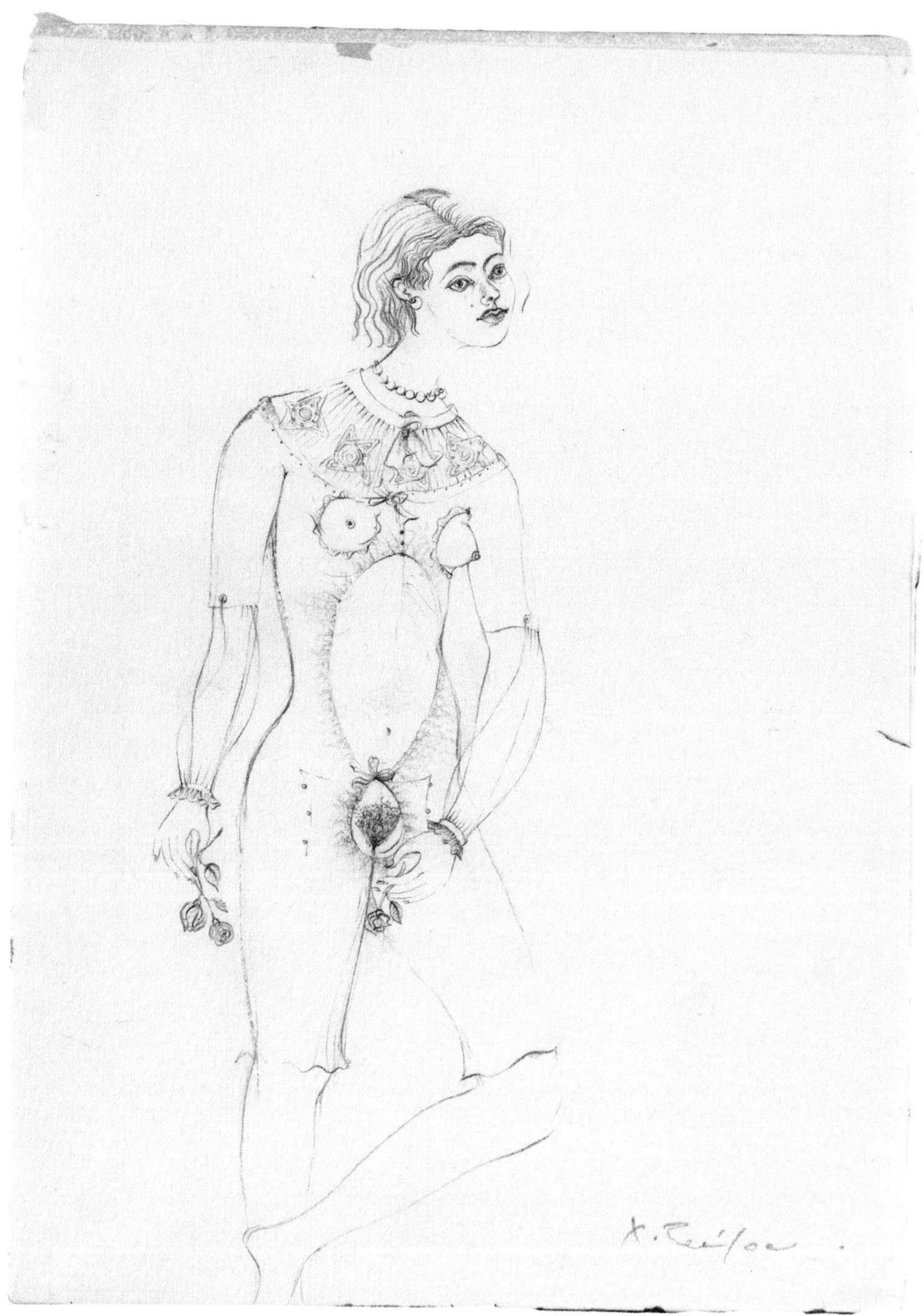

Untitled

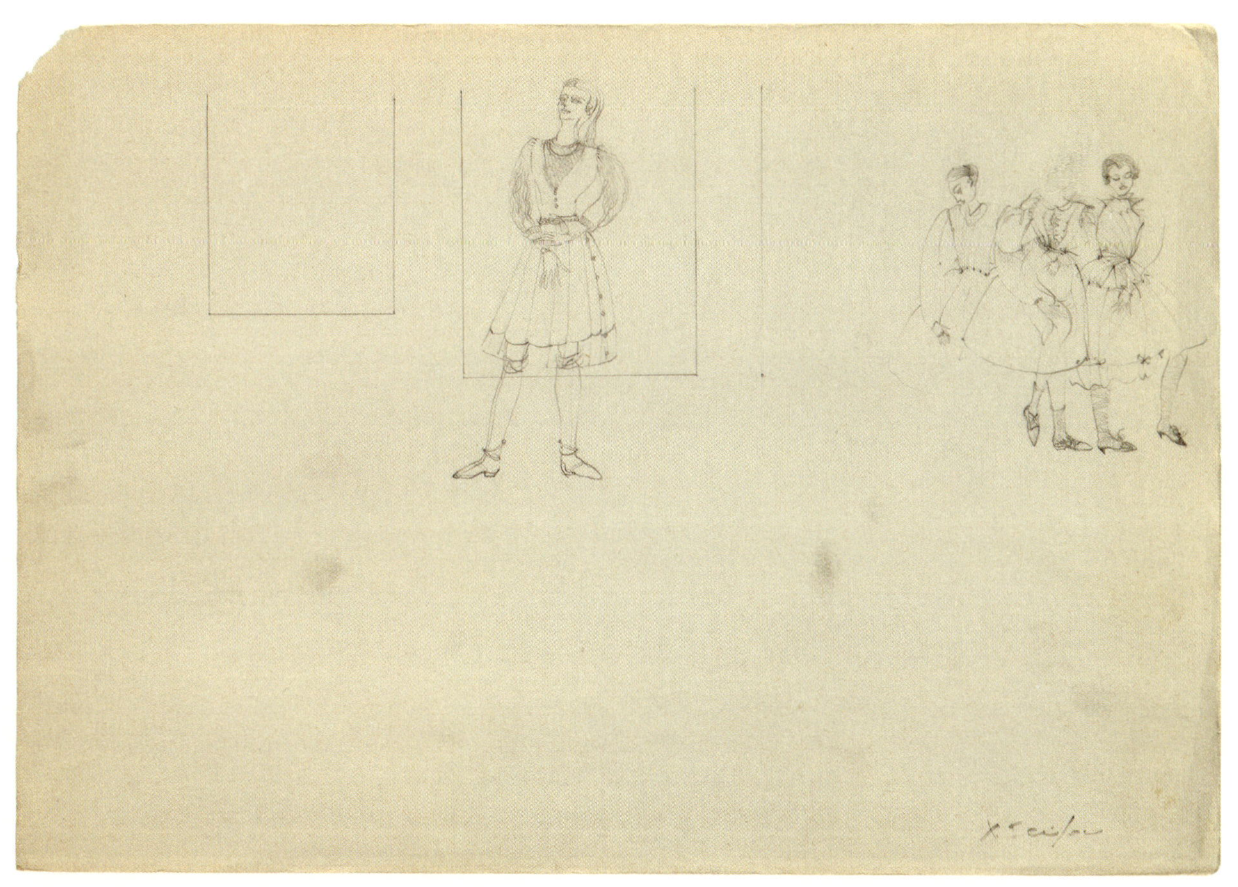

Untitled

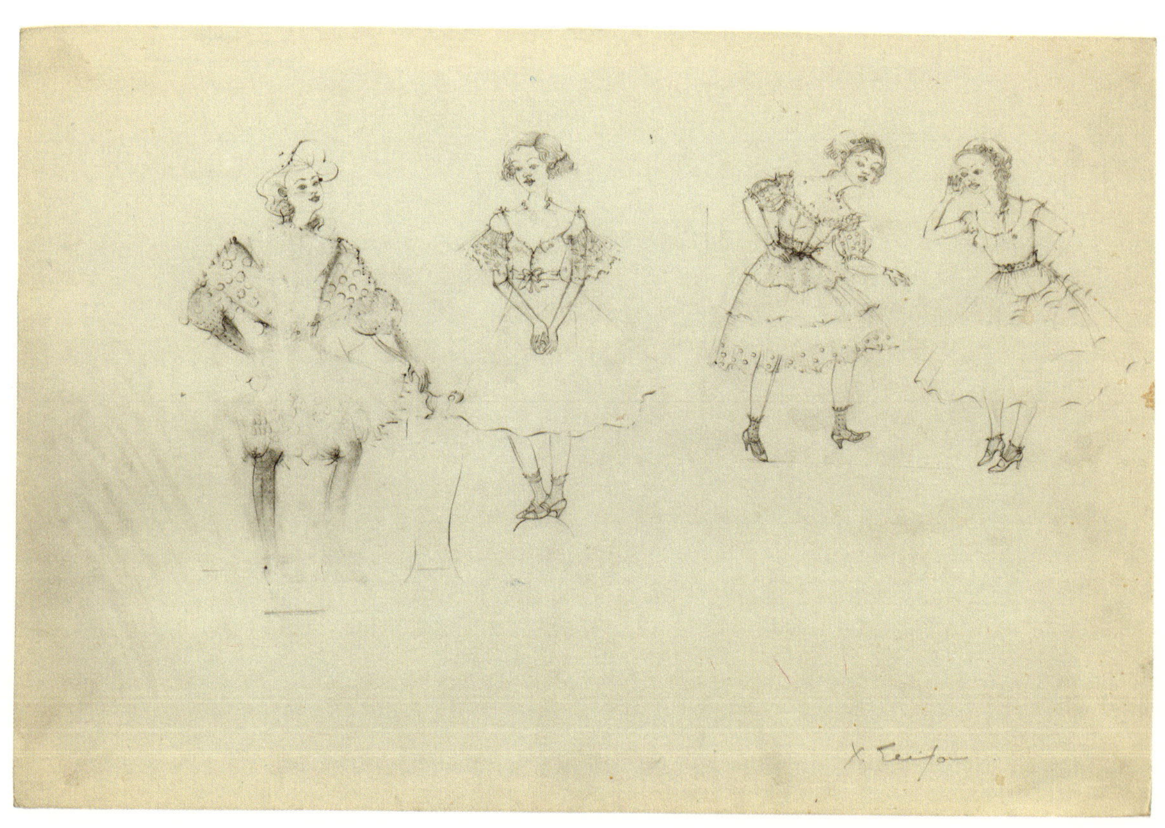

Untitled

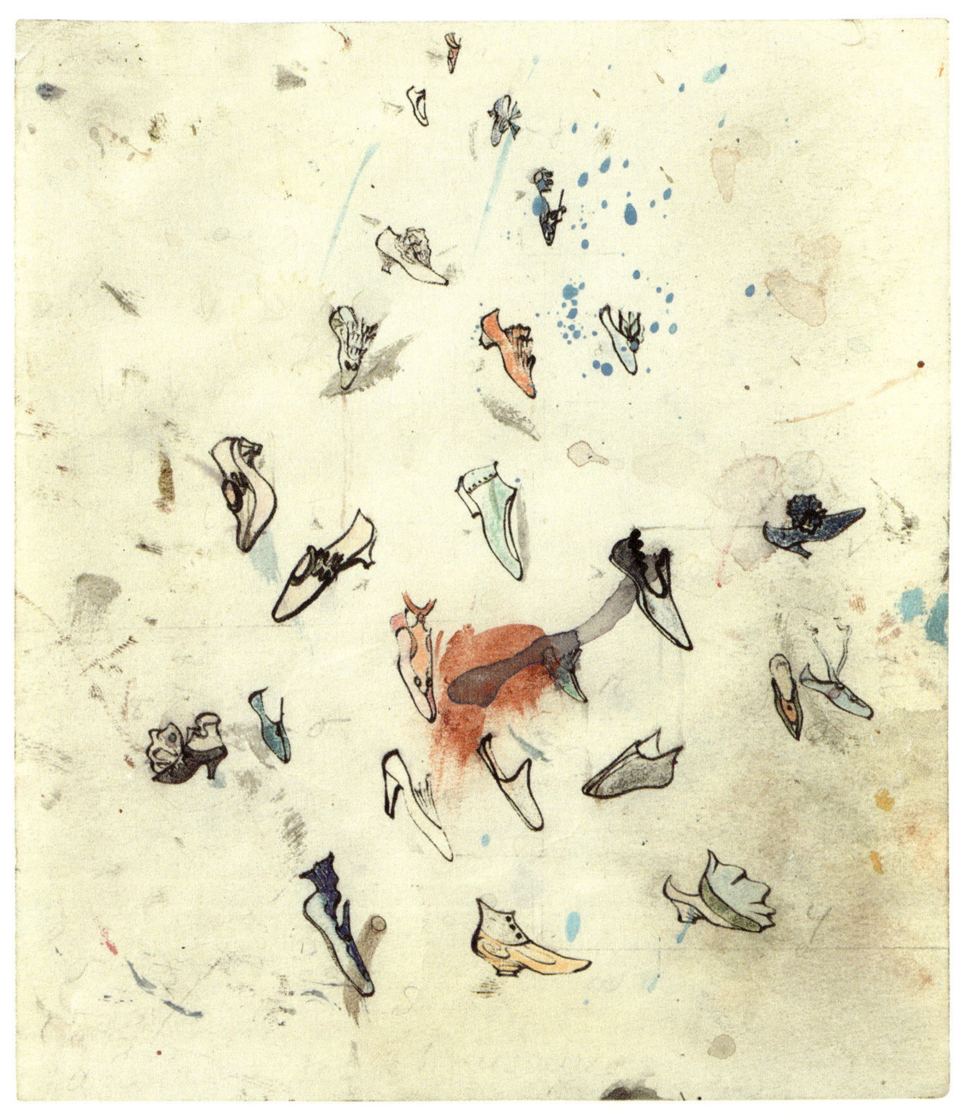

Untitled

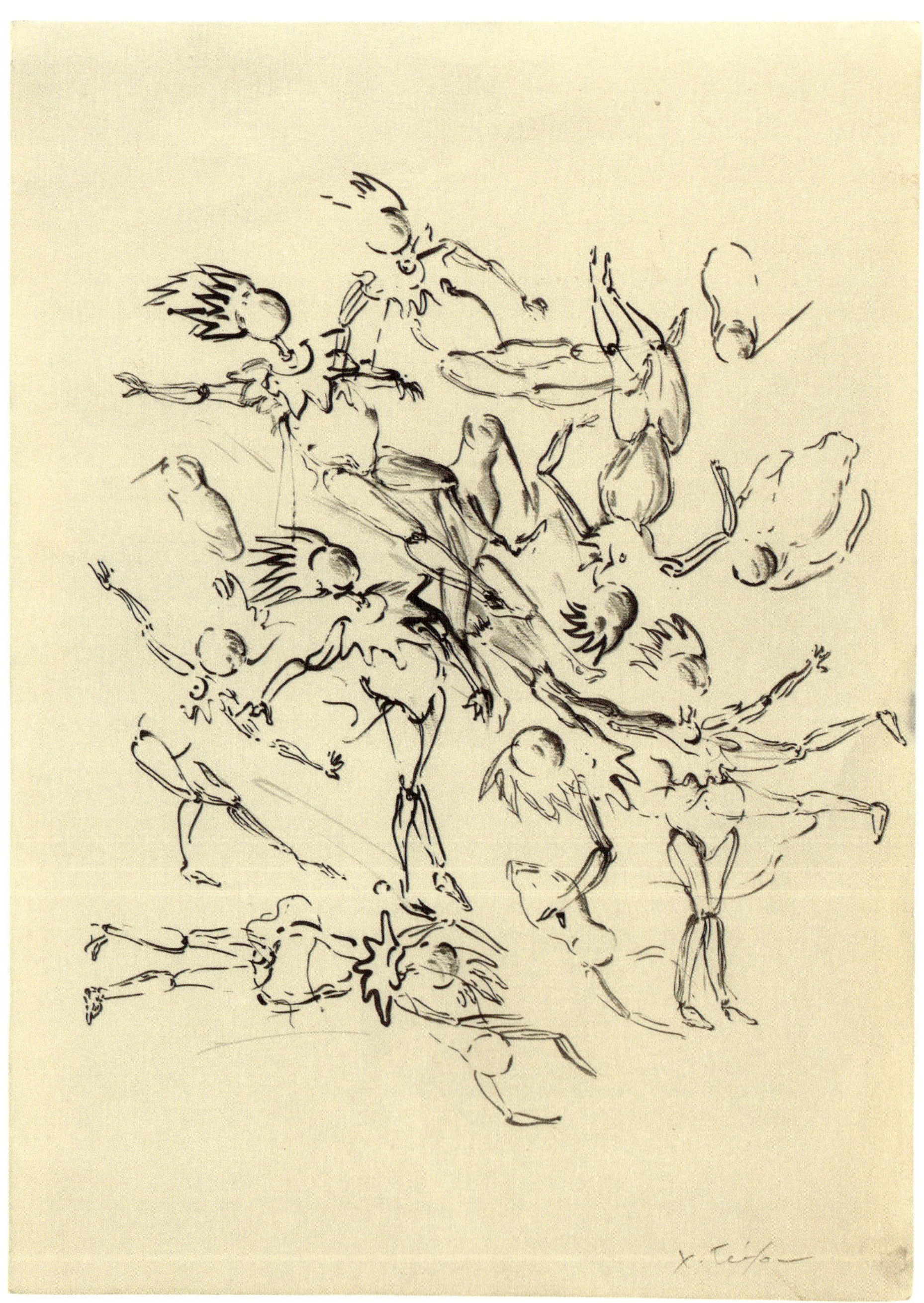

Untitled

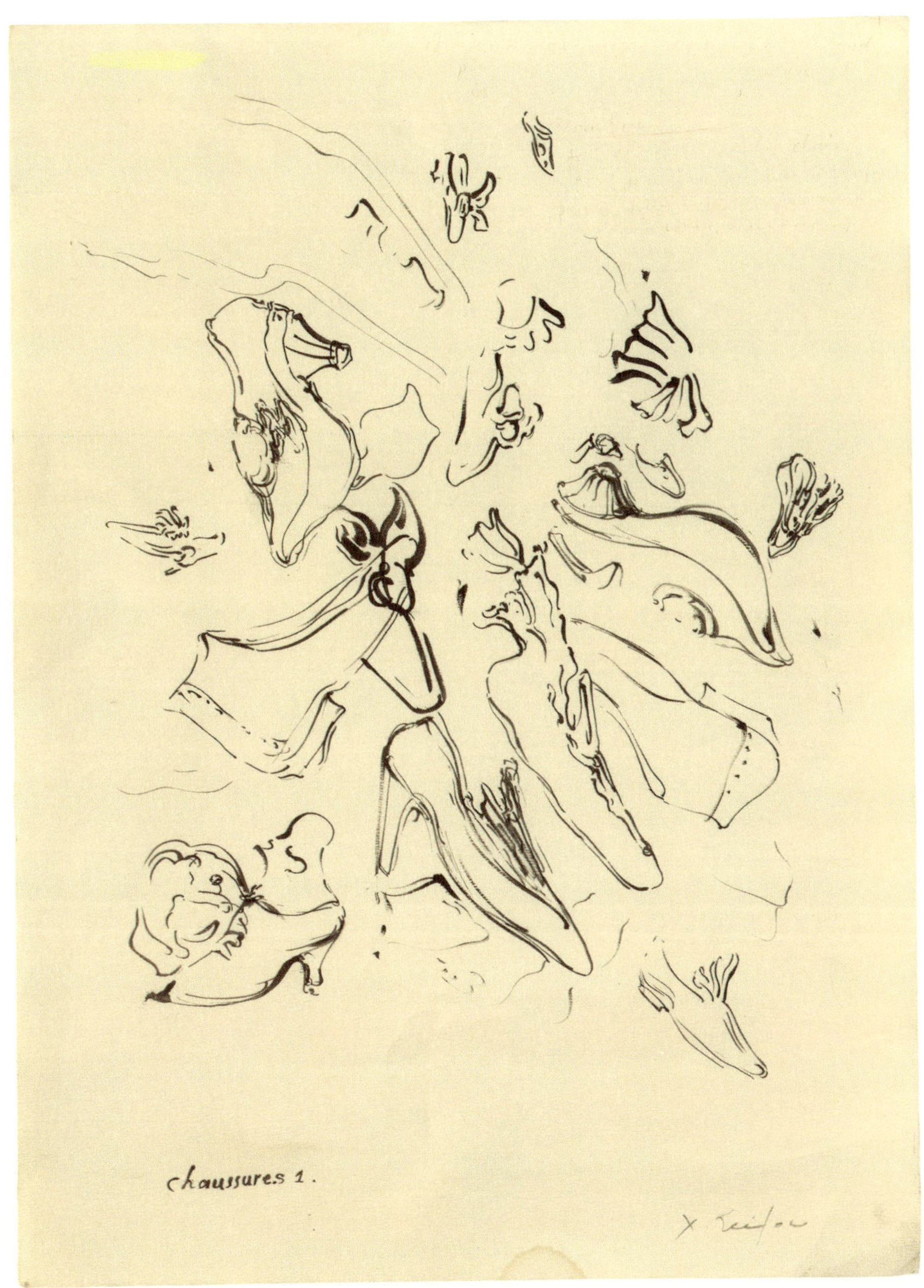

Untitled

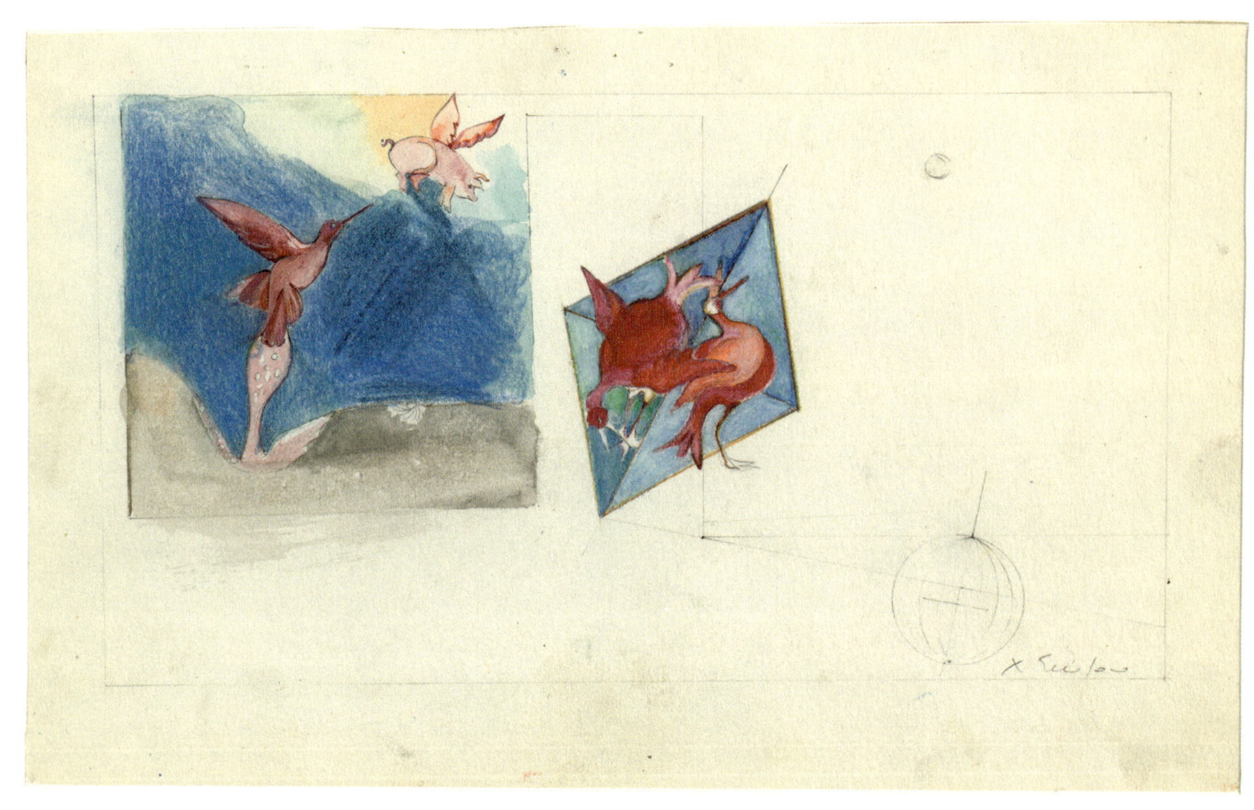

Untitled

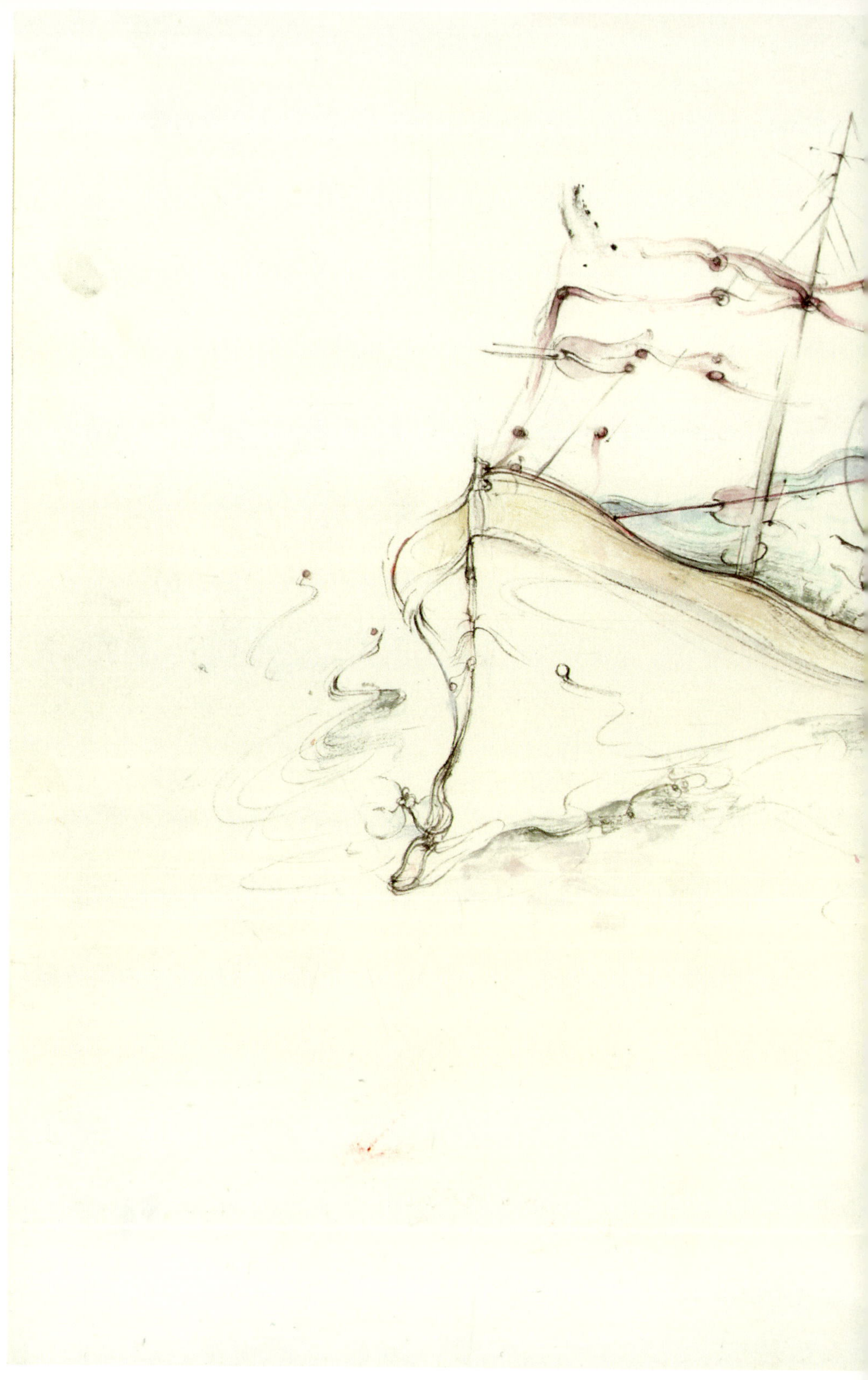

Shipwrecked—Amorgos/N. Gatsos, 2005

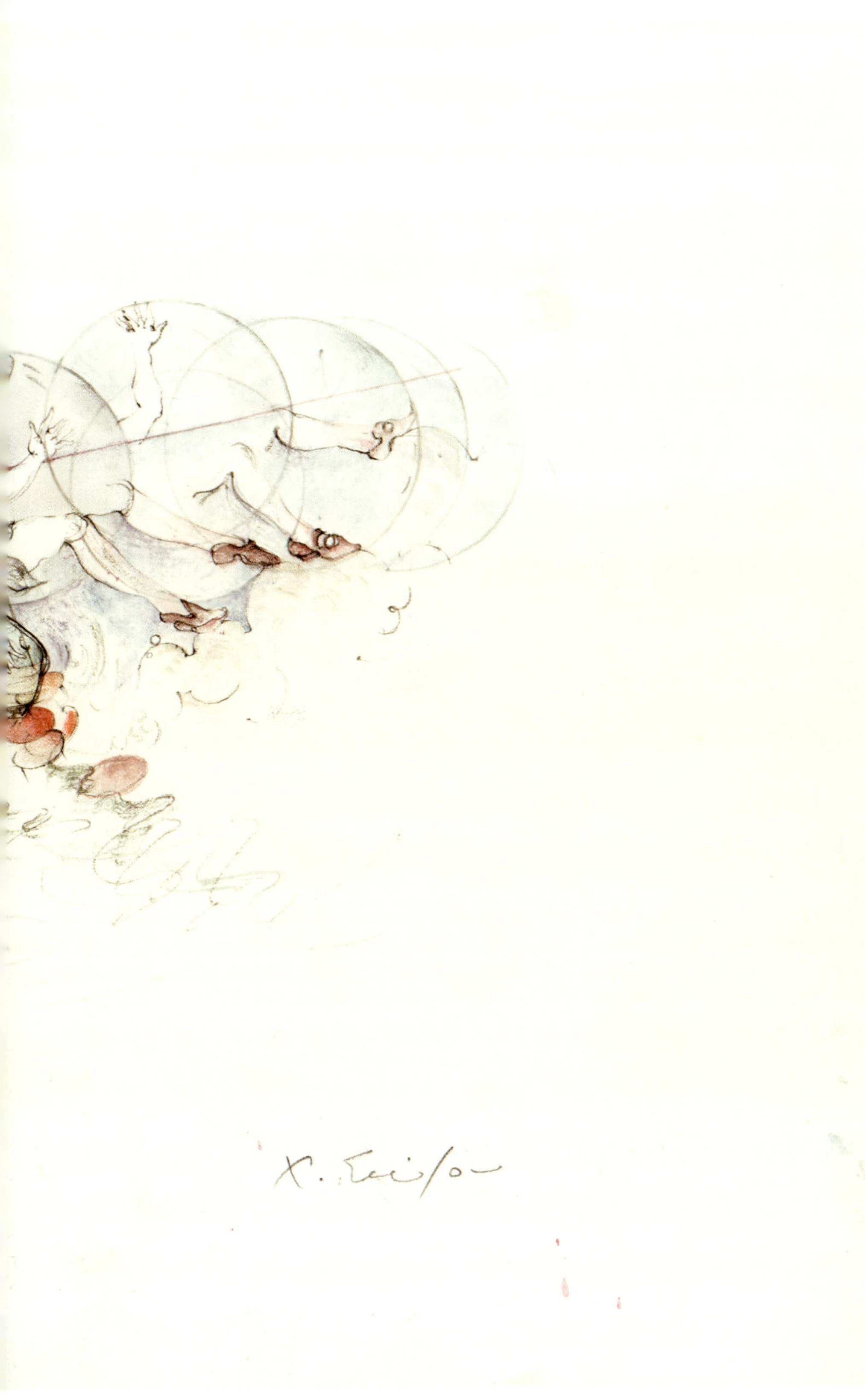

Laying the Ground with Stars—Amorgos/N. Gatsos, 2005

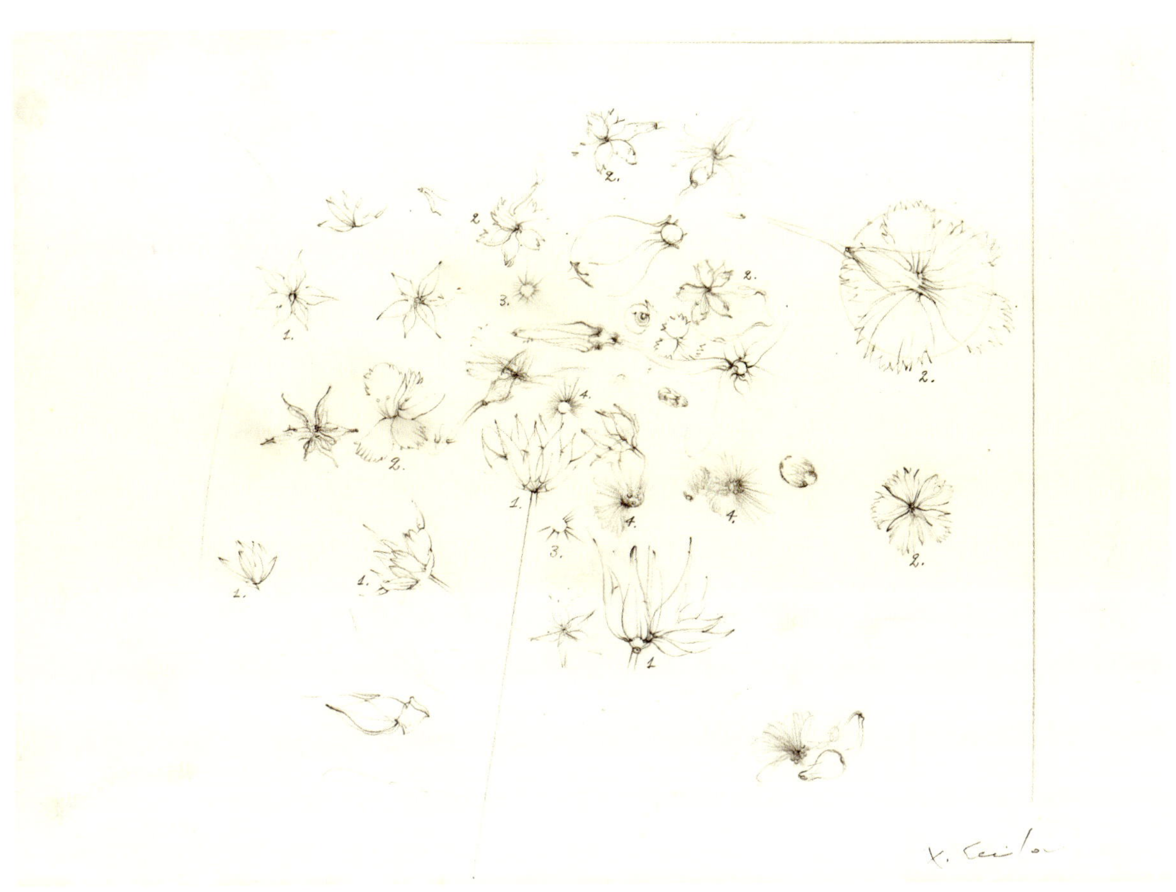

At the House of the Mournful Man—Amorgos/N. Gatsos, 2005

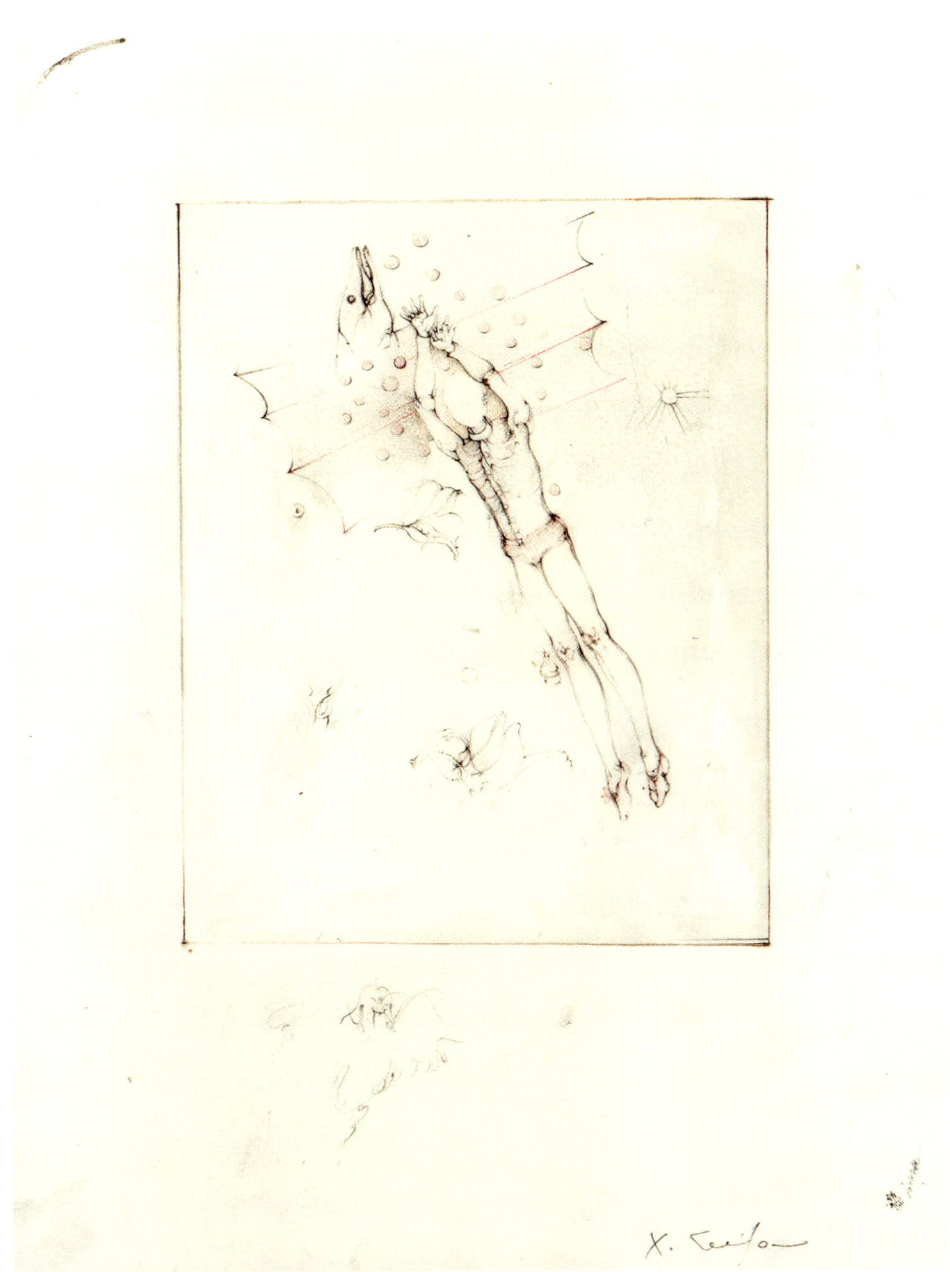

At the House of the Mournful Man, 2005

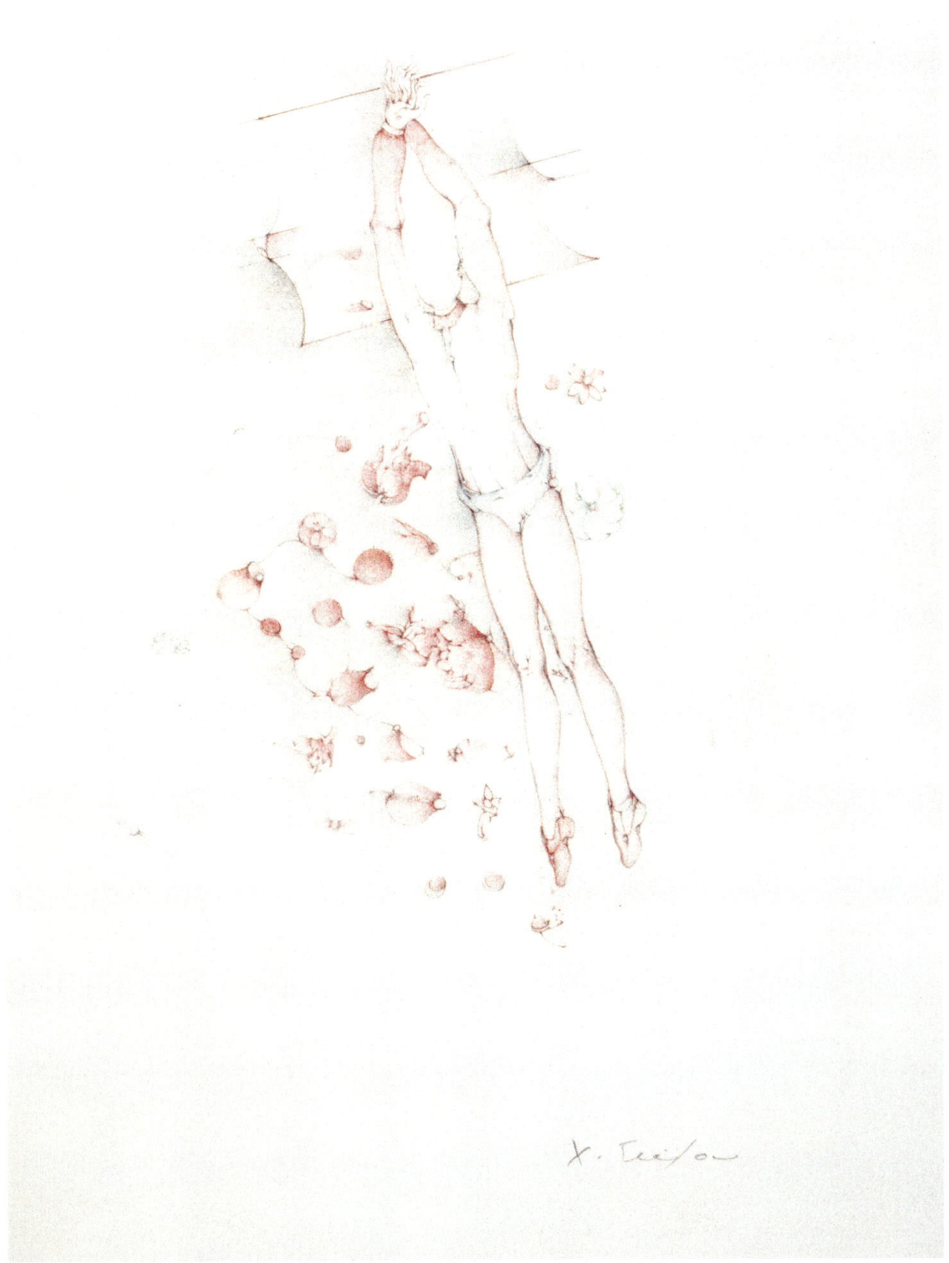

The Man during the Course of His Mysterious Life—Amorgos/N. Gatsos, 2005

The Frog of Communication, 2005

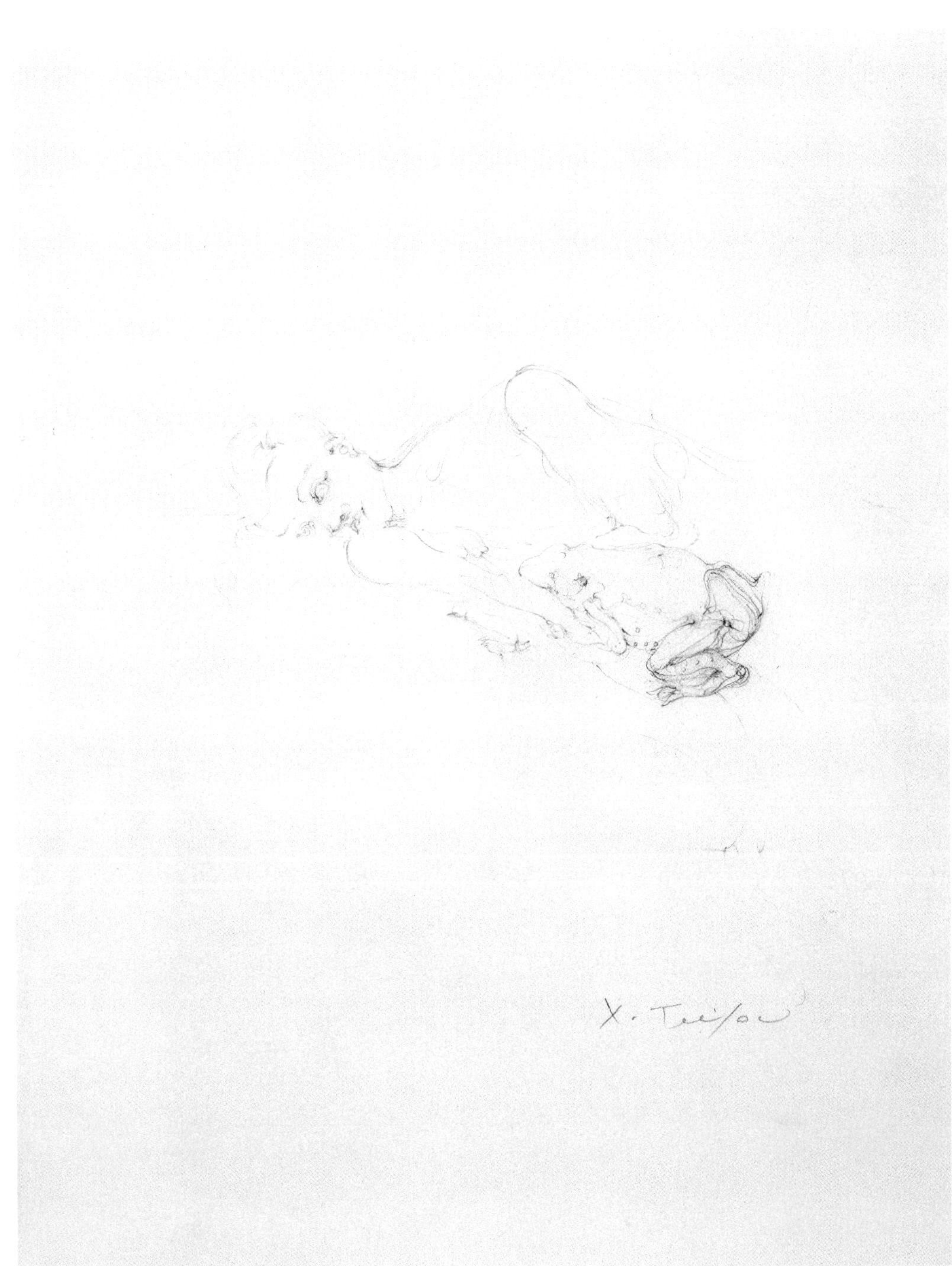

Untitled, 2005

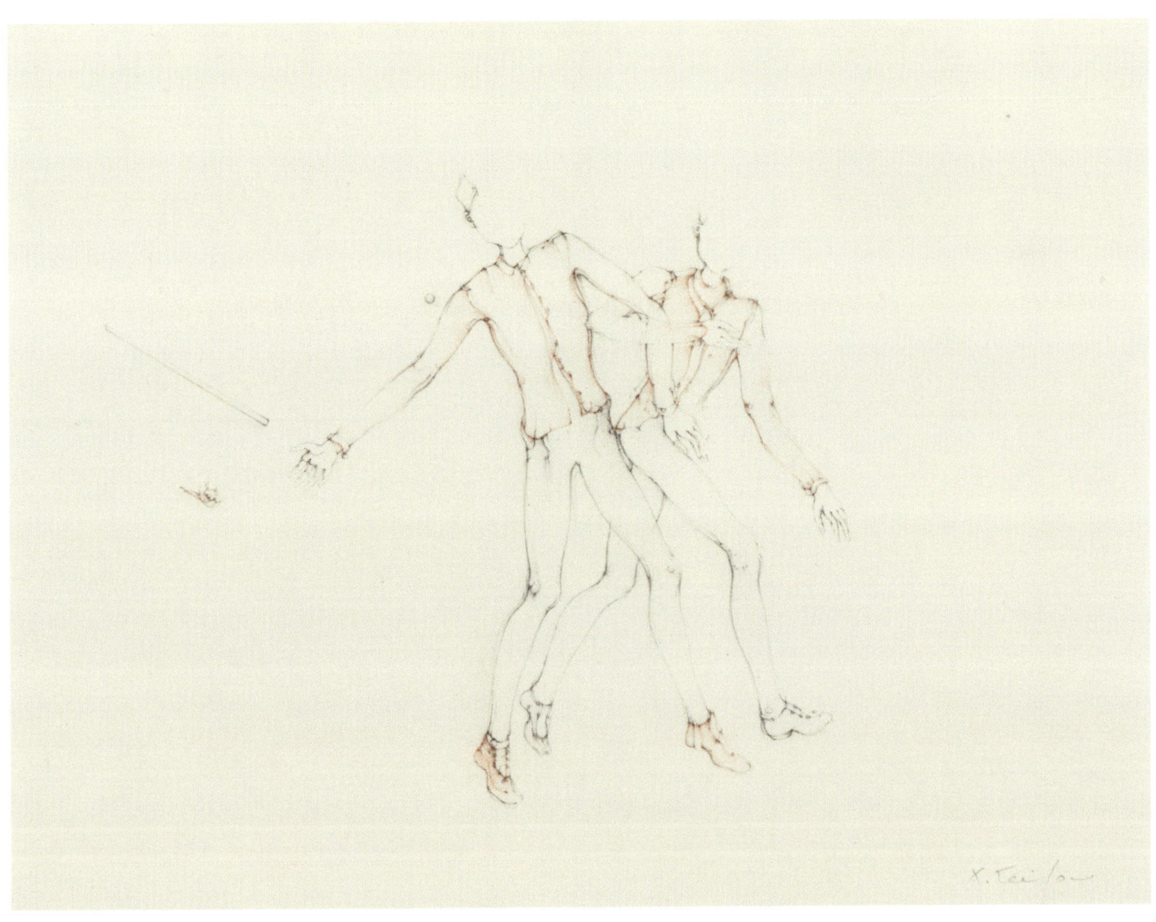

She Is Sleeping, 2005

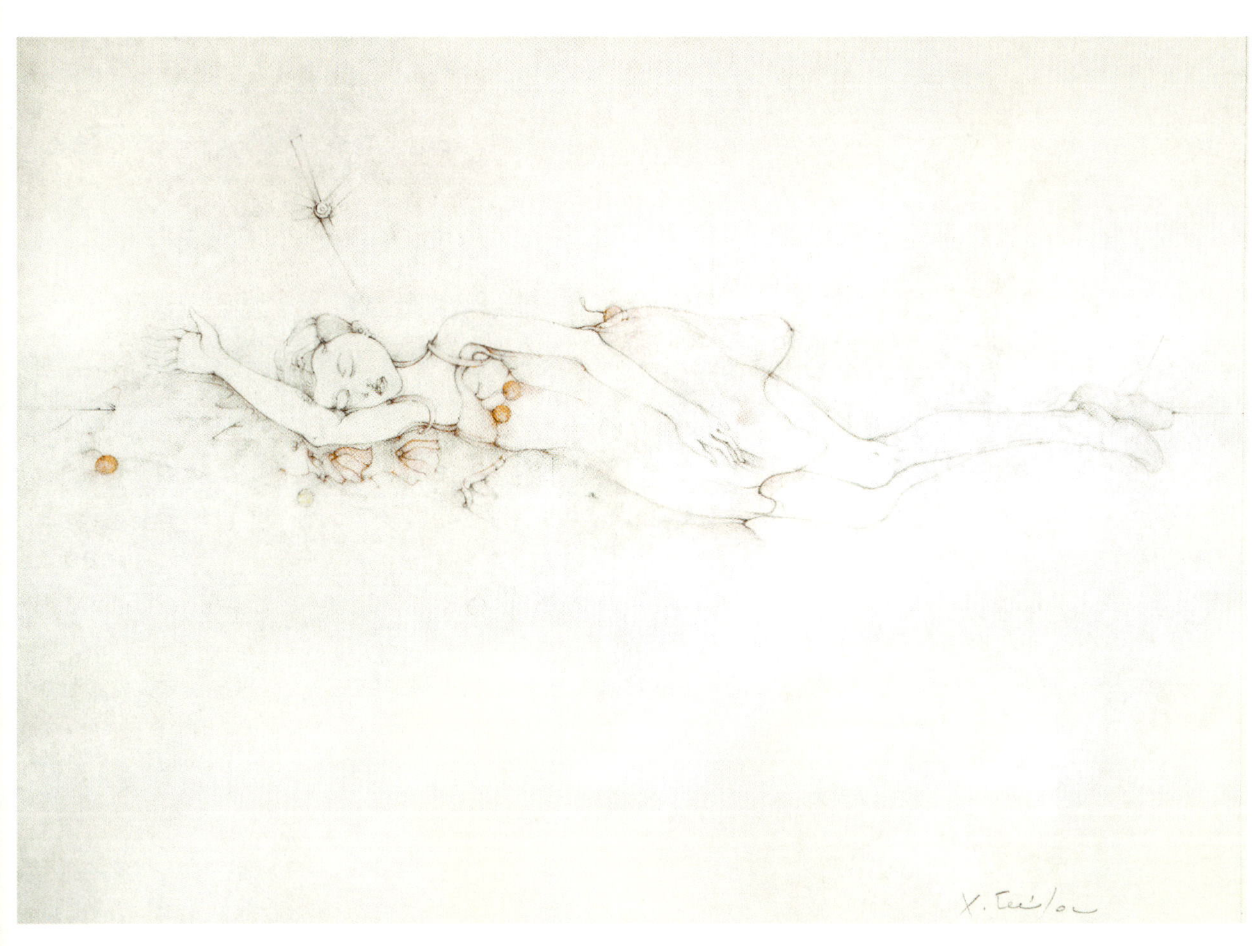

Only I Know How Very Much I Loved You, 2005

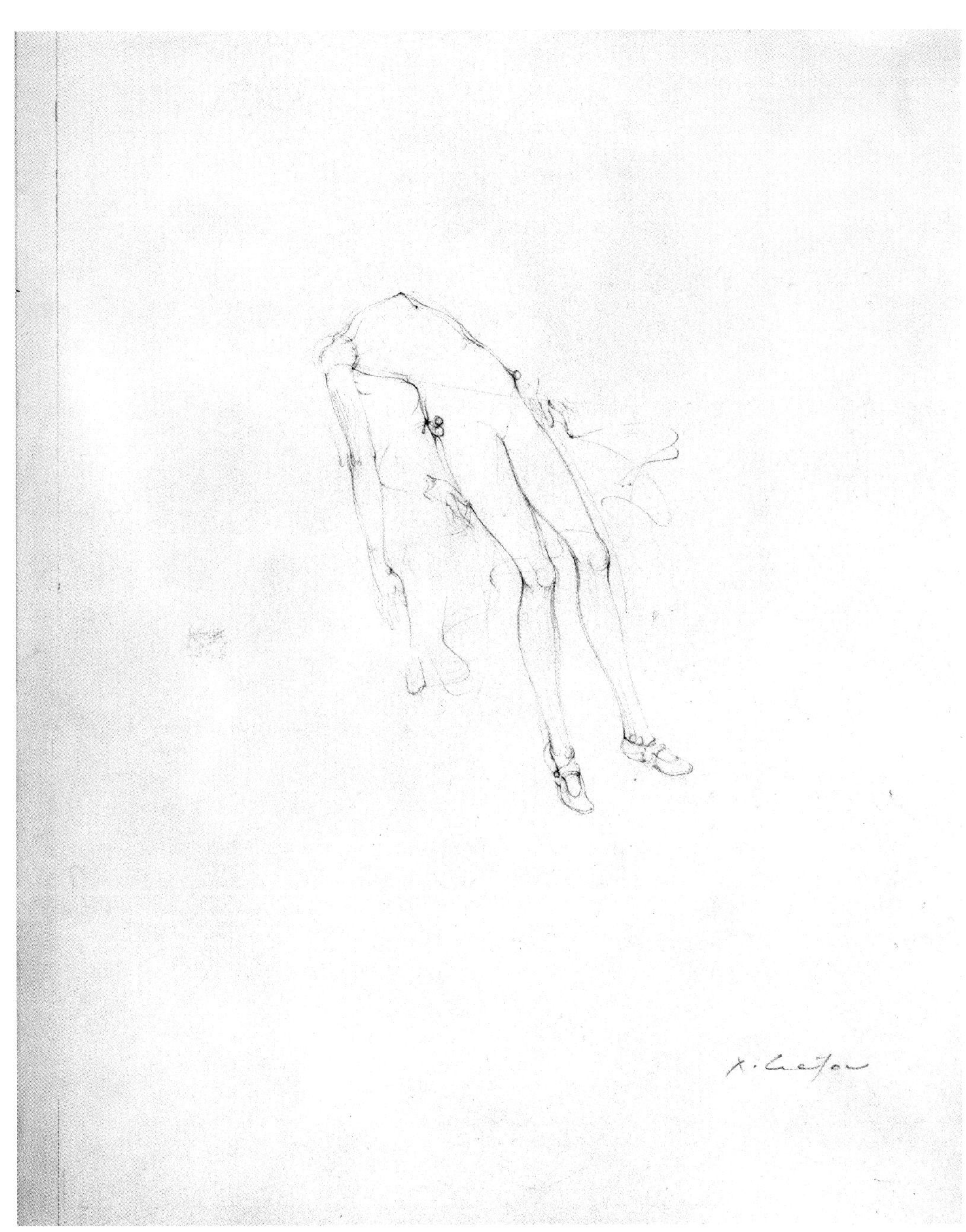

La Belle Dame sans Merci, 2006

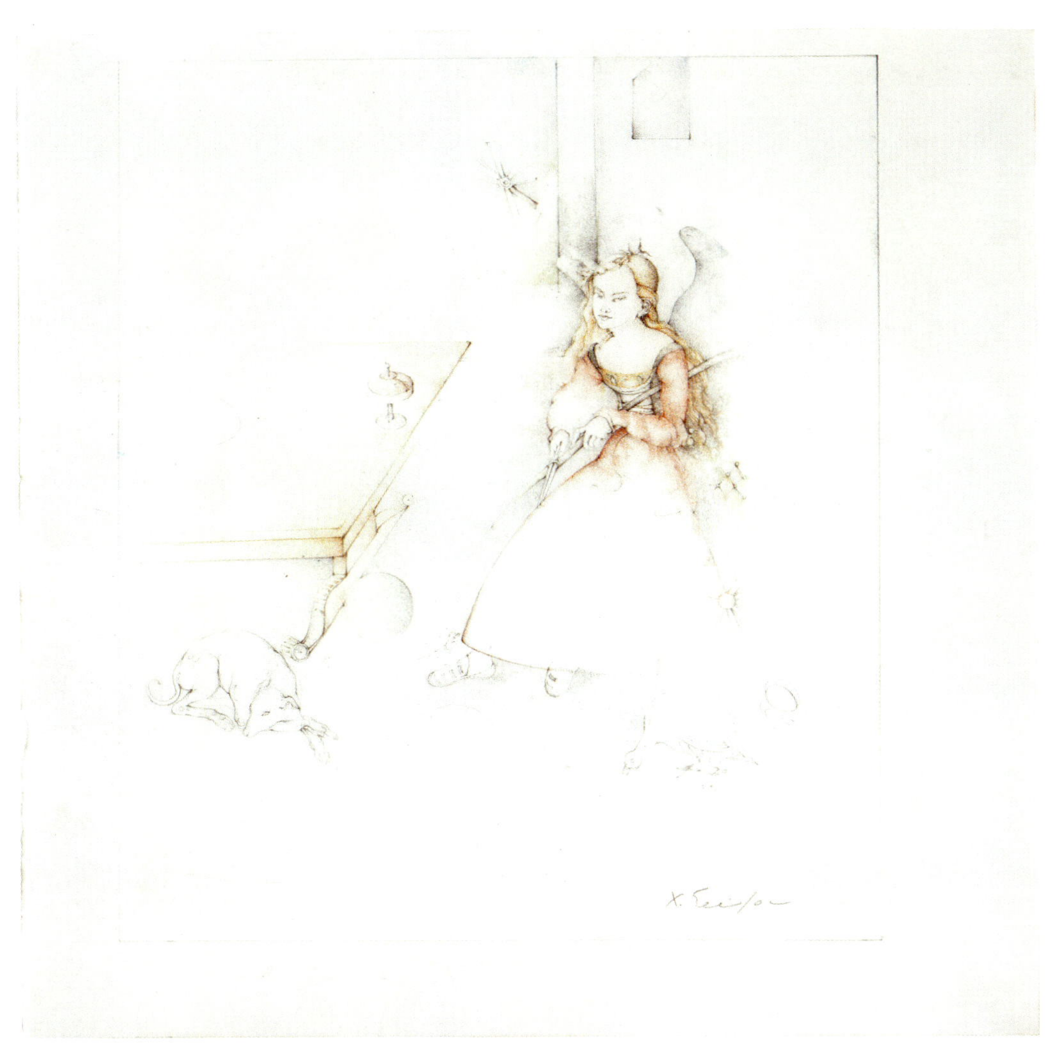

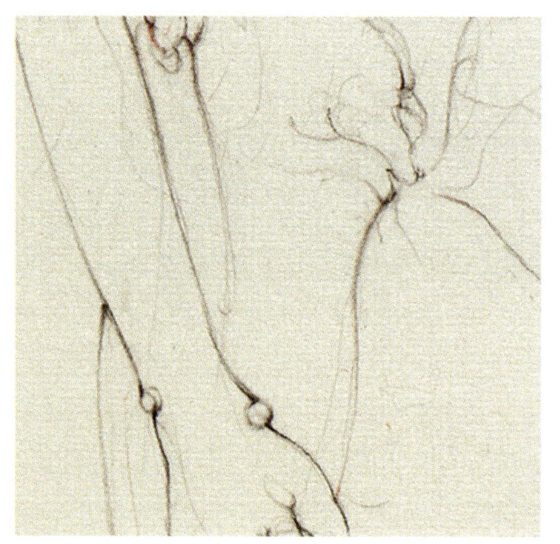

Nu, 2007

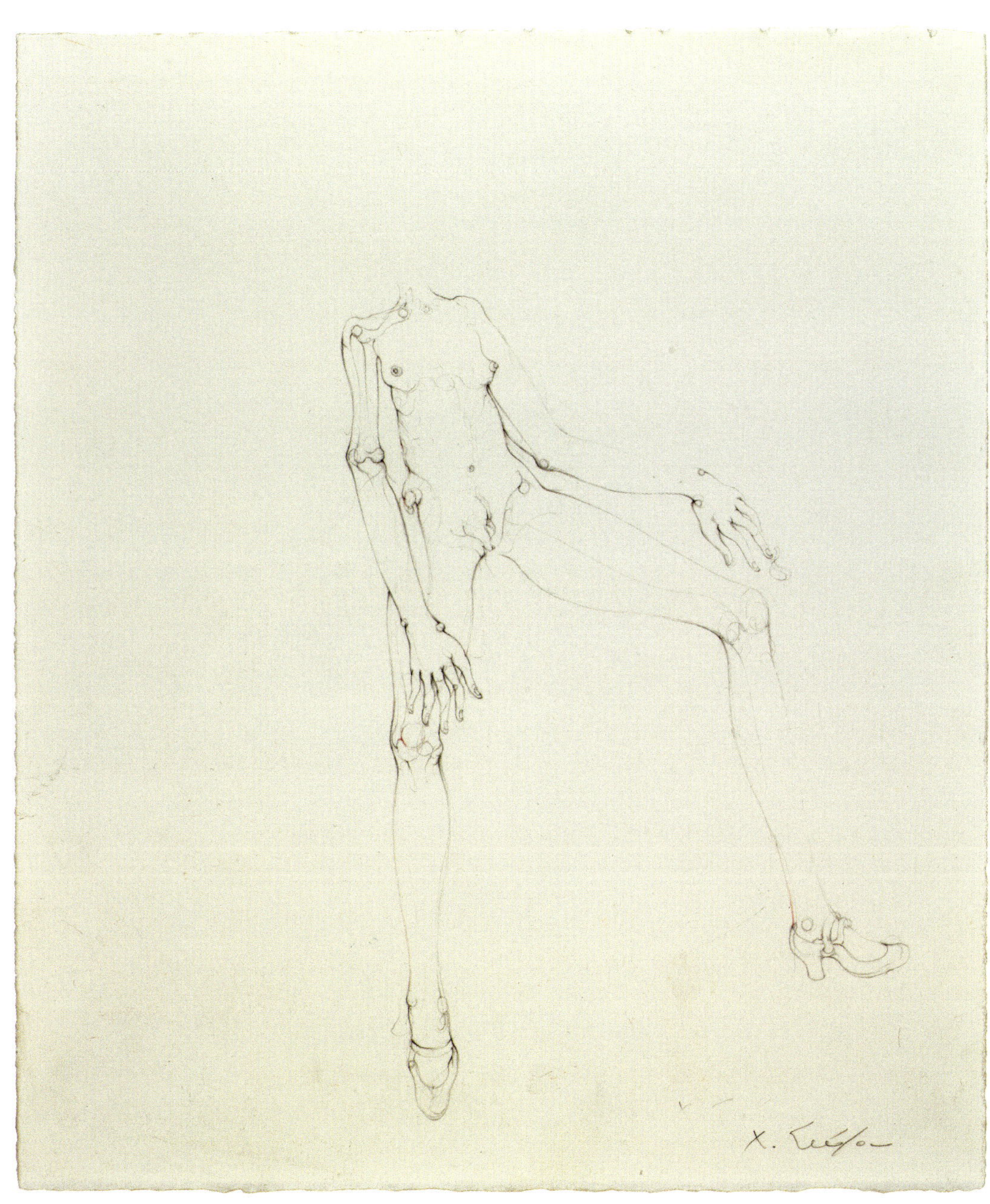

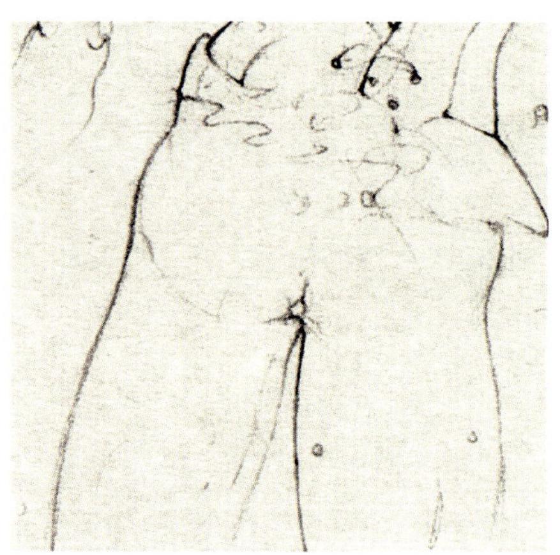

Domenico Scarlatti, Sonate K209, 2007

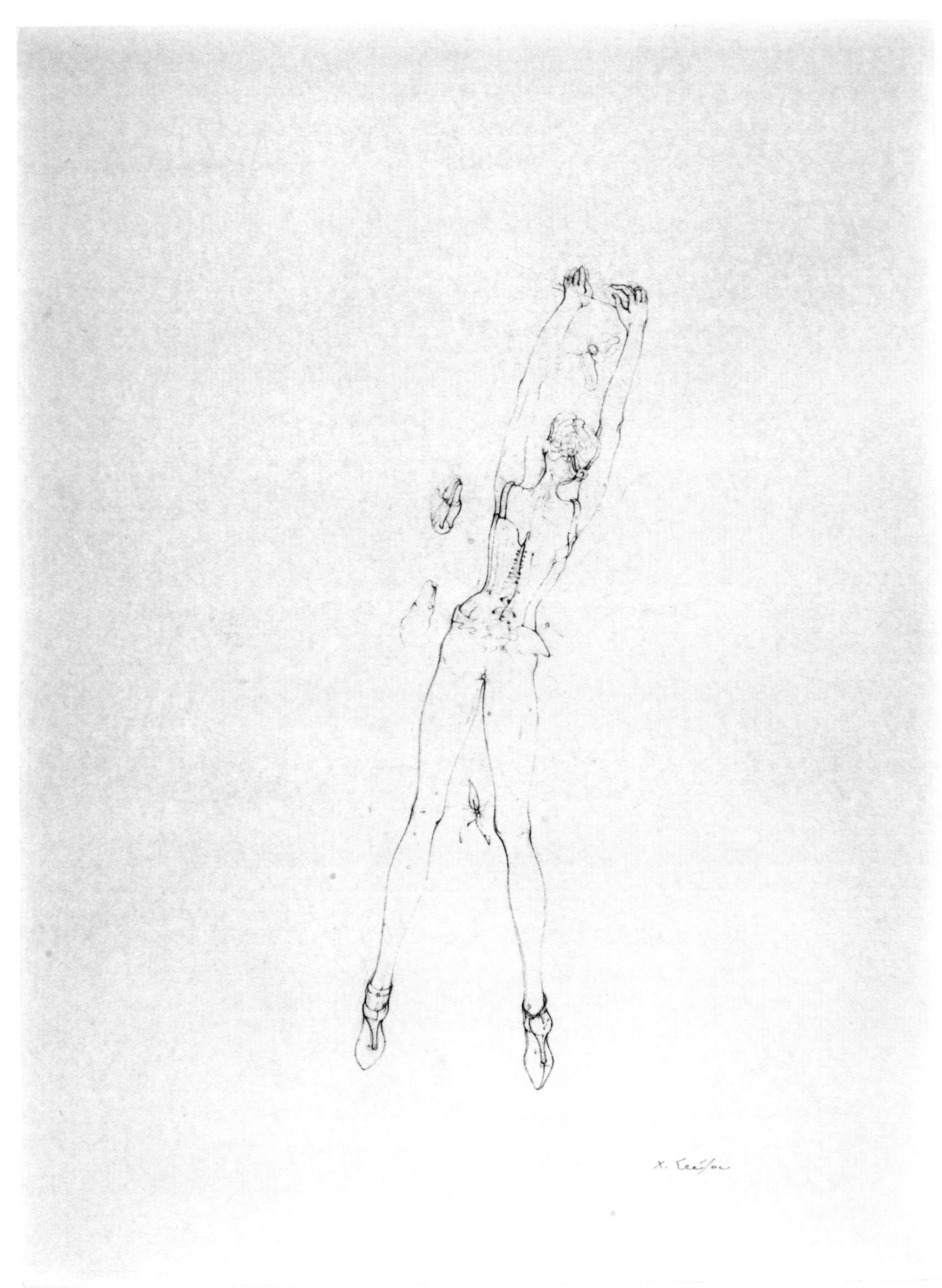

On my work on Tarot Cards

When I decided to work on the Tarot Cards, I said
I was tempted by the variety and the depth of the ideas,
of the names of the cards, of subjects featured as specific
names: The fool, the Emperor, Justice or Death, are
some of the host of really interesting themes to work .
on. Most of all, the idea of having assembled into a
paquet, such an ensemble of diverse themes/figures,
so essentially different between them and yet so alike,
since they all together form a single game.
That was my first idea and yet I knew that what really
was in my head, shaped under the curious "pretexte" of
a tarot game, was my attempt to prove throughout the
context of a very concrete system (tarot game), the
absolute ambiguity of meanning, significance and
possible definition of each figure.
What better example than to choose diverse titles, to
finally bring them all towards a common end?
Because all those cards, despite their different names
(fool, magician, justice e.t.c.) that differenciate them
in terms of meanning and significance, share between
them common essential features. My work on the
Tarot Cards is mainly a judgement (a critic) on
human qualities.
It is a work on characters and I should like to
introduce you here the "dramatis personae"
of my work;

Characters	Qualities
1. The Magician	magic
2. The High Priestess	strong, settled, committed
3. The Emperor	young, proud, arrogant, not pretentious, sweet, cute, sly, cunning, handsome, foolish, charming, intelligent.
4. The Empress	obviously royal, sly, cunning.
5. The Hierophant	young, pretentious, impertinent, trickster, cheat, promising, ambitious.
6. The Lovers	
7. The Chariot	
8. Strength	
9. The Hermit	fool, committed, indecisive, sad.
10. Wheel of Fortune	
11. Justice	strong, reserved, devoted, settled, committed, determined honest, loyal
12. The Hanged Man	hanged
13. Death	un ultimate lost
14. Temperance	strong, reserved, devoted
15. The Devil	a poor devil
16. The Tower	
17. The Star	
18. The Moon	
19. The Sun	
20. The Last Judgement	pensive
0. The Fool	young, wise, dreamer
21. The World	

Conclusion

The magician is the only to be magic, unlike the emperor who is young, proud, arrogant, not pretentious, sweet, cute, sly, cunning, handsome, foolish, charming and intelligent. High Priestess, Justice and Temperance are strong. High Priestess, the Hermit and Justice are committed. Justice and Temperance are reserved. They are also both devoted. Justice is also determined and loyal and among all characters, she is the only to possess those qualities. The Emperor is young, so is the Hierophant and the Fool. But the Fool is wise and dreamer, unlike the hierophant who is trickster, promising and ambitious.

Some qualities represent 'ensembles' that comprise many characters. What makes a character being defined by its own quality, is either when he is the only to possess one (see the magician), or when one or more qualities, exceed the ensemble of common qualities shared with other characters (see justice), or when a composition of qualities, even if part of them, are already comprised into some other character, they still form a unique shape (see temperance).

My attempt was to show what makes the Difference that shapes every character into its own unique quality.

How difference can be discrete?

Finally in my story, the fool is wise, the Emperor is foolish and the Hermit is fool. Ressemblance is not to be found in similarity but in difference.

Christiana Soulou

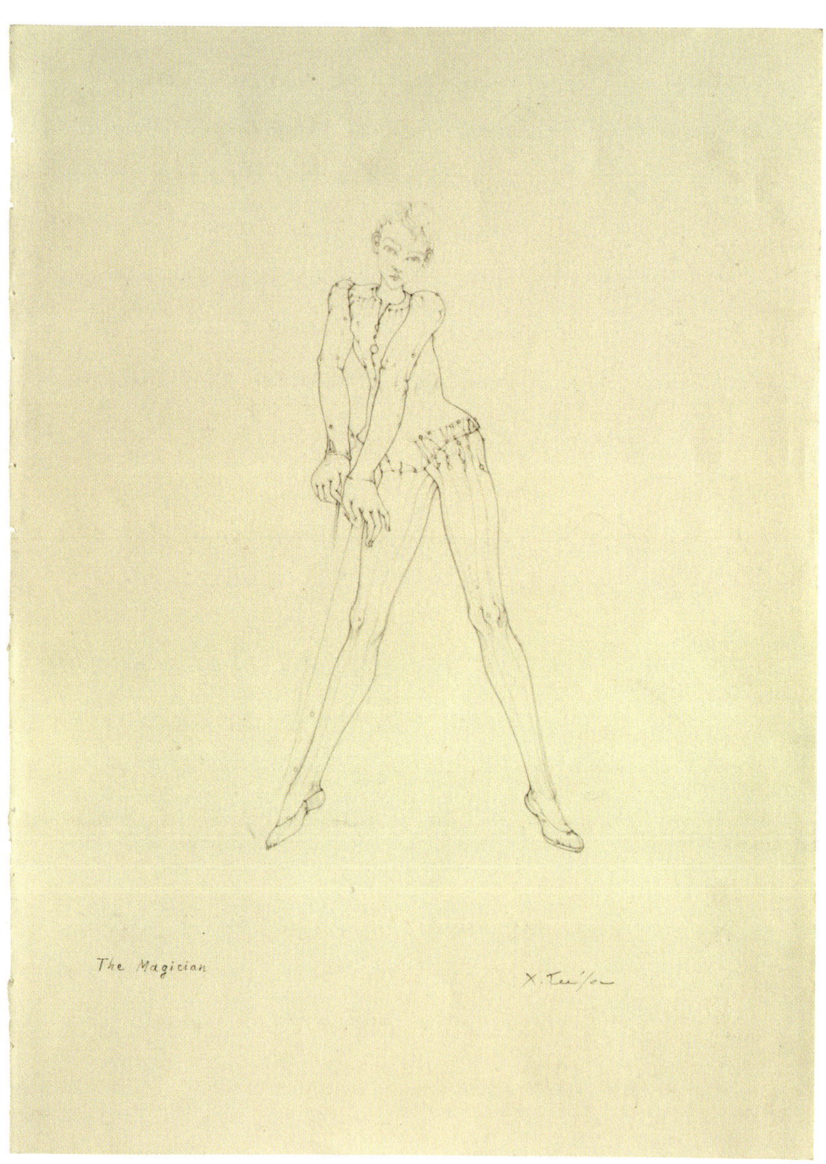

Tarot (The Magician), 2009

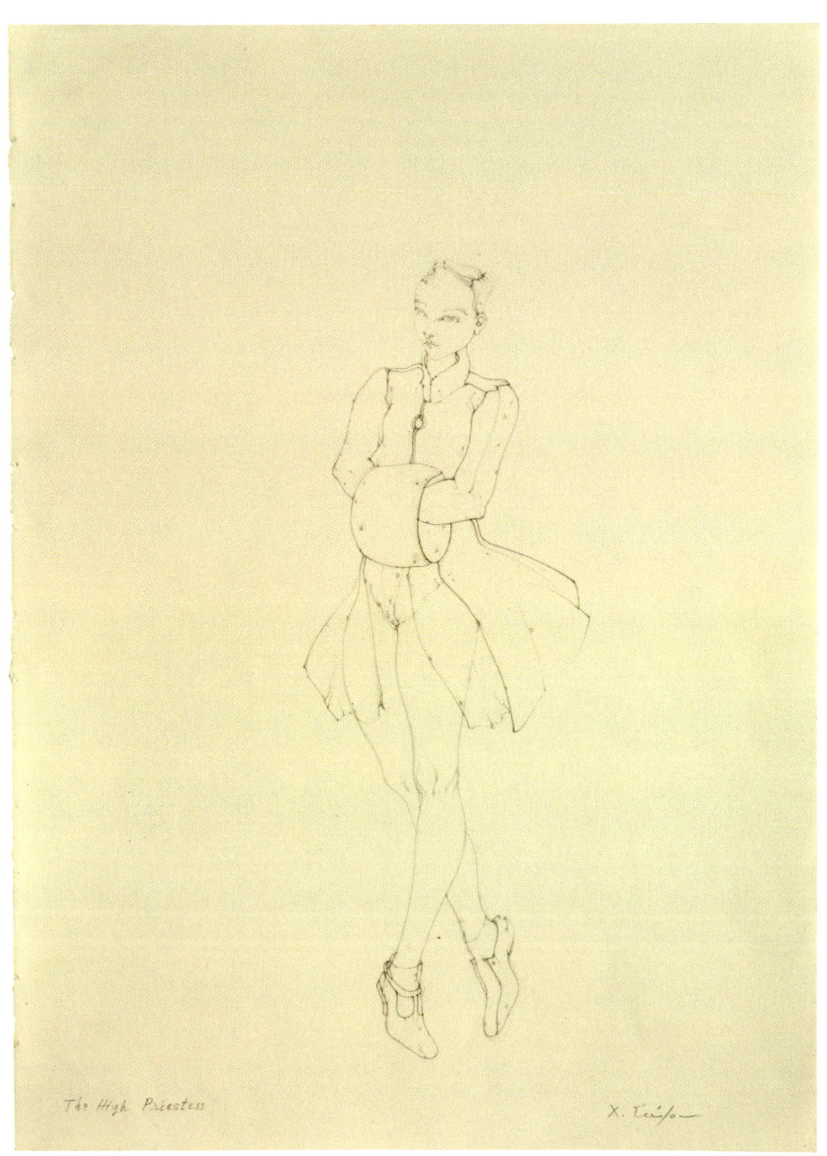

Tarot (The High Priestess), 2009

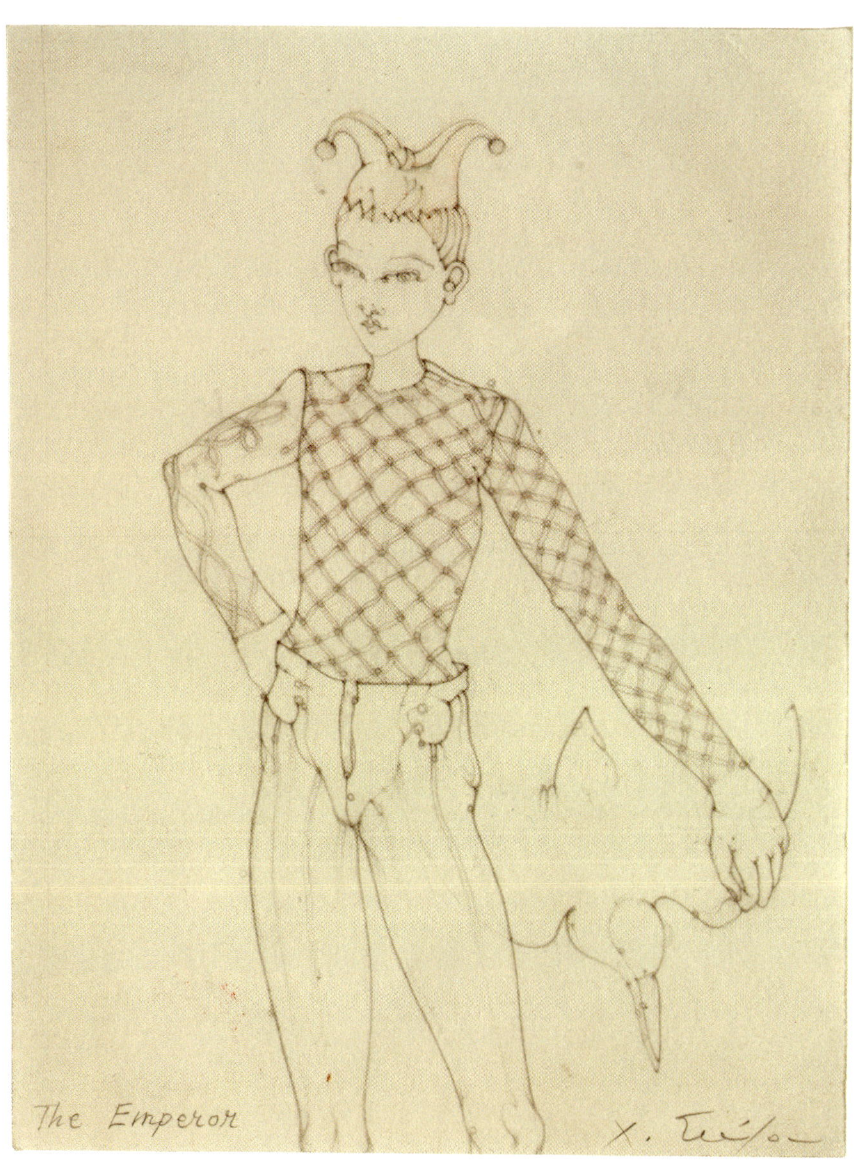

Tarot (The Emperor), 2009

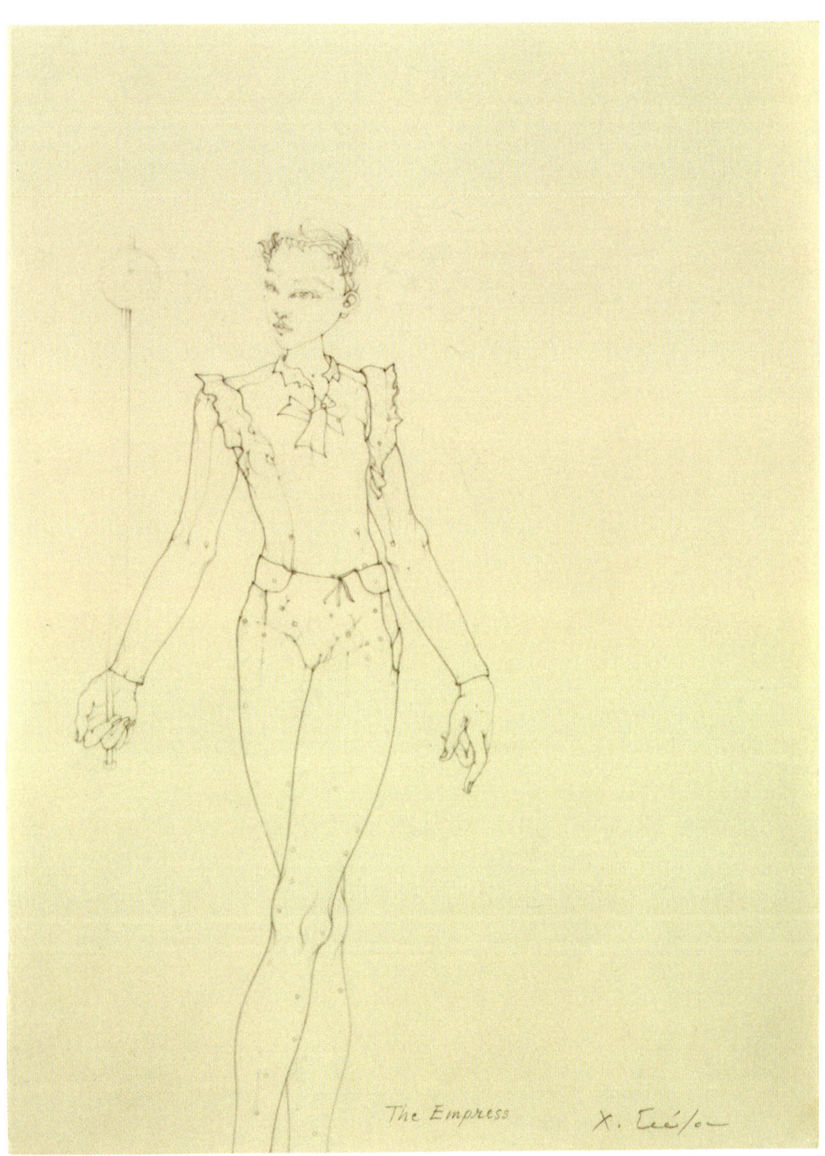

Tarot (The Empress), 2009

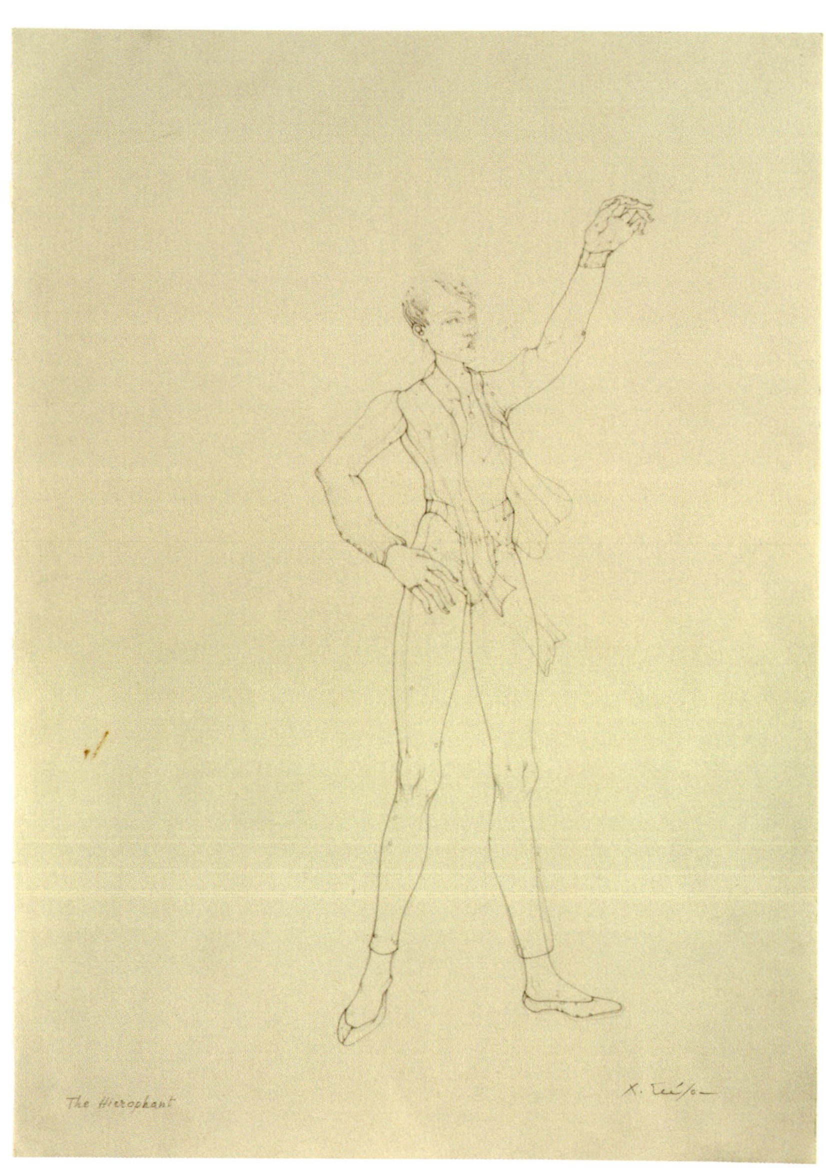

Tarot (The Hierophant), 2009

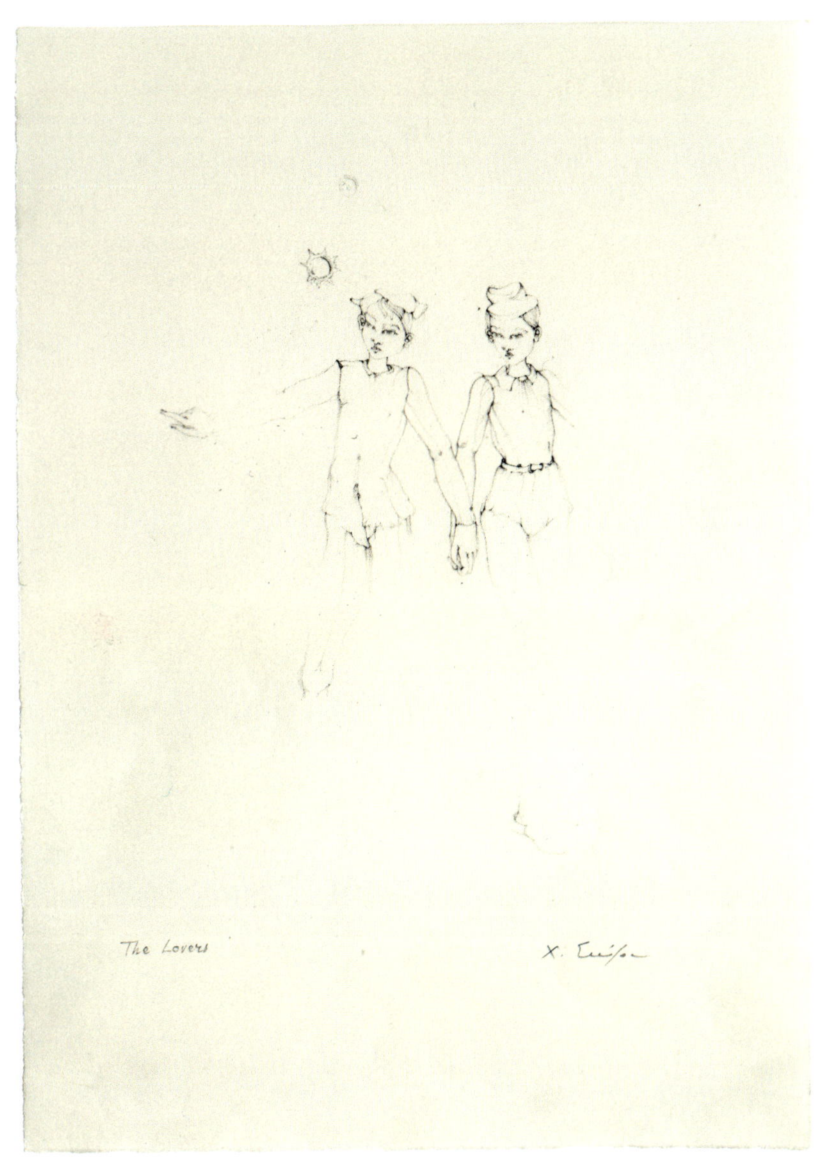

Tarot (The Lovers), 2009

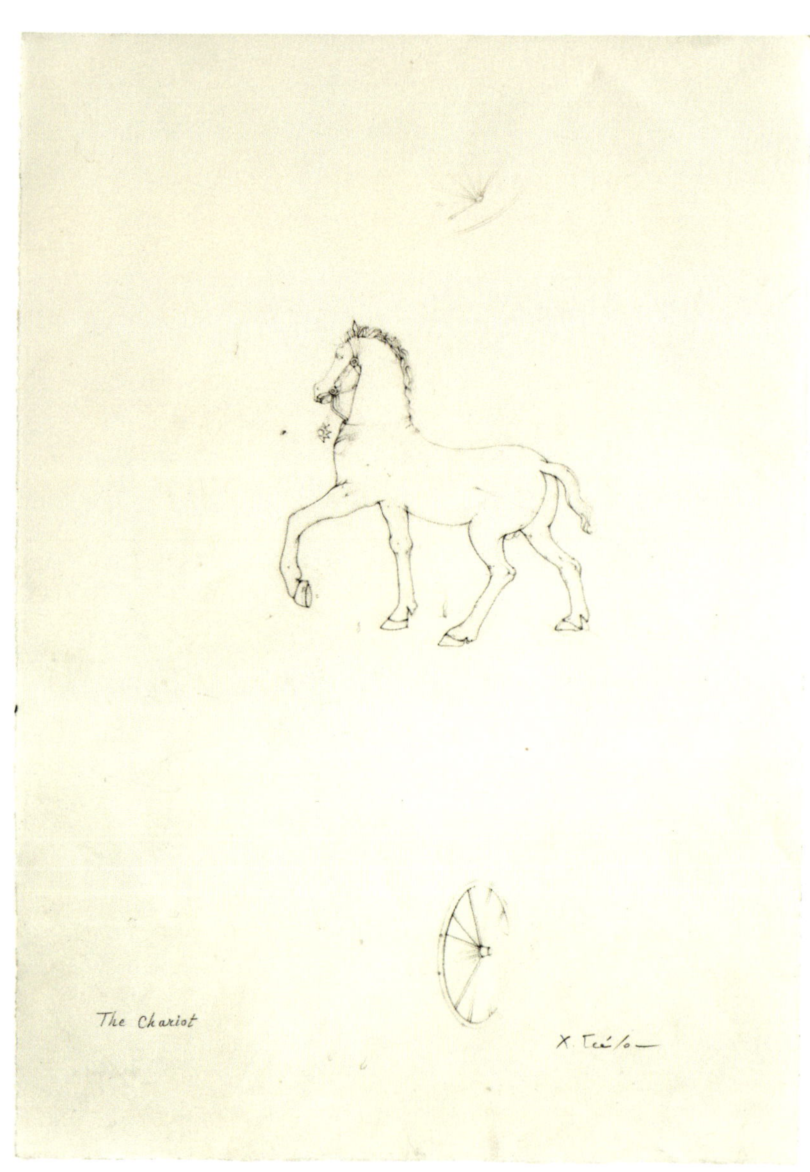

Tarot (The Chariot), 2009

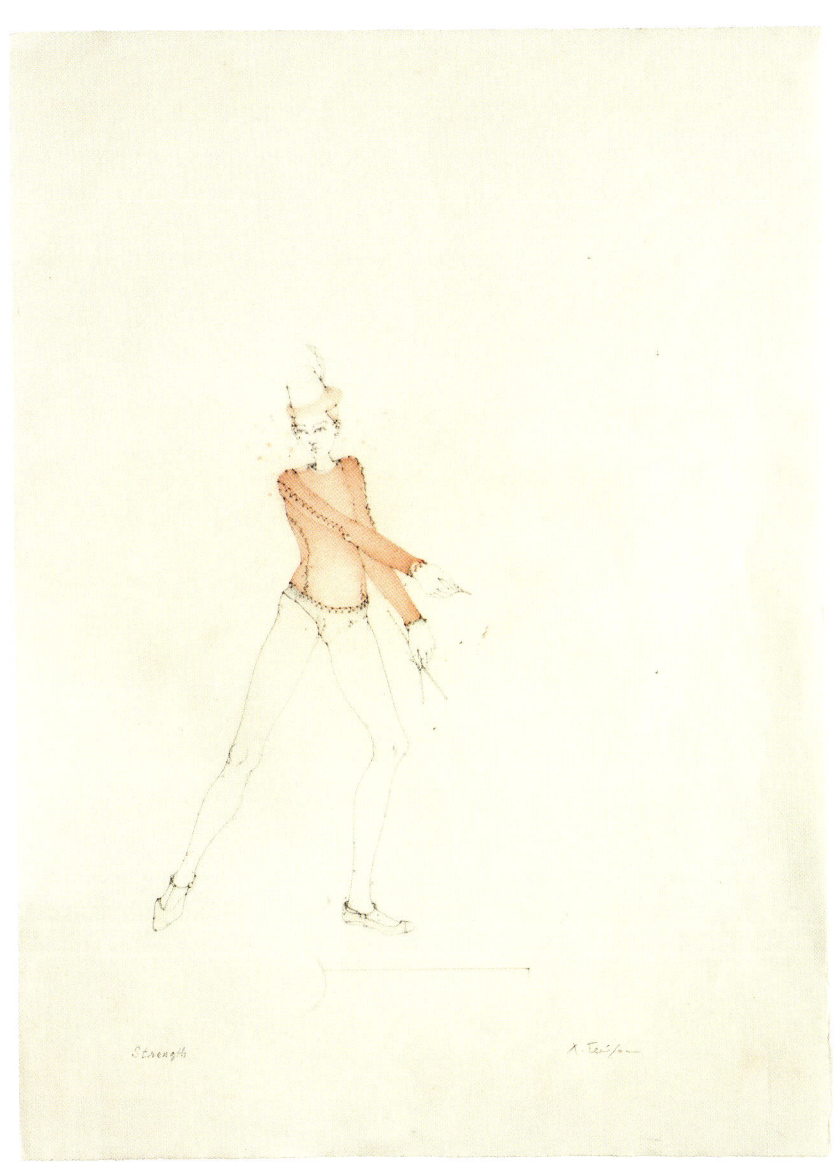

Tarot (Strength), 2009

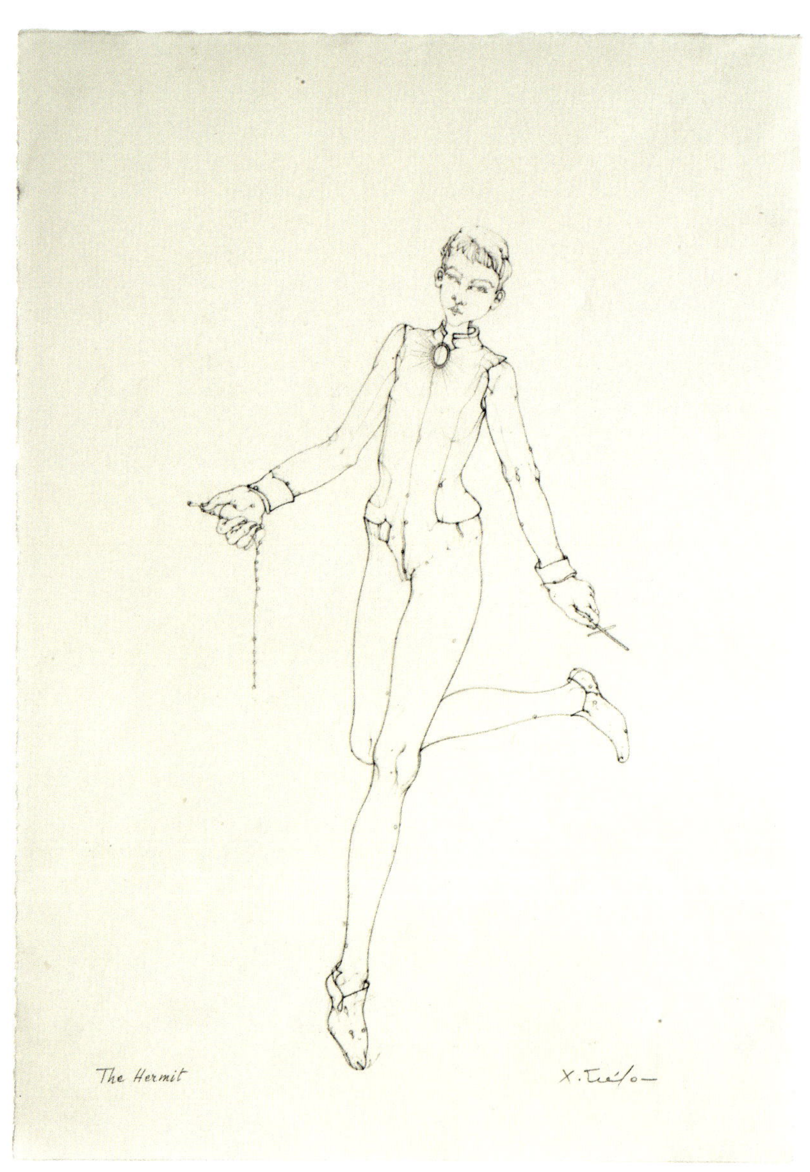

Tarot (The Hermit), 2009

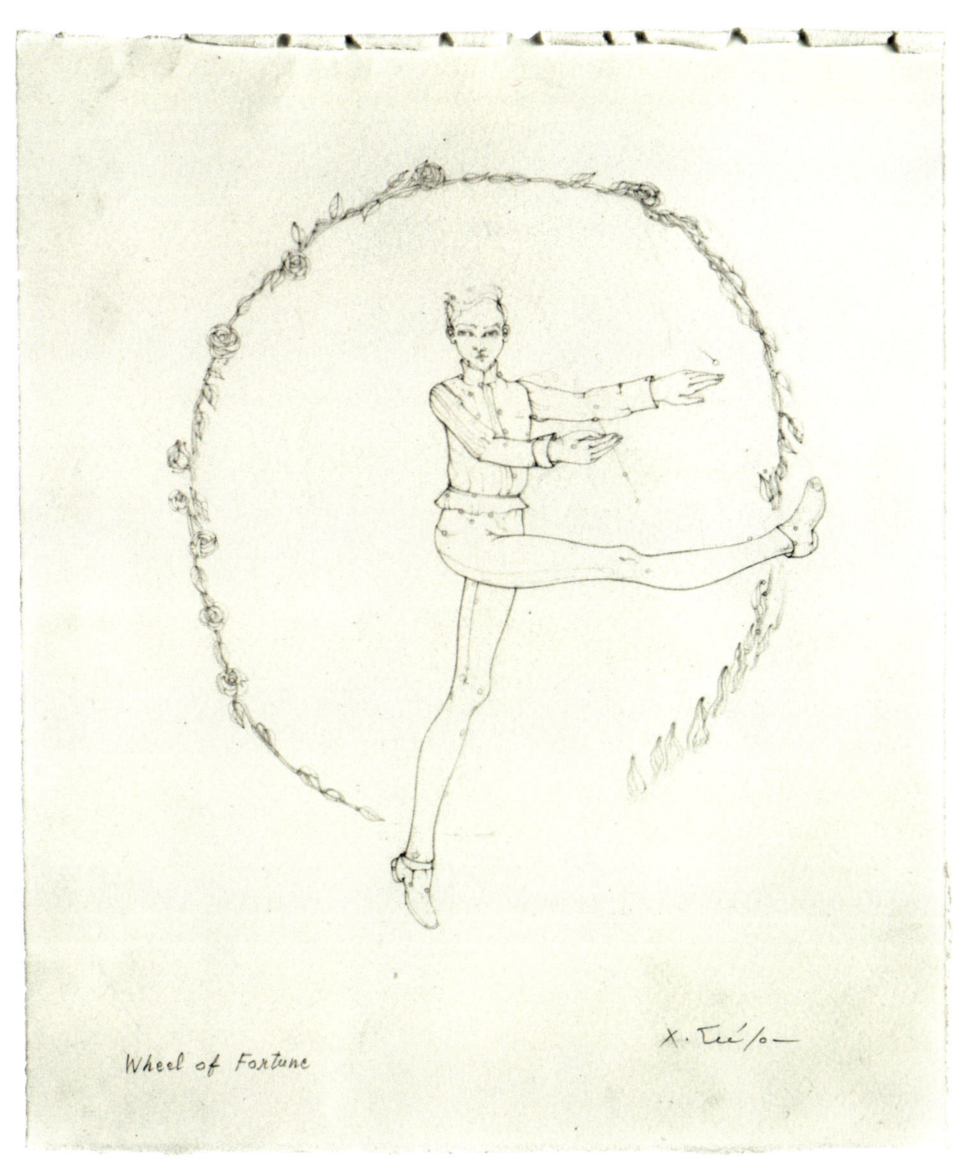

Tarot (Wheel of Fortune), 2009

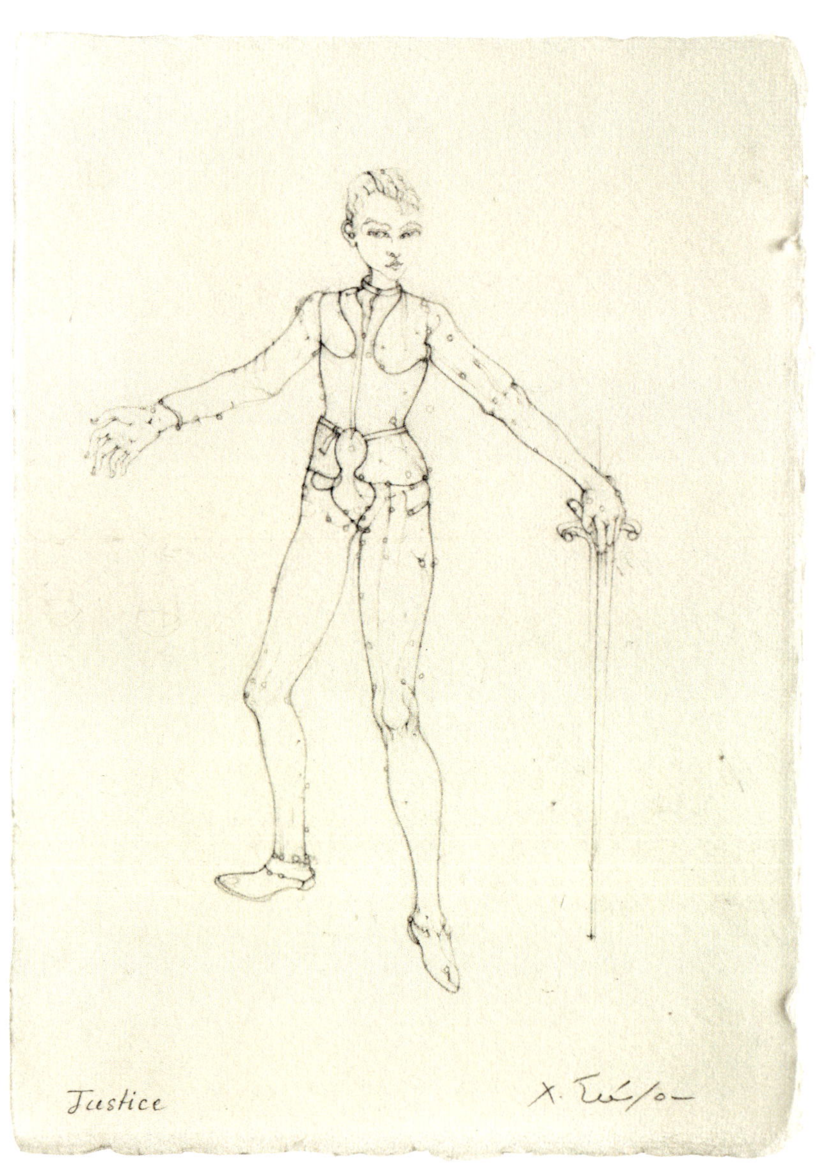

Tarot (Justice), 2009

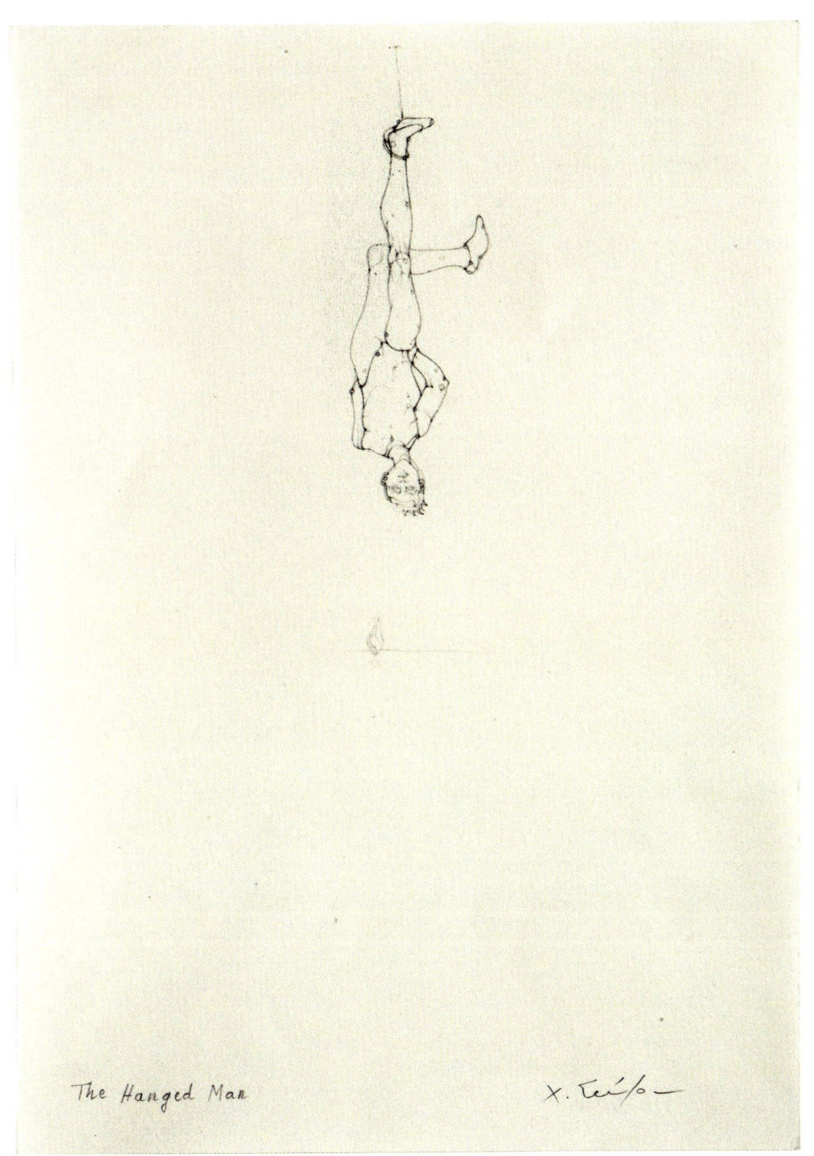

Tarot (The Hanged Man), 2009

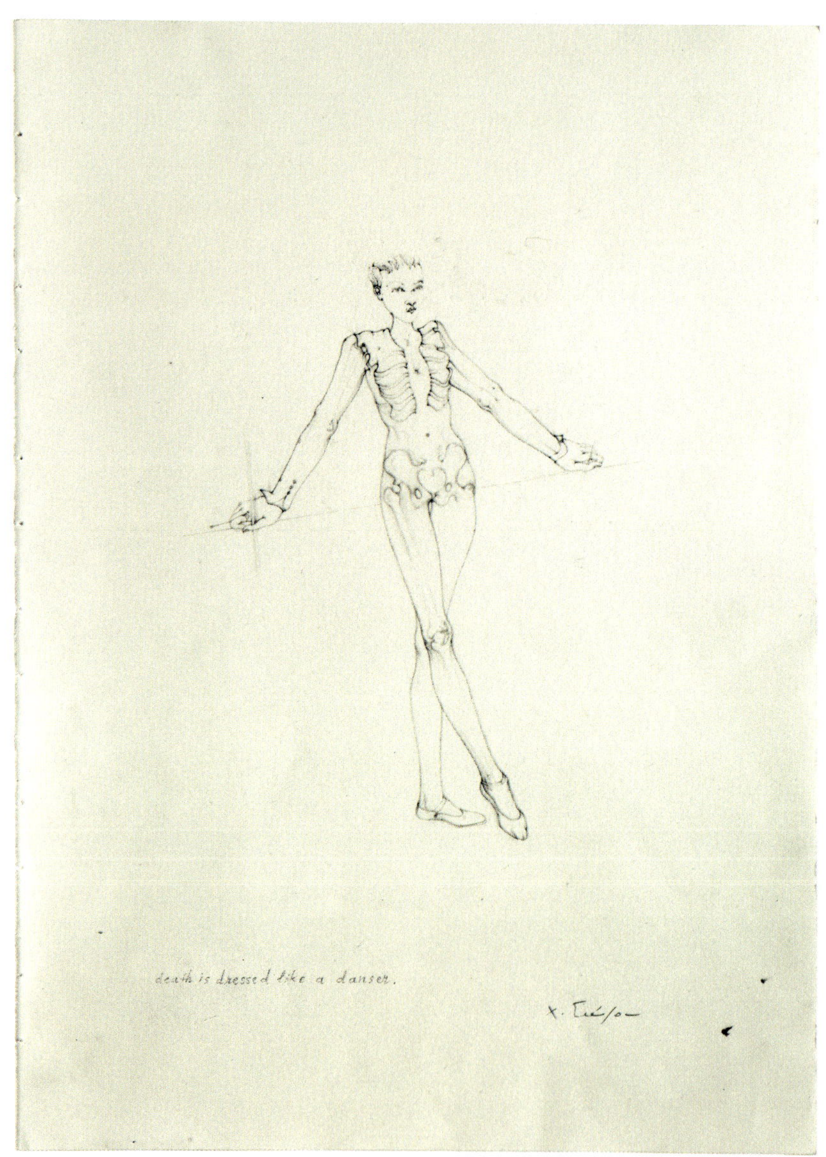

Tarot (Death), 2009

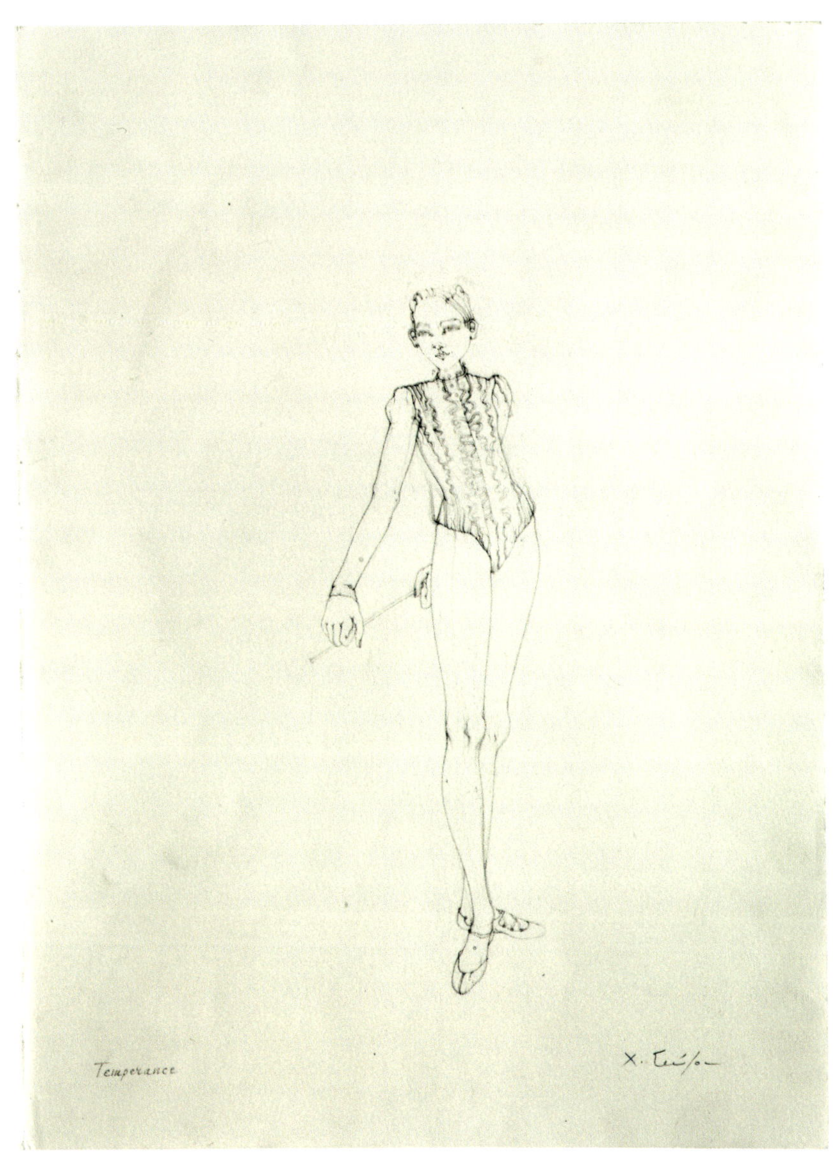

Tarot (Temperance), 2009

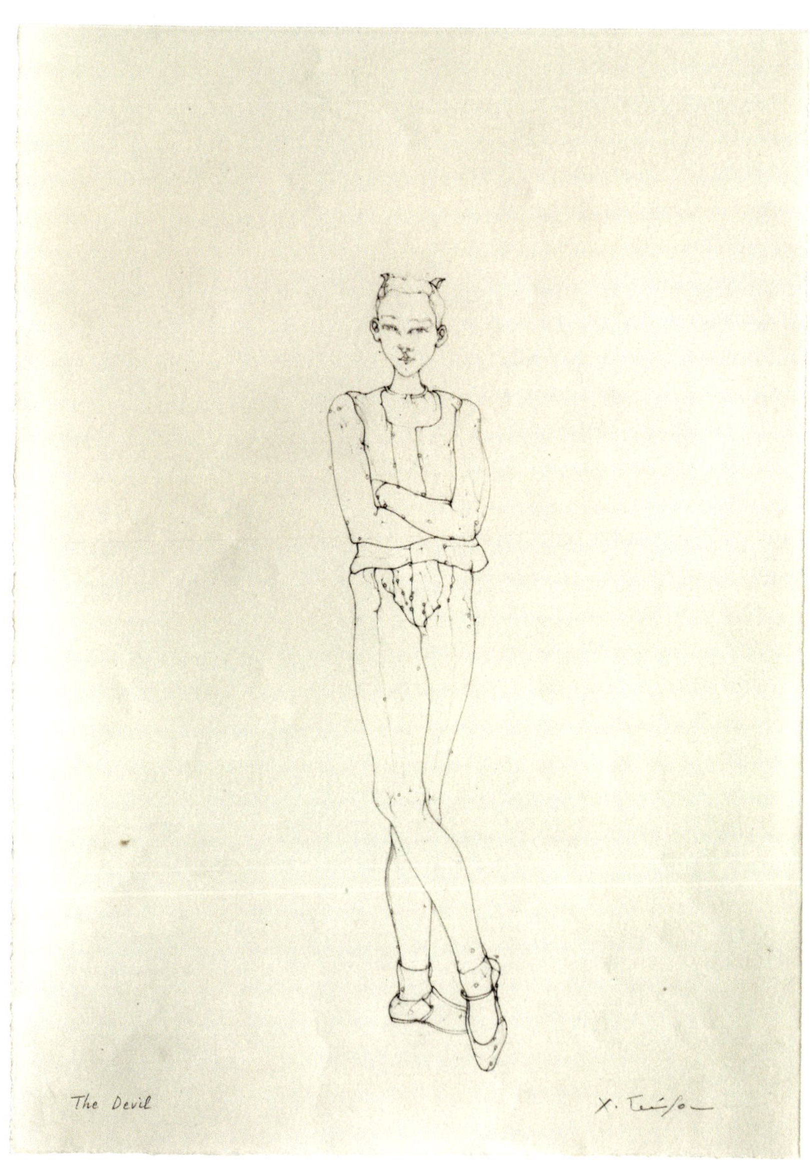

Tarot (The Devil), 2009

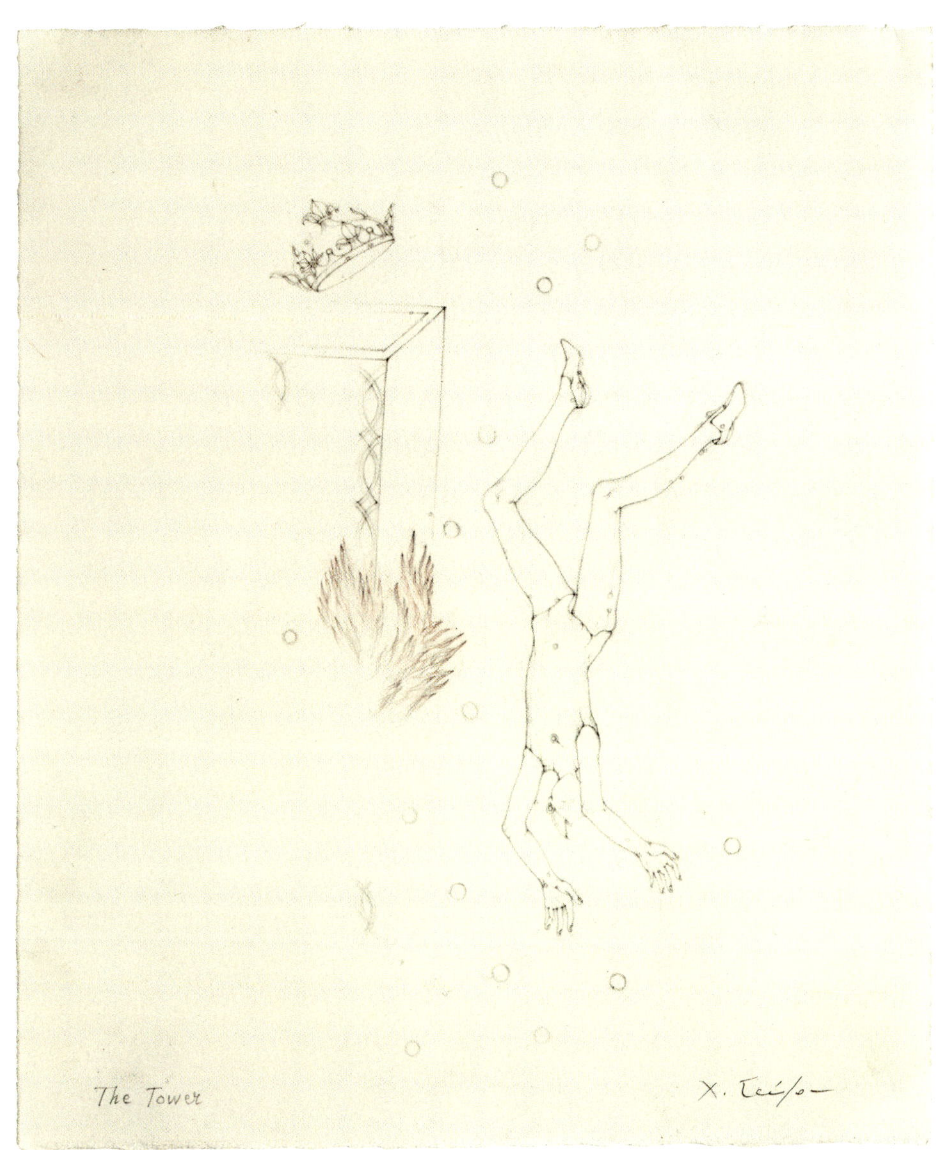

Tarot (The Tower), 2009

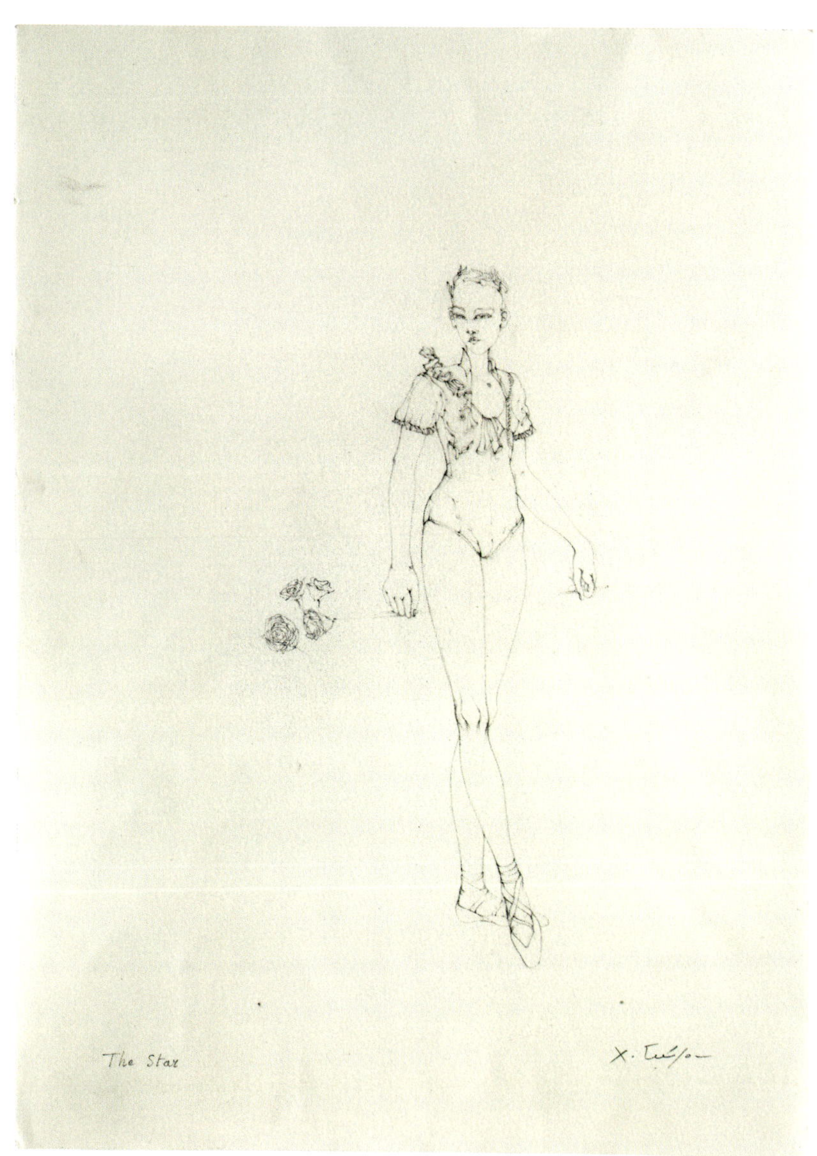

Tarot (The Star), 2009

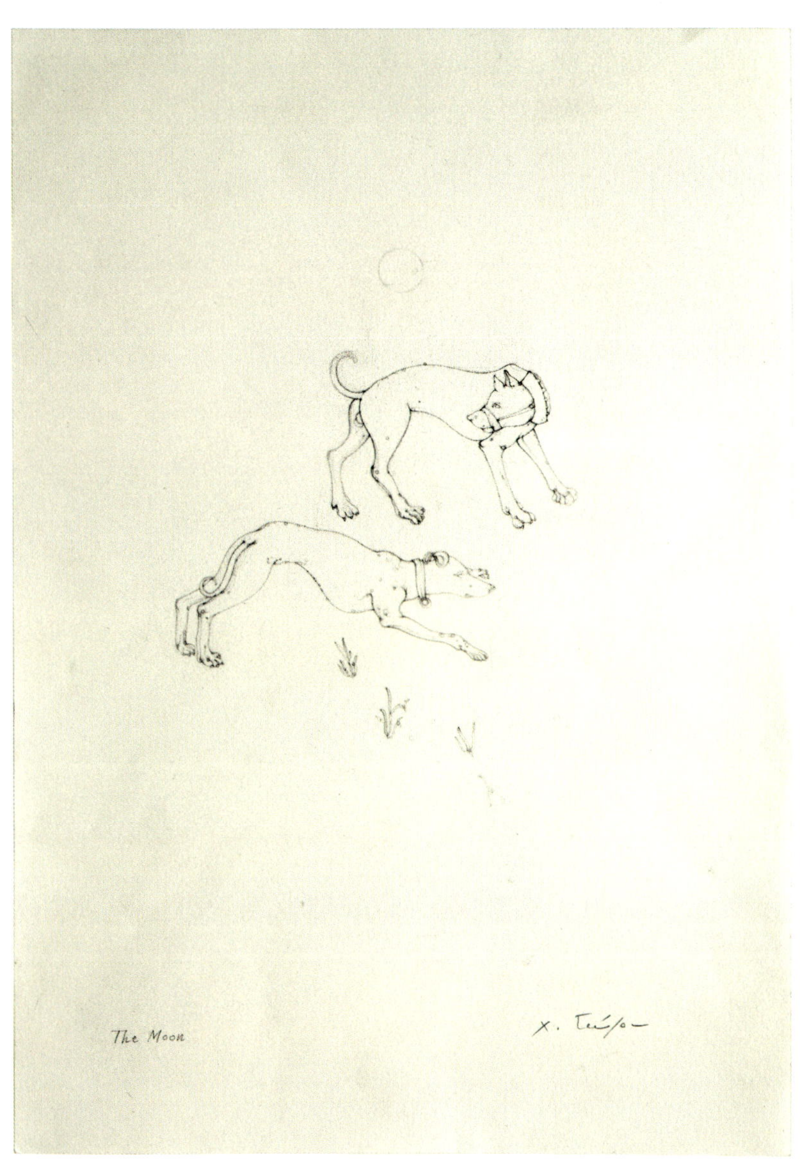

Tarot (The Moon), 2009

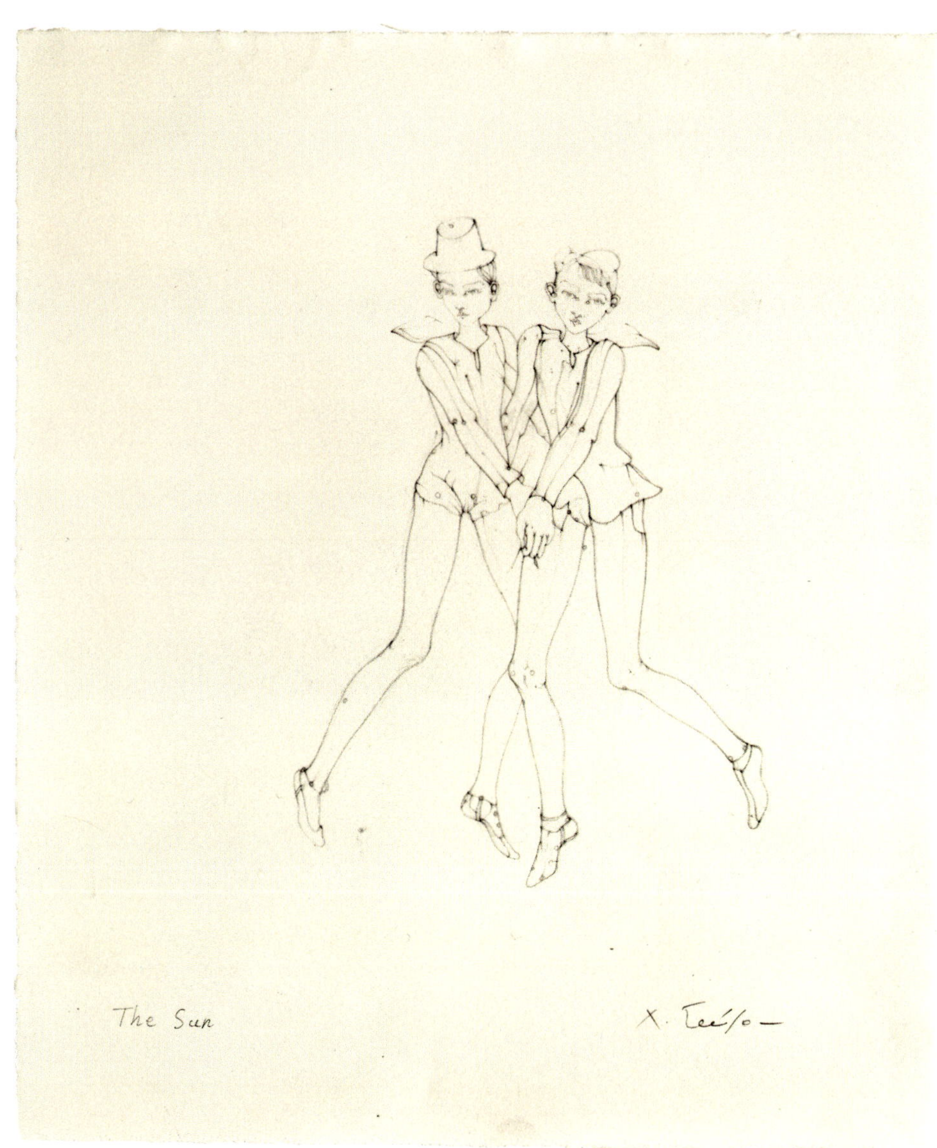

Tarot (The Sun), 2009

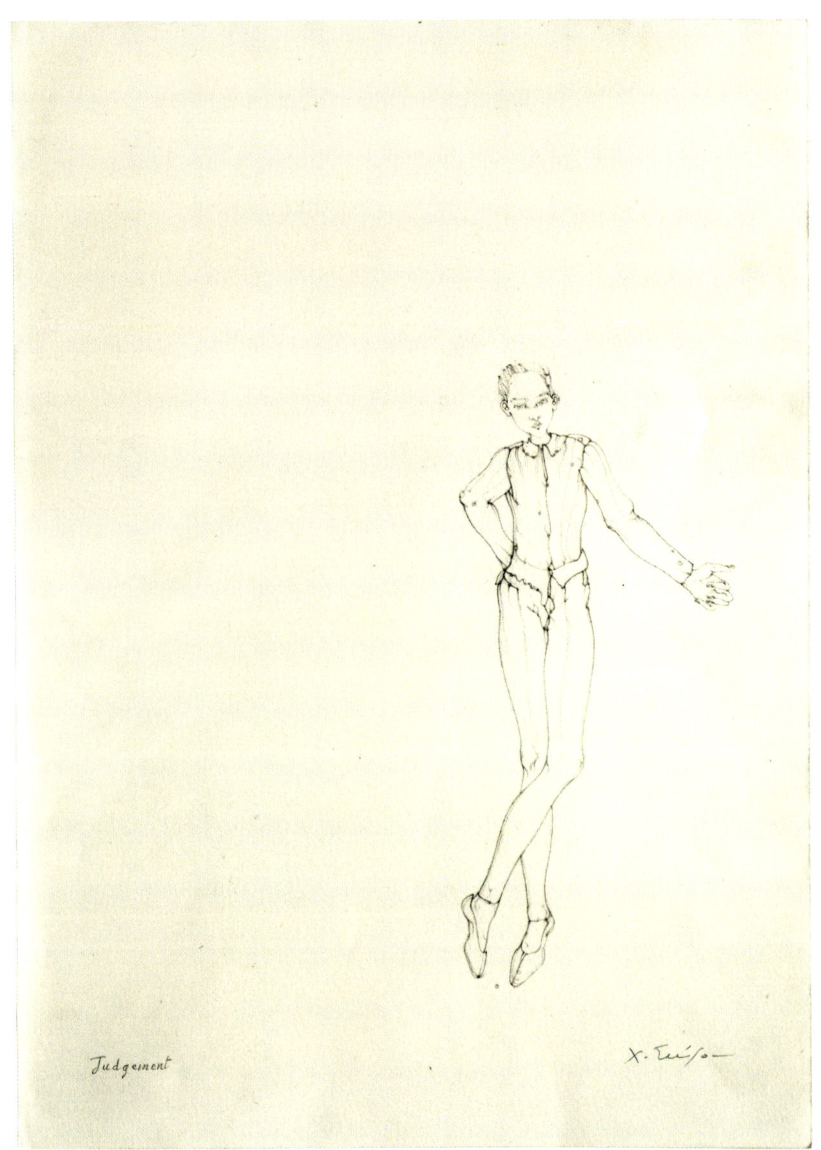

Tarot (Judgment), 2009

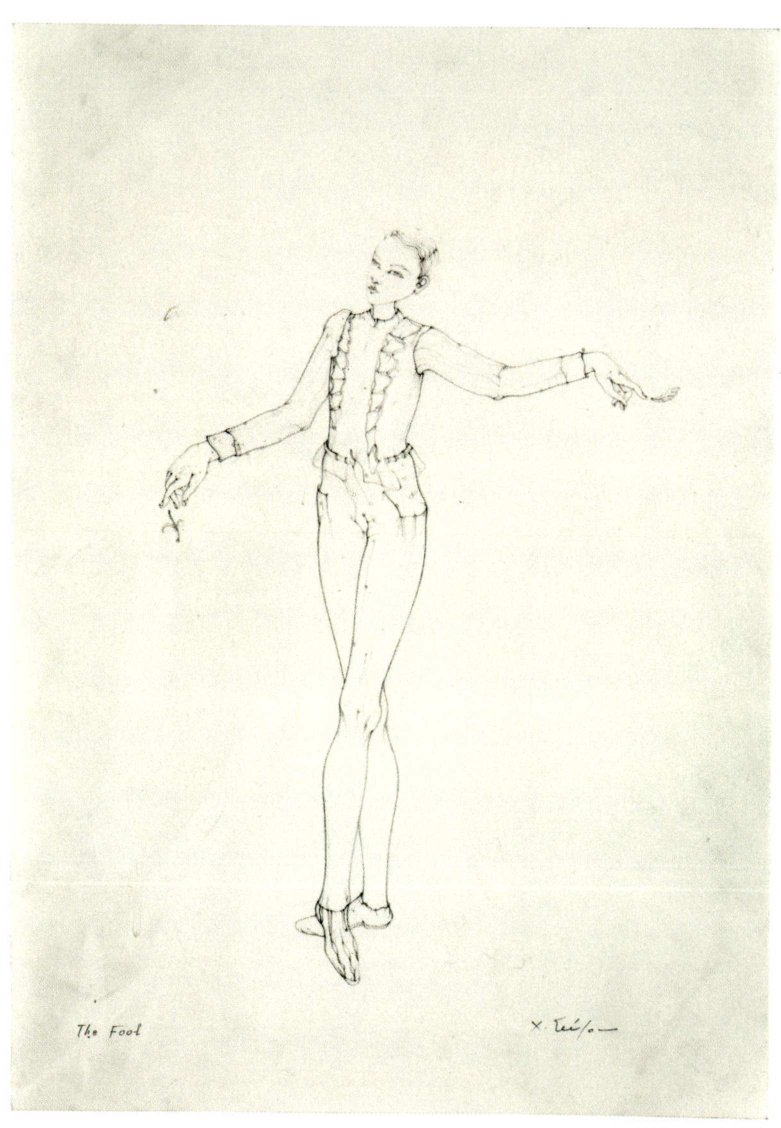

Tarot (The Fool), 2009

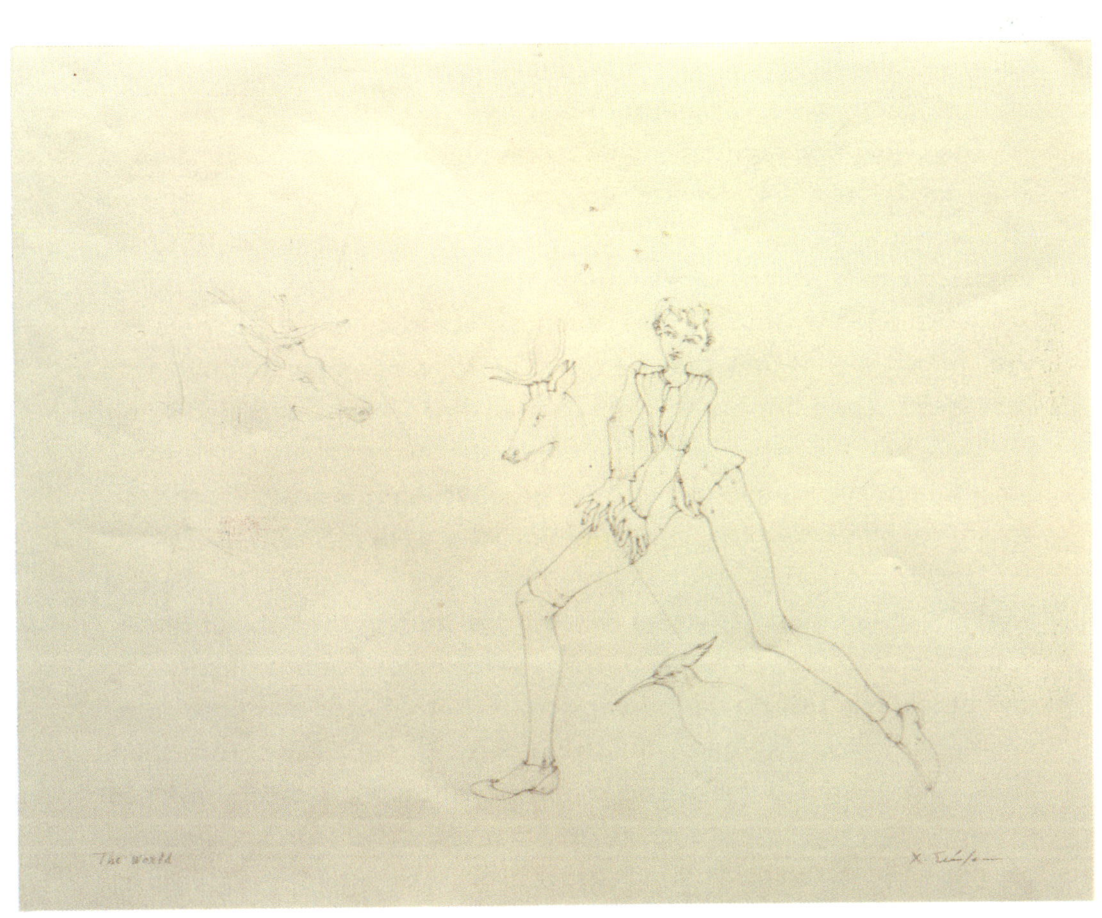

Tarot (The World), 2009

About My Work on Georges Bataille's *The Dead Man*

The Dead Man is to me a work of Doric starkness, purged of linguistic flourishes and anecdotes. It is an *elementary* work in which the element narrates itself. The element being the words—the discourse, as it were—a writer's only true material.

The work, the real work done by the author of *The Dead Man*, is an edifice he constructs with words: a terrific achievement of meticulous, anatomical precision *(rigueur)* of discourse.

The Dead Man contains no doctrines, ideologies, or ideas to be embraced. There are no extraneous elements that might turn the work into something else. The work is what it is in all its rawness. This rawness is the only worthy way of contending with the concept of beauty.

In Bataille's writing, phrases such as "she slid her long fingers into the crack," even if they may be taken literally, open perspective onto a vast space. *Long* fingers—as well as the word "crack," dropped into the phrase without further qualification—open the possibility not simply for a schematic image, but also for an abyss that is precisely the elementary part on which, in my opinion, the work is based.

The work's Doric aspect—I can't find a better word for it—the sobriety of it, lies in its structure much more than in the subject itself, in the architecture of the text, which determines notions of space and time while testing our perception of them. Bataille imposes an austere, immovable framework that operates much like commitment does. And it is this point of *commitment* that is the starting point for my own drawings: the stand I take. After *The Dead Man* I can no longer draw like I used to; I cannot draw an inn scene because this is not what the work is about. I cannot illustrate a pornographic scene, even with all the charm of a Klossowski, because the work is situated well past the point of "promise." I must then focus on the *vibrations* the work emits: *Time had just negated the laws to which fear subjects us. / An emptiness opened inside her, a prolonged shudder went through her and bore her upward like an angel. / Her bare breasts were rising in a church seen in a dream. / What is more, Edward drops dead.*

What is the work's time and space? Bataille proposes a certain geometry. He seems to be creating a space outside the space of the work: the dead man—the book's main subject that is also its title— lies outside the book itself. He is *eccentric*, has been left outside the frame, beyond the piece of paper that holds my own drawing. The dead man lies beyond the book, and beyond the drawing, in some other space, and yet his power is tremendous, because he operates like the light that shines upon and lights the drawing page. Maria's drawings are lit by the light of the dead man...

The space of *The Dead Man* may be no other than the boundless realm of our imagination, where we may take as much time as we need to envisage the dead Edward. Where? It matters not. That "where" belongs to a space outside the work and as such is hugely suggestive, as it looms above the entire work, a haunting presence or motive force. The dead man is everything. He momentarily returns—as a dead man—at the end of the book and "fills the room" so that we may be assured of his existence.

To put it differently, what stretches outside the work is an extension—an extension of the work itself in space and time.

If the artist's goal is to liberate such concepts as those of space and time from their material contingency and conventional restraints, then it may be said that the work of *The Dead Man* renders time and space perennial.

In the place that remains, in that part which remains, the book that is, there is but one real space: the void—an emptiness opened inside Maria that bears her upward like an angel.

Bataille's work is a work of pure form and as such may be of aesthetic interest to an artist. Its rawness is Maria's nakedness as much as it is the bareness, the clarity of form.

The absence of flowery language (and the presence of all that has been mentioned above) is conducive to one thing only: the artist's main concern, which is to base her work—whatever implications or symbolic readings this may prove to have in retrospect—in purely aesthetic-formal means. I believe this is exactly what Bataille does. He works and reworks the same thing until he reaches the climax he is looking for, the clarity he desires. It is as if his language were carved out of crystal. He deals with clarity as if it were death itself.

Christiana Soulou
(2013)

The time had come to deny the laws to which fear subjects us, 2012

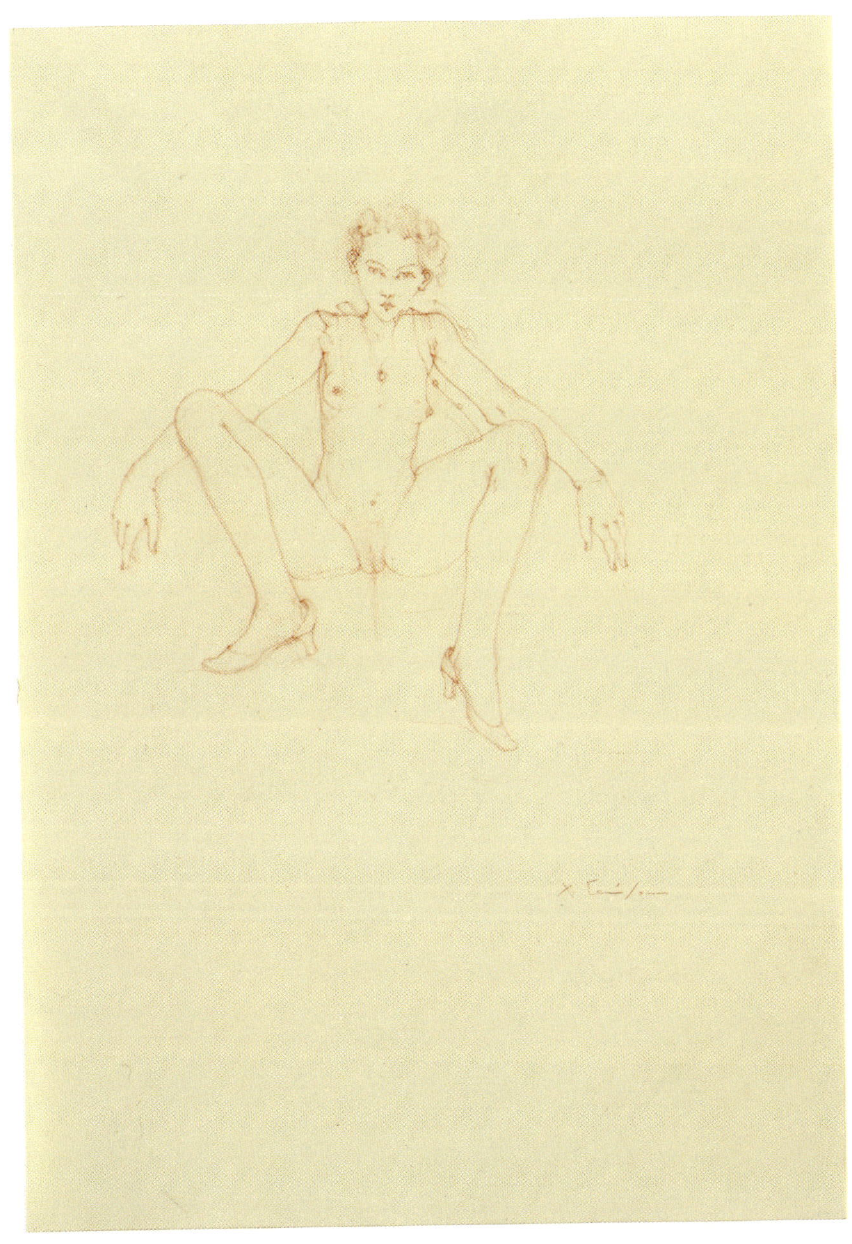

Dazed, 2012

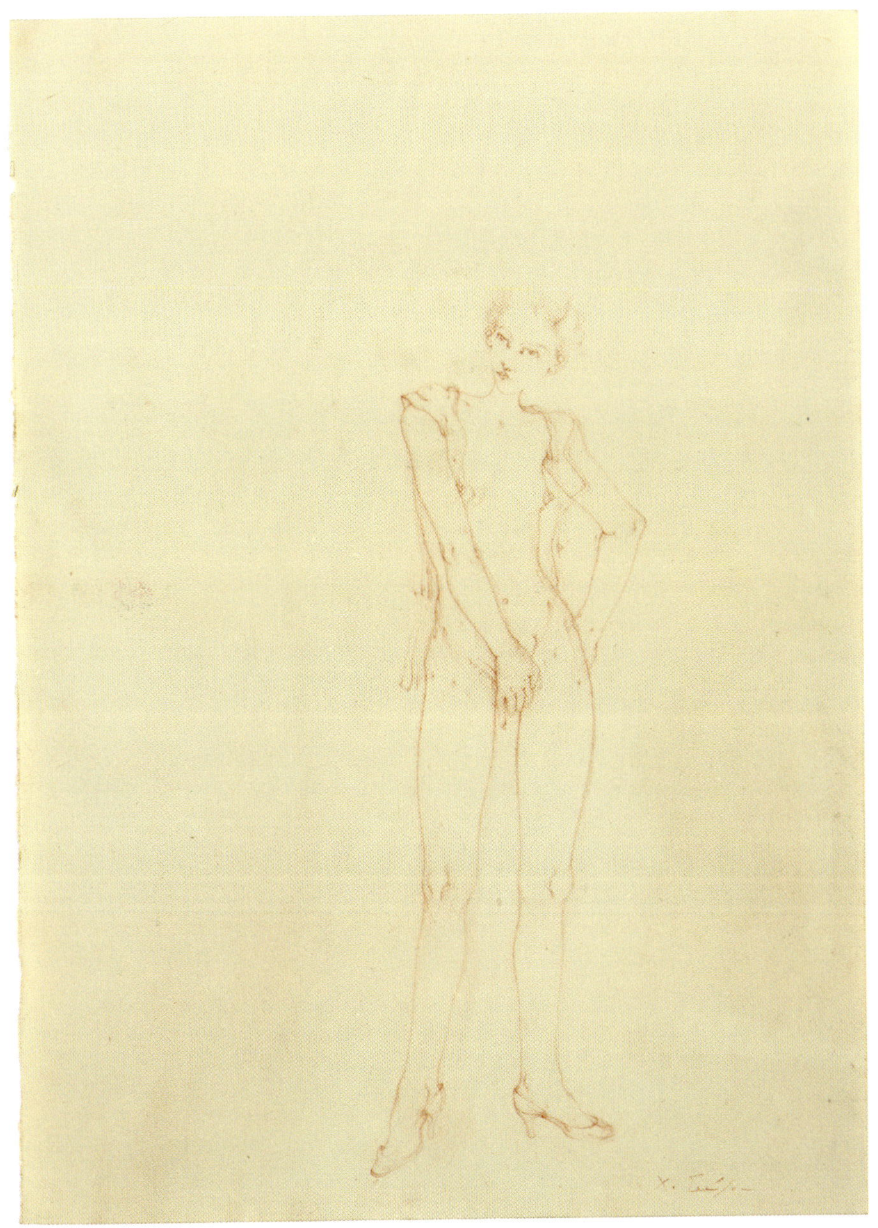

Farmboy (farm-boy), 2012

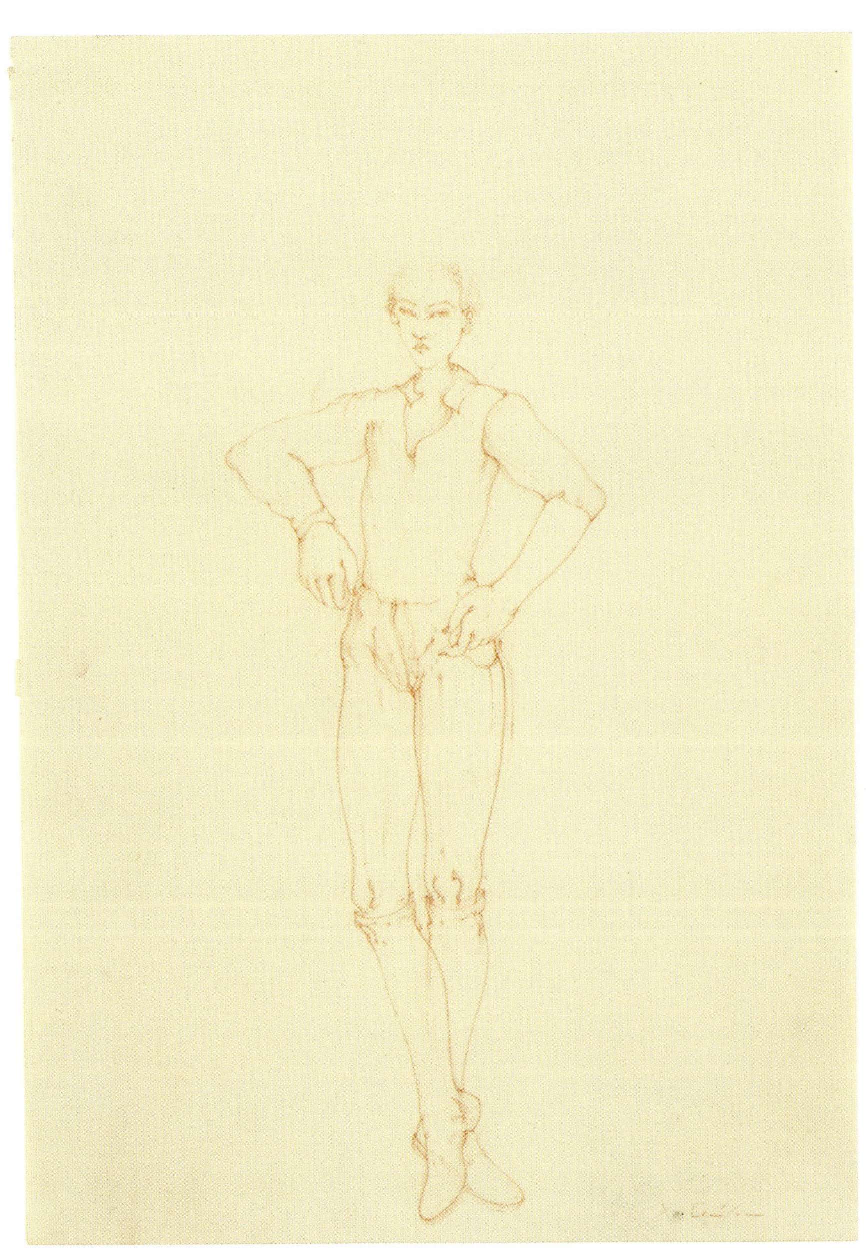

They danced an obscene java, 2012

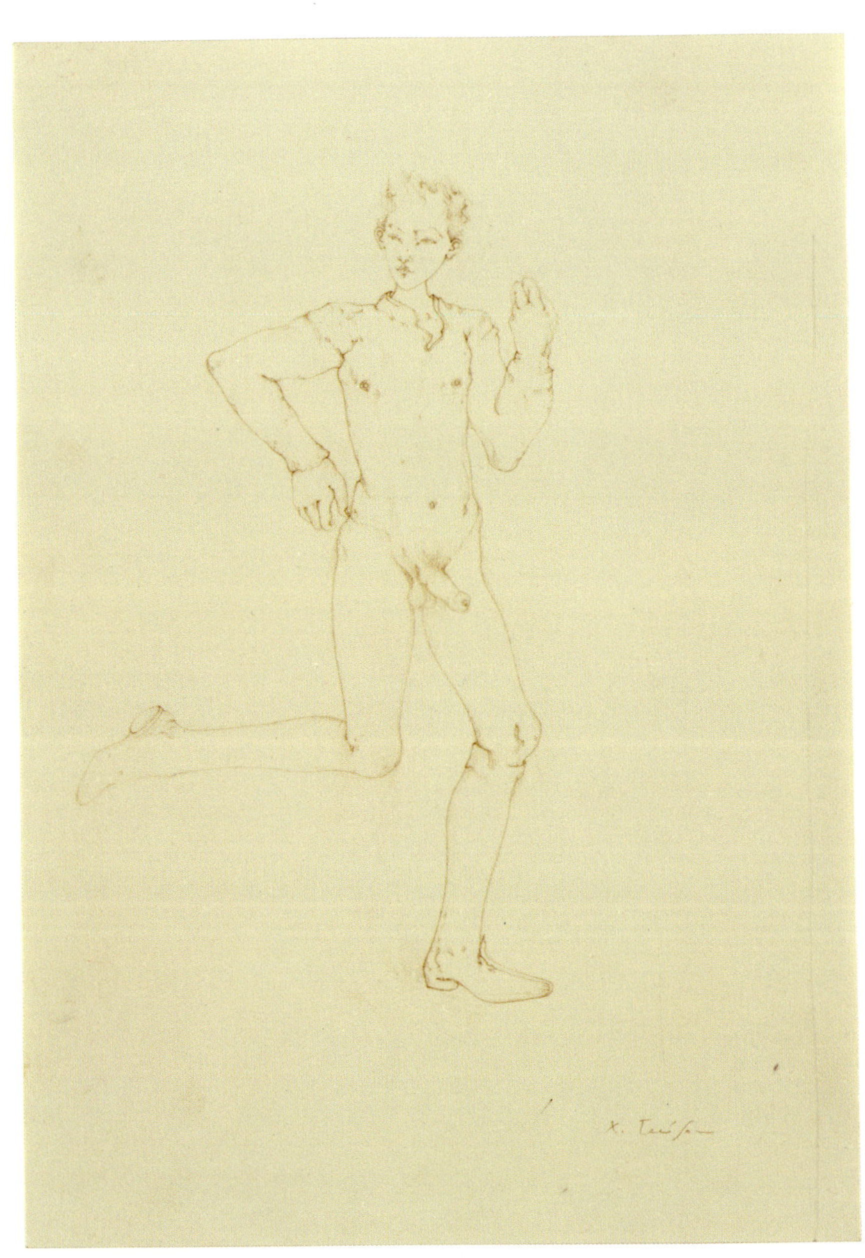

The Count, 2012

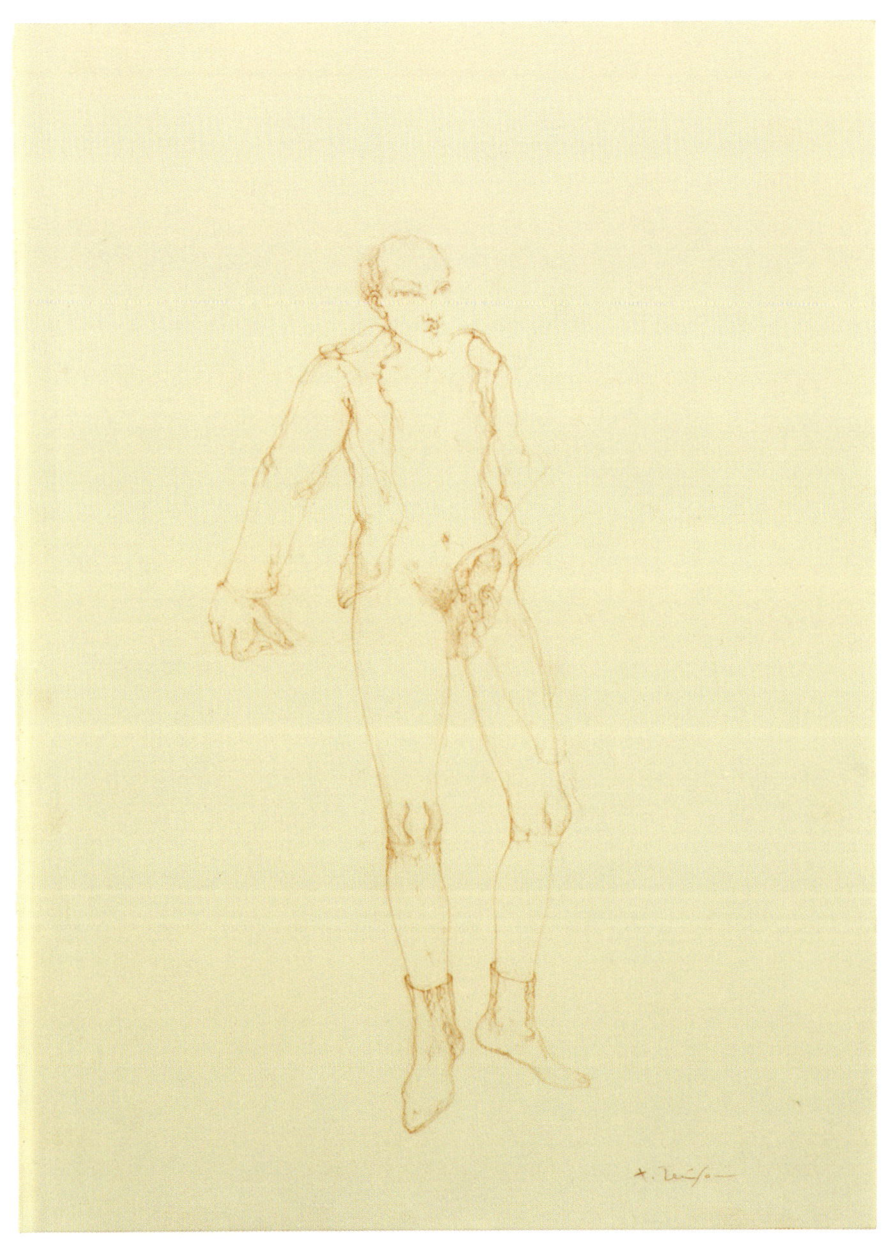

Marie falls onto the Count, 2012

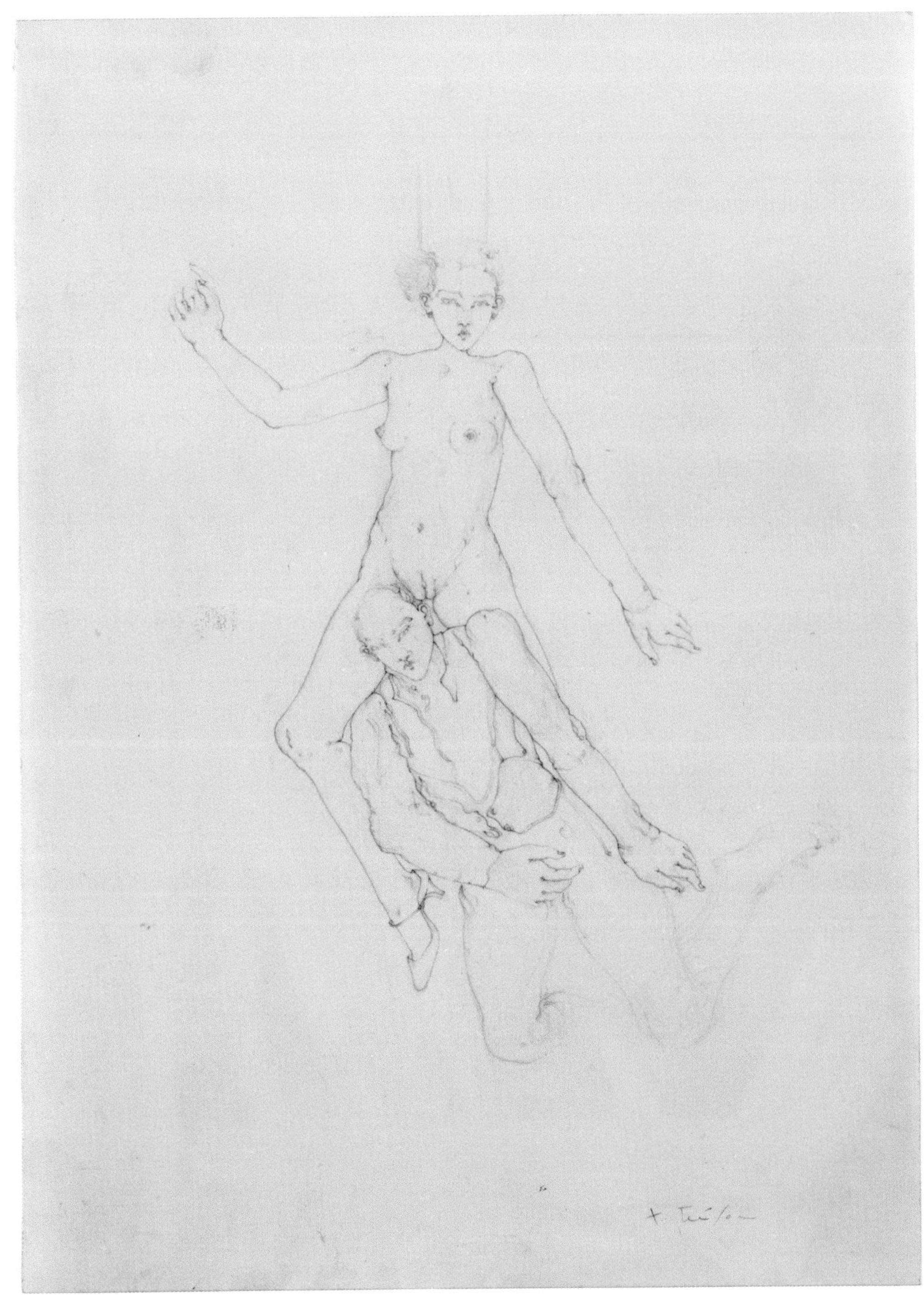

Sick, lit-up, Marie seemed happy, 2012

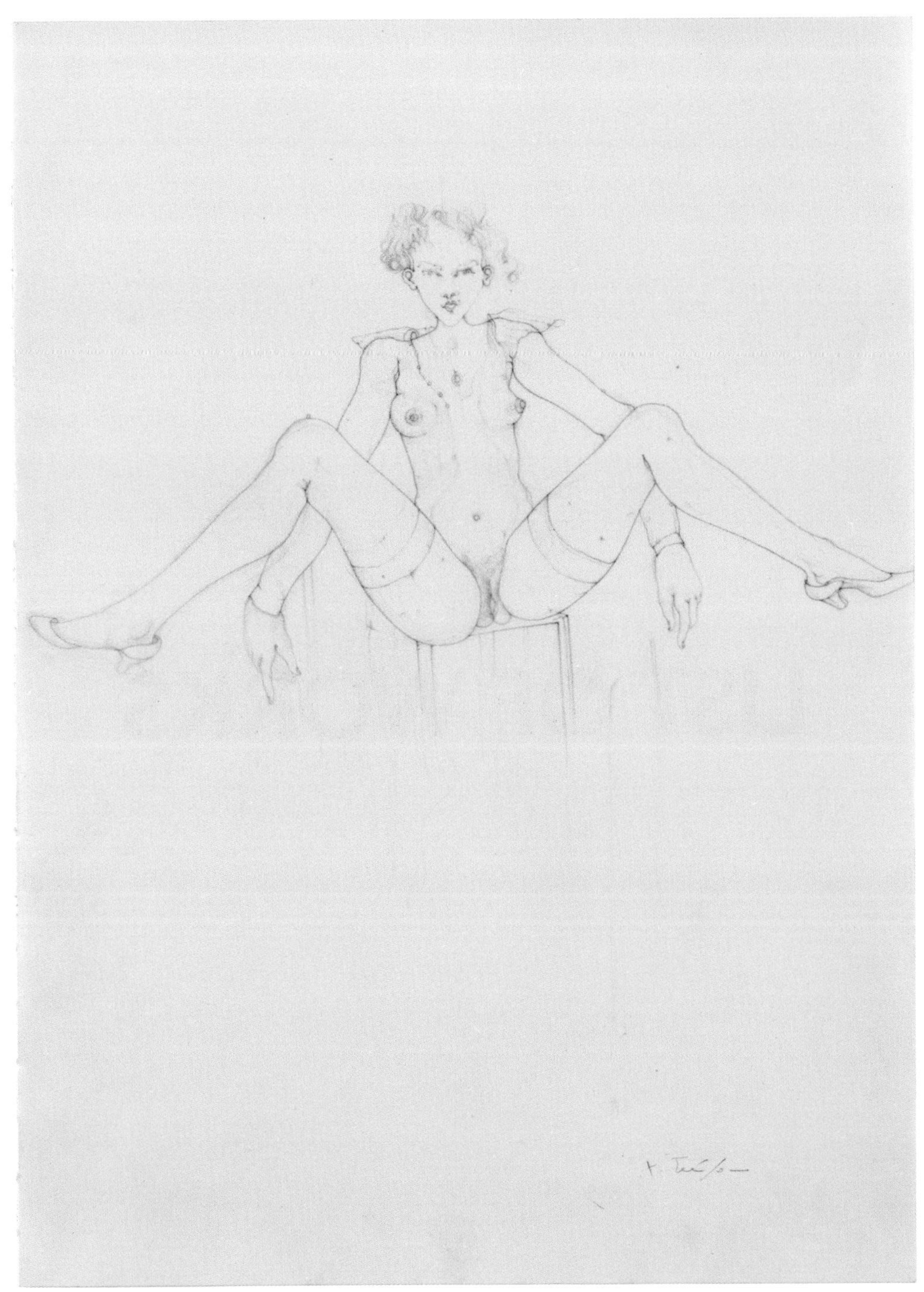

LIST OF WORKS

I Accept, If You Can Tolerate Me Silently, 1982
Colored pencil on paper
25 x 18 cm

Girl, 1982
Pencil on paper
19 x 15 cm

Girl, 1982
Pencil on paper
21 x 15 cm

Montre ta montre monstre, 1982
Colored pencil on paper
21 x 15 cm

The Letter, 1982
Pencil on paper
18 x 28 cm

... And You a Coffee House – The Nut in the Cage, 1982
Pencil on paper
17 x 11.5 cm

L'escamoteur (after Hieronymus Bosch) 1–4, 1982
Gouache and ink on paper
24 x 34 cm

Water, 1983–1985
Pencil, colored pencil, ink, charcoal, and watercolor on
paper
70 parts:

Artemis Polumastos
24.2 x 15.7 cm

Untitled
24.4 x 11.6 cm

Untitled
24.3 x 18.2 cm

Untitled
24.4 x 17 cm

Untitled
17.5 x 13.8 cm

The Spring Doors Open
24.2 x 24.4 cm

Untitled
17.6 x 13.8 cm

Reference to Lucas Cranach's Venus
17.6 x 13.2 cm

Untitled
17.6 x 24.5 cm

Vault
17.6 x 25.3 cm

The Spoon, an Object
17.6 x 25.3 cm

Untitled
17.6 x 25.3 cm

Untitled
17.6 x 24.5 cm

1. Poppy or Mushroom, 2. Butterfly, Hand, Doll, 3. Compass
17.6 x 24.5 cm

Untitled
17.5 x 24.5 cm

Untitled
16.5 x 22 cm

Untitled
20.7 x 29.5 cm

Untitled
17.6 x 25.3 cm

Untitled
17.6 x 25.3 cm

Untitled
17.6 x 25.3 cm

Untitled
17.6 x 25.3 cm

Untitled
17.6 x 25.3 cm

Untitled
20.8 x 29.4 cm

Untitled
21 x 26.6 cm

The Open Dancer, the Knight
20.5 x 29.2 cm

Gorgo (Gargoyle Mermaid)
20.8 x 29.4 cm

Untitled
24.3 x 34.1 cm

Untitled
24.5 x 34.1 cm

Untitled
17.6 x 25.3 cm

Untitled
17.6 x 25.3 cm

Untitled
17.6 x 25.3 cm

Untitled
17.6 x 25.3 cm

Untitled
24 x 32 cm

Untitled
23.9 x 32 cm

Untitled
24 x 32 cm

Untitled
17.6 x 25.3 cm

Untitled
17.6 x 25.3 cm

Untitled
17.6 x 25.3 cm

Untitled
17.6 x 25.3 cm

Untitled
24.2 x 34.3 cm

The God of Money
24.2 x 28.5 cm

Untitled
18.3 x 14.8 cm

Untitled
24.4 x 17.1 cm

Untitled
22.5 x 28.7 cm

The Spinning Top
21 x 29.8 cm

The Little Fisherman
31.9 x 23.6 cm

After Yves Bonnefoy's On the Motion and Immobility of
Douve
25.2 x 17.5 cm

Untitled
25.2 x 17 cm

The Cyclist
23.9 x 29.5 cm

Untitled
24.2 x 34.5 cm

Priests
25.2 x 35.2 cm

Untitled
19.2 x 29.3 cm

Untitled
18.6 x 29.4 cm

Untitled
18.7 x 29.5 cm

Untitled
19.2 x 29.3 cm

Girl in the Red Box
17.6 x 24.5 cm

Untitled
17.9 x 23.6 cm

Untitled
19.2 x 29.2 cm

Untitled
19.2 x 29.2 cm

Untitled
17.9 x 23.5 cm

Untitled
17.9 x 23.5 cm

Untitled
23.5 x 17.5 cm

Untitled
24.9 x 17.5 cm

Untitled
25 x 17.5 cm

Untitled
24.3 x 34 cm

Untitled
24 x 34.5 cm

Untitled
16.5 x 14.1 cm

Untitled
41.7 x 29.5 cm

Untitled
41.7 x 29.5 cm

Untitled
18.7 x 29.3 cm

Shipwrecked—Amorgos/N. Gatsos, 2005
Aquarelle and pencil on paper
23 x 30.5 cm

Laying the Ground with Stars—Amorgos/N. Gatsos, 2005
Pencil on paper
23 x 30.5 cm

At the House of the Mournful Man—Amorgos/N. Gatsos,
2005
Aquarelle, pencil, and colored pencil on paper
30.5 x 23 cm

At the House of the Mournful Man, 2005
Colored pencil on paper
28 x 25.5 cm

The Man during the Course of His Mysterious Life—
Amorgos/N. Gatsos, 2005
Pencil on paper
32 x 22 cm

The Frog of Communication, 2005
Pencil on paper
25 x 19 cm

Untitled, 2005
Pencil and colored pencil on paper
25 x 30 cm

She Is Sleeping, 2005
Colored pencil on paper
22 x 39 cm

Only I Know How Very Much I Loved You, 2005
Pencil on paper
39 x 27 cm

La Belle Dame sans Merci, 2006
Colored pencil on paper
29.5 x 30 cm

Nu, 2007
Graphite on paper
28 x 23.2 cm

Domenico Scarlatti, Sonate K209, 2007
Graphite on paper
57.5 x 41.5 cm

Tarot (The Magician), 2009
Pencil on paper
41.9 x 29.5 cm
54.5 x 42 x 3.8 cm, framed

Tarot (The High Priestess), 2009
Pencil on paper
41.9 x 29.5 cm
54.5 x 42 x 3.8 cm, framed

Tarot (The Emperor), 2009
Pencil on paper
16.5 x 11.8 cm
29 x 24.6 x 3.8 cm, framed

Tarot (The Empress), 2009
Pencil on paper
29.9 x 20.6 cm
42.5 x 33.5 x 3.8 cm, framed

Tarot (The Hierophant), 2009
Pencil on paper
41.9 x 29.9 cm
54.5 x 42 x 3.8 cm, framed

Tarot (The Lovers), 2009
Pencil on paper
38.1 x 26.7 cm
51 x 39 x 3.8 cm, framed

Tarot (The Chariot), 2009
Pencil on paper
38.1 x 26.7 cm
51 x 39 x 3.8 cm, framed

Tarot (Strength), 2009
Pencil on paper
53 x 38.1 cm
65.5 x 51 x 3.8 cm, framed

Tarot (The Hermit), 2009
Pencil on paper
38.1 x 26.7 cm
51 x 39 x 3.8 cm, framed

Tarot (Wheel of Fortune), 2009
Pencil on paper
27.9 x 22.9 cm
40.5 x 35.5 x 3.8 cm, framed

Tarot (Justice), 2009
Pencil on paper
21.6 x 15.2 cm
34 x 27.5 x 3.8 cm, framed

Tarot (The Hanged Man), 2009
Pencil on paper
29.9 x 20.6 cm
42.5 x 33.5 x 3.8 cm, framed

Tarot (Death), 2009
Pencil on paper
41.9 x 29.9 cm
54.5 x 42 x 3.8 cm, framed

Tarot (Temperance), 2009
Pencil on paper
41.9 x 29.9 cm
54.5 x 42 x 3.8 cm, framed

Tarot (The Devil), 2009
Pencil on paper
38.4 x 26.7 cm
51 x 39 x 3.8 cm, framed

Tarot (The Tower), 2009
Pencil on paper
27.9 x 22.9 cm
40.5 x 35.5 x 3.8 cm, framed

Tarot (The Star), 2009
Pencil on paper
41.9 x 29.9 cm
54.5 x 42 x 3.8 cm, framed

Tarot (The Moon), 2009
Pencil on paper
41.9 x 28.9 cm
54.5 x 42 x 3.8 cm, framed

Tarot (The Sun), 2009
Pencil on paper
27.6 x 23.5 cm
40.5 x 35.5 x 3.8 cm, framed

Tarot (Judgment), 2009
Pencil on paper
41.9 x 29.9 cm
54.5 x 42 x 3.8 cm, framed

Tarot (The Fool), 2009
Pencil on paper
41.9 x 29.2 cm
54.5 x 42 x 3.8 cm, framed

Tarot (The World), 2009
Pencil on paper
45.7 x 36.8 cm
58 x 49.5 x 3.8 cm, framed

*The time had come to deny the laws to which fear
subjects us,* 2012
Pencil on paper
41.7 x 28.8 cm

Dazed, 2012
Pencil on paper
41.7 x 29.5 cm

Farmboy (farm-boy), 2012
Pencil on paper
41.8 x 29.4 cm

Pierrot with a hateful look on his face, 2012
Pencil on paper
41.3 x 28.5 cm

They danced an obscene java, 2012
Pencil on paper
41.7 x 28.7 cm

The Count, 2012
Pencil on paper
41.8 x 29.4 cm

Marie falls onto the Count, 2012
Pencil on paper
41.8 x 29.3 cm

Sick, lit-up, Marie seemed happy, 2012
Pencil on paper
41.8 x 29.4 cm

ARTIST BIO

Christiana Soulou was born in Athens, Greece, in 1961 and studied at the École nationale supérieure des Beaux-Arts in Paris. In dialogue with the work of writers such as Antonin Artaud and Heinrich von Kleist, she has developed a rigorous drawing practice that explores narrative, identity, and storytelling.

Soulou has exhibited internationally, with solo shows at Capitain Petzel, Berlin (2012), Sadie Coles HQ, London (2011), Friedrich Petzel Gallery, New York (2010), and Bernier/Eliades, Athens (2010). She has shown her work in numerous group exhibitions, including the 55th Venice Biennale (2013); *Skin Fruit* at the New Museum of Contemporary Art, New York (2010); *Alpha Omega* at the DESTE Foundation for Contemporary Art, Athens (2010); *Heaven* at the 2nd Athens Biennale (2009); *In Praise of Shadows* at the Istanbul Museum of Modern Art, IMMA, Dublin, and the Museum Benaki, Athens (2009); *Dream & Trauma* at the Kunsthalle Wien and mumok, Vienna (2007); *Panic Room* at the DESTE Foundation (2006–07); and *Of Mice and Men* at the 4th Berlin Biennale for Contemporary Art (2006). Capitain Petzel published Soulou's *Selected Writings* in 2012. *Fractures*, a book of the artist's writings, poems, and drawings, was published by DESTE during the group exhibition *Fractured Figure* (2008). *Water*, a book of her early drawings from 1983 to 1985, was published by Sadie Coles HQ the same year.

Christiana Soulou lives and works in Athens.

AUTHOR BIO

Claire Gilman is curator at the Drawing Center in New York, where she has organized *Drawing Time, Reading Time* (2013), *Dickinson/Walser: Pencil Sketches* (2013), *Giosetta Fioroni: L'Argento* (2013), *Alexandre Singh: The Pledge* (2013), *Ishmael Randall Weeks: Cuts, Burns, Punctures* (2013), *José Antonio Suárez Londoño: The Yearbooks* (2012), and *Drawn from Photography* (2011).

Gilman has taught art history and critical theory at Columbia University, New York; the Center for Curatorial Studies at Bard College, Annandale-on-Hudson; Corcoran College for Art + Design, Washington, D.C.; the Museum of Modern Art, New York; and the School of Visual Arts, New York. She has written for *Art Journal, CAA Reviews, Documents, Frieze,* and *October,* and has authored numerous essays for art books and museum exhibitions. Gilman earned her PhD in art history at Columbia University.

A warm thank you to Christiana Soulou, whose ethereal drawings of mysterious creatures haunt my imagination. I would also like to thank Claire Gilman, whose essay casts new light on the artist's private creative universe. Thank you to Massimiliano Gioni for bringing Christiana and Claire together and for his continued dedication to the *2000 Words* series. And special thanks to Karen Marta and Sue Medlicott for the great care they have put into each *2000 Words* book. And lastly, thanks to Brendan Dugan for the great design concept for the series and to Vanessa Antoniadou for designing this particular volume.

—Dakis Joannou

Christiana Soulou
2000 Words

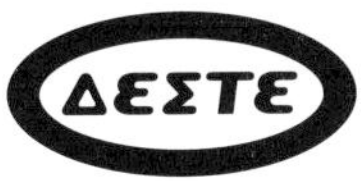

Commissioning Editor: Massimiliano Gioni
Editor: Karen Marta
Design concept and cover: An Art Service
Design: idteam
Editorial Assistant: Quinn Lewington
Coordinators: Regina Alivisatos and Dustin Cosentino
Registrar: Natasha Polymeropoulos
Copy Editor: Miles Champion
Production: The Production Department

Published by:
The DESTE Foundation for Contemporary Art
Filellinon 11 & Em. Pappa St.
N. Ionia 142 34, Athens
www.deste.gr

Cover: Christiana Soulou, *Girl in the Red Box*, from *Water*, 1983–1985
Thank you to James Cahill and Brinda Roy at Sadie Coles HQ and
Svenja Schuhbauer at Capitain Petzel, Berlin. Special thanks to
Stavros Petsopoulos and Agra Publications for granting permission
to include works from the *Dead Man* (2012) series.

Reproductions of *Water*, *Domenico Scarlatti*, *Sonate K209* (2007),
and *Nu* (2007) courtesy Sadie Coles HQ, London. "Notes on
I Accept, If You Can Tolerate Me Silently" is adapted from Christiana
Soulou's *Selected Writings* (Berlin, 2012: Capitain Petzel).

Distributed in the Americas by:
ARTBOOK | D.A.P.
155 Sixth Avenue, 2nd Floor
New York, NY 10013
www.artbook.com

Distributed in Europe by:
Buchhandlung Walther König
Ehrenstrasse 4
50672 Köln
www.buchhandlung-walther-koenig.de

Printed in Greece by Alta Grafico S.A. Printing and Graphic Arts

ISBN: 978-618-5039-06-6

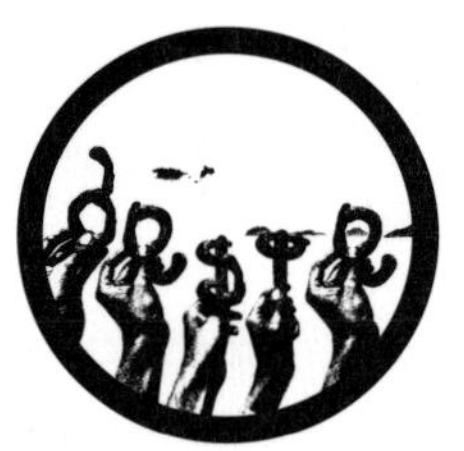